One of God's special gifts to Christian families has been Dr. Ted Baehr, who has shared wise and helpful counsel through *MovieGuide®*. Now Ted has teamed with Pat Boone to share a book that will help us understand the present media culture and how we can both survive and thrive as Christians who share the light of Christ into the darkness of our culture.

Dr. Paul Cedar
Chairman, Mission America Coalition

We have come to expect Dr. Baehr's writing to be informed by the core issues of the culture war and directed to the pressure points where Christians willing to fight this war can have the most impact. In *The Culture-Wise Family,* he has again hit the most salient point, namely that our children must be equipped to know the issues and strategies in media in order for us to win the culture war. As president of one of the fastest growing evangelical universities in America, I can tell you that students who come to us from families who informed them about these issues integrate their faith with rigorous learning much more easily than those who had no family nurturing in these great cultural issues. The family is God's ultimate weapon against the erosion of all that has come to define Western civilization and America as a Christian nation. The Church, school and university will never win this battle without the family.

Dr. David W. Clark
President, Palm Beach Atlantic University

I've admired and respected Pat Boone for more than four decades, and I have worked with Ted Baehr on various projects for nearly a decade now. I know of no better mentors for the vast majority of us who need help in becoming more culture-wise and media-wise, and thus more faithful Christians.

Joseph Coleson
Professor of Old Testament, Nazarene Theological Seminary
Translation Team member, *New Living Translation*

Perhaps the greatest challenge for evangelical Christians in the twenty-first century is the culture war. As a nation, our Christian values are under attack as never before. *The Culture-Wise Family* will be a great help to all who hold dear our Christian history and heritage. I heartily recommend it.

Larry Lewis
National Facilitator, Mission America Coalition

The Culture-Wise Family is a must-read for any family—especially Christian families. If you know what is feeding your mind, you can keep the trap door shut against those things that are wrong. This book shows you how.

Terry D. Porter
Writers Guild of America
Agent, Agape Productions

A corrupt and corrupting mass media violates the American people on a daily basis. Kudos to Dr. Baehr and Pat Boone for arming us with a coherent, unambiguous and forceful guide to being culture wise.

Judith A. Reisman, PhD
The Institute for Media Education
Author, *Kinsey, Crimes and Consequences*

THE
CULTURE-WISE
FAMILY

*Upholding Christian Values in
a Mass Media World*

TED BAEHR
PAT BOONE

Regal

**From Gospel Light
Ventura, California, U.S.A.**

Published by Regal Books
From Gospel Light
Ventura, California, U.S.A.
Printed in the U.S.A.

Regal Books is a ministry of Gospel Light, a Christian publisher dedicated to serving the local church. We believe God's vision for Gospel Light is to provide church leaders with biblical, user-friendly materials that will help them evangelize, disciple and minister to children, youth and families.

It is our prayer that this Regal book will help you discover biblical truth for your own life and help you meet the needs of others. May God richly bless you.

For a free catalog of resources from Regal Books/Gospel Light, please call your Christian supplier or contact us at 1-800-4-GOSPEL *or* www.regalbooks.com.

Portions of the material in this book written by Pat Boone are reprinted courtesy of WorldNet Daily.com Inc., Pat's favorite news source (www.wnd.com).

Library of Congress Cataloging-in-Publication Data
Baehr, Theodore.
The culture-wise family / Ted Baehr, Pat Boone.
p. cm.
ISBN 0-8307-4305-7 (hardcover) — ISBN 0-8307-4355-3 (international trade paper)
1. Christianity and culture. 2. Mass media—Influence. 3. Mass media—Religious aspects—Christianity. I. Boone, Pat. II. Title.
BR115.C8B335 2007
261—dc22   2006034900

1 2 3 4 5 6 7 8 9 10 / 10 09 08 07

Rights for publishing this book in other languages are contracted by Gospel Light Worldwide, the international nonprofit ministry of Gospel Light. Gospel Light Worldwide also provides publishing and technical assistance to international publishers dedicated to producing Sunday School and Vacation Bible School curricula and books in the languages of the world. For additional information, visit www.gospellightworldwide.org; write to Gospel Light Worldwide, P.O. Box 3875, Ventura, CA 93006; or send an e-mail to info@gospellightworldwide.org.

No, in all these things we are more than conquerors through him who loved us. For I am convinced that neither death nor life, neither angels nor demons, neither the present nor the future, nor any powers, neither height nor depth, nor anything else in all creation, will be able to separate us from the love of God that is in Christ Jesus our Lord.

ROMANS 8:37-39, *TNIV*

For though we walk in the flesh, we do not war after the flesh: (for the weapons of our warfare are not carnal, but mighty through God to the pulling down of strong holds;) casting down imaginations, and every high thing that exalteth itself against the knowledge of God, and bringing into captivity every thought to the obedience of Christ.

2 CORINTHIANS 10:3-5, *KJV*

Finally, brothers, whatever is true, whatever is noble, whatever is right, whatever is pure, whatever is lovely, whatever is admirable—if anything is excellent or praiseworthy—think about such things.

PHILIPPIANS 4:8

Among you there must not be even a hint of sexual immorality, or of any kind of impurity, or of greed, because these are improper for God's holy people. Nor should there be obscenity, foolish talk or coarse joking, which are out of place, but rather thanksgiving. For of this you can be sure: No immoral, impure or greedy person—such a man is an idolater—has any inheritance in the kingdom of Christ and of God.

EPHESIANS 5:1-5

Those who are wise will shine as bright as the sky, and those who turn many to righteousness will shine like stars forever.

DANIEL 12:3, *NLT*

Do not conform any longer to the pattern of this world, but be transformed by the renewing of your mind. Then you will be able to test and approve what God's will is — his good, pleasing and perfect will.

ROMANS 12:2

The Spirit of the LORD will rest on him—the Spirit of wisdom and of understanding, the Spirit of counsel and of power, the Spirit of knowledge and of the fear of the LORD and he will delight in the fear of the LORD. He will not judge by what he sees with his eyes, or decide by what he hears with his ears.

ISAIAH 11:2-3

This book is joyfully dedicated to:

Jesus, our Lord and Savior;
Lili, my beautiful wife;
Peirce, James, Robert and Evelyn, my wonderful children.

—Ted Baehr

Our loving God, who has led me all the way;
my dear wife, Shirley;
and our incredible brood:
Cherry, Lindy, Debby, Laury and our 15 grandchildren.

—Pat Boone

Father Almighty,

*Thank You for Your magnificent Creation.
Thank You for reigning over all things. Thank You for redeeming us
and bringing us into Your kingdom through the shed blood
of Your Son, Jesus the Christ. Thank You for civilization, culture,
entertainment, joy and imagination.*

*Please bless all who read this book. Please guide our words
and open our ears. Please grant us, as Your people, the wisdom to
liberate our culture, family and friends from the bondage to the lust of
the eyes, the lust of the flesh and the pride of life and so to take every
thought captive for Jesus Christ in whom there is perfect freedom.
Please give us the discernment, courage and wisdom to choose the
good in our culture and to reject and rebuke the bad.*

*Please help us communicate this discernment to our friends
and our families. Help us most of all to lift up Your Holy Name,
Jesus, through the power of Your Holy Spirit.
Thank You for the blessings You have bestowed upon us.
Amen.*

CONTENTS

PART IV
Values, Principles and Worldviews

PART V
How to Develop Discernment

PART VI
Understanding the Answers

Some Thoughts on a Culture-Wise Family

Janet Parshall, National Radio Host

The Culture-Wise Family is the clear, concise, comprehensive guide to becoming more than overcomers in the midst of an increasingly toxic culture. While most books focus on the almost apocalyptic problems facing believers in a neo-pagan society and the secular news theology and fear mantra "If it bleeds, it leads," *The Culture-Wise Family* helps concerned readers understand the problems and develop discernment and wisdom. This wisdom allows them to become more than overcomers who are not only able to live their faith and values within the neo-pagan world without being corrupted by it but also able to lead others out of the darkness into the light and truth of the gospel of Jesus Christ and thereby to help Him transform the culture into a vibrant civilization.

We live in the best of times of abundance and liberty, and the worst of times of gluttony and license. *The Culture-Wise Family* looks into the abysmal future possibilities of where the current collapse of civilization may lead and also into the hope offered by renewed rededication to biblical wisdom, knowledge and understanding. Furthermore, *The Culture-Wise Family* helps the reader understand what must be done, why it must be done and how it can be done. This understanding will stem the tide of toxic culture, redeem the time, and transform not only our lives but also the lives of our families and friends.

As Ted Baehr notes, the biblical pattern of civilizations informs us that prosperity often precedes judgment. Although God says that He wants to prosper us, He does so when we follow the pattern outlined in the Bible to love our neighbor as ourselves—the homeless, the orphans, the weak, the defenseless and the needy—and remember to love God instead of following after the false gods of our selfish desires. Those familiar with the Word of God know that the end of the story of history is great news, but in the meantime, we face trials and tribulations as our civilization ebbs and revival flows to new areas of the globe.

Many people of faith and values are deeply troubled by the collapse of civility. They bemoan the problem and see their children being lost to the world, the flesh and the devil; yet they have no idea how to protect the eyes and ears of innocence and to help their children to be more than overcomers.

Building on the proven principles presented in the *Media-Wise Family*™ book, tapes and videos, *The Culture-Wise Family* helps the reader understand from a biblical perspective the social ills we face and how to be media-wise in the midst of the conflicting and often toxic messages from the mass media of entertainment and contemporary culture. It looks beyond the so-called culture wars to help readers acquire the skills to recognize and decipher what is being communicated to them. It is a helpful book that every parent, teacher and person of faith and values will want to read and reread.

Extensive research indicates that most Christians and conservatives have the same media diet as other demographic groups, including non-Christians, though many conservatives and Christians consistently complain about the entertainment media. In the past, Western civilization, otherwise known as Christendom, promoted civilization by encouraging salvation for the lost, promoting love and truth, healing the sick, feeding the hungry, clothing the poor, and creating art to worship a just and loving Creator. Now, our culture is shaped by the mass media of entertainment in many ways that are destructive to those same ideas.

The Culture-Wise Family will help Christians understand the clash of worldviews, the influence of the entertainment industry, and how to develop media wisdom.

This is more than just another book about the media and the culture. This study will help turn you and your children's hearts away from the negative and addictive influences that are bombarding you and will bend your hearts toward God and family.

You will learn step by step how to teach your children to develop discernment and understanding about the culture and the media of entertainment and communication. Such learning will enable your children to use and enjoy entertainment media without succumbing to the vain imaginings and temptations of the media mind-set.

The approach in *The Culture-Wise Family* has been tested on children and parents for more than three decades, and more than 90 percent of those who have been taught this method of discernment have found it effective.

Our families, especially our youth, are being corrupted and destroyed by the powerful influences of the mass media. Even our churches have been unable to give their members, especially their youth, help in dealing with the emotive images and idols of our entertainment culture. In fact, many churches are clueless about the extent of the problem in their congregations, while other churches have opted for an anything-goes approach. As a result, children suffer, and parents are confused and often clueless as to how to deal with the problem.

Like most books that have addressed the problem, many leaders have no solution except for parents to rearrange the furniture in their houses, or play Scrabble with their children rather than watch TV. These are fine ideas, but they do not offer a comprehensive solution.

This book will clearly set forth the practical tools needed to teach children discernment. While other books have presented the problem eloquently, *The Culture-Wise Family* differs because it presents the solution in a comprehensive, intelligible way to help your children learn to use the media for entertainment, information and even education—without being conformed and addicted to it.

As one friend noted when he came to faith in Jesus Christ, "God gave me back my mind." God wants us to think clearly, so He tells us in His Word to develop discernment, get wisdom, and acquire knowledge. This book will do just that by giving the reader the media awareness and biblical discernment skills to overcome the powerful influences and artificial peer pressure of the entertainment media.

The Culture-Wise Family presents clear, concise teachings and conversational insights into the mass media of entertainment and the contemporary culture. Therefore, I am happy to commend to you this book: *The Culture-Wise Family*.

PART I

THE INFLUENCE OF THE CULTURE AND THE MASS MEDIA OF ENTERTAINMENT

CHAPTER 1

We Are Not in Kansas
or Kiev Anymore

When I am in my office, I am about 45 miles west of the heart of the entertainment industry in Hollywood, California. The drive takes an hour . . . or two or three, if there's traffic.

Increasingly, I am called to speak around the world in far away places such as Poland, India, Japan or the border of Laos. When I step on the plane, I find Hollywood movies and television programs. When I go into the jungle of the highlands of Thailand, I find satellite dishes run by generators connected by exposed wires that bring Hollywood entertainment into the flimsy grass huts. The children in these villages try to dress like the Hollywood stars they idolize and try to mimic their lives—right down to the smoking, drinking and sexual promiscuity.

Hollywood is not a geographic place anymore, but an entertainment industry that reaches the world. It is the United States of America's voice to people everywhere, especially the youth. As Jesus told the leading spokespeople of His day, "It's not what goes into the mouth that defiles a man, but what comes out of the mouth, this defiles a man" (Matt. 15:11, *CSB*). All too often, what comes out of the mouth of our entertainment-oriented culture are movies such as *Kill Bill* and *Saw 3*.

When I drive to Hollywood to preview a movie at a screening, I visit studio executives to help them understand the influence that they are having on the children and grandchildren of the United States and the world. The good news is that many of them are listening. The type of entertainment being produced is gradually moving away from salacious, ultra-violent R-rated movies to family films with faith—movies such as *The Nativity Story; Charlotte's Web; The Lion, the Witch and the Wardrobe* and *The Pursuit of Happyness*. Even Rocky Balboa has found faith in Jesus Christ. Now, every studio is pursuing the Christian faith-based audience.

But even so, there remains a large residue of movies with rotten values in the bloodstream of the culture, and a significant number of rotten movies and television programs are still being produced. So while so much contributes to establishing society's mores, Hollywood no doubt has a secure foothold as the epicenter of what is popular and what is not. Clearly, what happens in Hollywood does not stay in Hollywood. What Lindsay Lohan wears, Justin Timberlake sings and George Clooney articulates will ripple its way not only to the heartland of America but well beyond. Indeed, the culture clash thrives from Kansas to Kiev.

Ready to Collide

Sometimes, the influence of the mass media of entertainment on far away places helps us to reflect on our own problems and vulnerabilities as well as our influence on the culture of the world. Recently, I spoke in Kiev, a city in the Ukraine that's emerging from totalitarian suppression. The pastor of the church where I preached told me that his father had been tortured for his outspoken faith in Jesus Christ in the very hotel where I was staying. Now this pastor has a megachurch of over 1,000 and a growing group of almost 200 churches. The mayor of Kiev is his Spirit-filled Christian friend. The president, whose wife is from America, is a thoughtful Christian. Business is booming.

Yet on the other hand, the Ukraine has the highest rate of AIDS/HIV, prostitutes and women sold into white slavery in Europe, and at night the streets are filled with empty alcohol bottles. In 1994, there were only 183 registered cases of HIV, but by 2004 that number had grown to more than 68,000.[1] "[The] Ukraine . . . has replaced Thailand and the Philippines as the epicenter of the global business in trafficking women," an article from the *New York Times* noted.[2] While sin was no stranger when communism reigned in the Ukraine, one cannot help but notice how consumerism has adversely affected the nation's youth.

So it is the best of times and the worst of times for the people of Kiev. They asked me to teach them media wisdom to navigate the treacherous rapids of the changing culture—a culture that seems to be at war with itself. The communist oppressor of the East has left in disgrace and the materialistic pornography of Hollywood has blatantly and seductively taken its place. Two great rivers of conflicting cultural values have converged into a raging torrent of cultural confusion. A churning flood threatens to sweep aside a bright future for the precious next generation.

How do people navigate the cultural rapids? In Japan, a home-school conference has grown phenomenally in the past few years as families consider taking their children out of schools where materialism is so rapacious that young girls are selling themselves to buy iPods. These Japanese flocked to listen to my talks on cultural wisdom in search of guidance.

What is happening, why is it happening, and how do the messages of the mass media of entertainment influence us, our children, each society and the world as a whole? Is there any hope? Can we navigate a safe passage to reach the still waters and green pastures of Christ's kingdom?

The Decline of Nations

Observant pundits on all sides of the political spectrum have correctly noted a steady decline in the last century in the quality of culture. There has been a weakening of faith, an abandonment of values and an eroding of civility in our culture. The work of shaping our culture requires God's wisdom to use the right tools so that He will be glorified.

In their DVD *The Decline of Nations*, Dr. Ken Boa and Bill Ibsen point out three symptoms of decline: (1) *social decay*—the crisis of lawlessness, the loss of economic discipline and, finally, growing bureaucracy; (2) *cultural decay*—the decline of education, the weakening of cultural foundations, the increasing loss of respect for tradition, and the increase in materialism; and (3) *moral decay*—the rise in immorality, the decay of religious belief and the devaluation of human life.

Dr. Ken Boa and Bill Ibsen state that "symptoms of decline synergistically rot a nation from the inside out, making it vulnerable to attack from a variety of enemies." Then they ask the critical question: What objective measures of social and cultural health can be used to determine how America is doing? To answer this question, they cite a report published in 1993 by William J. Bennett, the former U.S. Secretary of Education, who notes that between the 1960s and the 1990s there was:

- A 966 percent increase in the rate of cohabitation
- A 523 percent increase in out-of-wedlock births
- A 370 percent increase in violent crime
- A 270 percent increase in children on welfare
- A 215 percent increase in single-parent families
- A 210 percent increase in teenage suicide
- A 200 percent increase in the crime rate
- A 130 percent increase in the divorce rate
- A 75 point decrease in the average SAT score

"Improvements were made in the violent crime rate, welfare and teenage suicide in the 1990s," Boa and Ibsen state. "However, the breakdown of the family remains of particular concern. Indicators point to nurturing relationships as a key factor to maintaining a stable society, while mass media entertainment often fills the voids left by family breakdown."[3]

Such a Time as This

All too often, the prosperity of God flows into fruitless endeavors as succeeding generations begin to disregard the root of their wealth. America's ancestors planted the seed of God's blessing and left a rich inheritance in this land. But God has no grandchildren. He has only first-generation descendents who yield to His Spirit, live in His grace and enter His kingdom. If those children become selfish, indolent or corrupt, they eventually stew in their own sin. As God warned the Israelites:

> Be careful that you don't forget the LORD your God by failing to keep His command—the ordinances and statutes—I am giving you today. When you eat and are full, and build beautiful houses to live in, and your herds and flocks grow large, and

your silver and gold multiply, and everything else you have increases, [be careful] that your heart doesn't become proud and you forget the LORD your God who brought you out of the land of Egypt, out of the place of slavery (Deut. 8:7-18, *CSB*).

It is true that God's kingdom will never end and that it is advancing into the far reaches of the world. But many cultures that once embraced the values of Christianity have turned away from the Word of God as the cornerstone of their civilization. When this happens—when people forget to love God and follow after the false gods of selfish desire—they fall from His blessing. Those familiar with the Word of God know that at the end of human history there is great news. In the meantime, we will face trials and tribulations as Christian civilization ebbs and flows to all areas of the globe.

Yet in the midst of such cultural collapse, it is important to remember that God has called His people to go on His adventure into the entire world. He has called them to preach the good news that will redirect the tidal wave of conflicting cultures. His people constitute His Body, the Church, which has braved paganism and persecution to build hospitals, schools, orphanages and loving homes that have civilized societies. The Church is here for such a time as this.

In the Ukraine, the church where I preached conducts street ministries to reach the unsaved, youth ministries to rescue the rebellious, and schools to lead the children out of darkness. Other ministries at the church reach orphans and vagrants and bring the good news to performing artists. This is the grand old story of Christian faith. In the midst of cacophony, the people of God proclaim good news and restore lost souls. Where the gospel takes root, faith and peace replace animosity. Where God's grace is lifted up, war-torn lands become green pastures where children and families can flourish.

To quote from a paper titled "Ethics in Communications" from the Pontifical Council for Social Communications, "Viewed in the light of faith, the history of human communication can be seen as a long journey from Babel, site and symbol of communication's collapse (cf. Gen. 11:4-8), to Pentecost and the gift of tongues (cf. Acts 2:5-11)—communication restored by the power of the Spirit sent by the Son. Sent forth into the world to announce the good news (cf. Mt 28:19-20; Mk 16:15), the Church has the mission of proclaiming the Gospel until the end of time. Today, she knows, that requires using media."[4]

Enough Already!

For the last few days, my e-mail box has been deluged by reviews from so-called evangelical Christian sources touting a New Age occult movie called *Conversations with God*. This movie was produced and directed by a man named Stephen Simon, who is a relentless proponent of New Age movies through his organization called the Spiritual Cinema Circle. What is strange is that this movie (to which *Movieguide*® gave only one star and a minus four) has received much praise from the reviewers of other evangelical movie sites. These reviews raise the question: Has the Evangelical Church gone the way of God's frozen chosen mainline denominations?

When I was in a mainline seminary in New York in the mid 1970s, the ecumenical Thursday night service was led by Hilda the White Witch, who was introduced by the bishop of New York. The Indian faker Sri Chinmoy, who claimed to be able to levitate, gave the Easter service, and the Lucifer Trust established their headquarters at the cathedral of St. John the Divine.

Most of the frozen chosen were oblivious to this occult takeover of the mainline churches. Those with a modicum of faith came to realize 25 years later (and too late) that these denominations were dead. They began to start splinter groups, which are now reviving the biblical faith.

The sea of e-mails I receive touting Luciferian movies such as *Conversations with God* is a heartbreaking déjà vu indicating that the Evangelical Church is turning into the Church of "do what you want" of Aleister Crowley. Like Telemachus, all we can say is, "Stop! And, wake up to the Good News and to the deliverance that only comes through Jesus Christ and His holy Word written."

What Can We Do?

One of the primary building blocks of the culture, the mass media, is a tool of communication, entertainment and art. Although anyone may

Good News, Bad News

Pat Boone

Lately, I've spouted off about things that concern me in the shifting, changing makeup of our culture. Countless other Americans share my concerns, and they've let me know so by a heavy volume of e-mail response.

Well, today I want to share some really good news. It's news you probably won't come across anywhere else, though it's readily available. That tribal rite, the Academy Awards, is approaching at warp speed, and we will not be able to avoid it, no matter how we might try. (You could be snowed in up in the Rockies with no phone or TV and some passing mountaineer will tap on your door to tell you who won for best actress or best film!)

Seriously, many of us have lost interest in the whole thing because we may not like *any* of the nominated films or people's performances. We really cringe when we see films and people fawned over and awarded Oscars. It troubles us greatly. I'm a guy who has actually made a few films and was in the Box Office Top Ten for about 10 minutes years ago. But that was back when families went to the movies together virtually every week, confident that nobody would need to sink down in the seat in embarrassment. We did not expect people to get up and walk out en masse.

I did that once. We had gone together to see a very popular musical film, *Paint Your Wagon*. It had been a celebrated Broadway smash with terrific music, and the movie version starred Clint Eastwood in a singing role! It was at the Cinerama Dome, a posh downtown theater in Hollywood. What could have been more ideal for a family outing?

But as the picture rolled along with its giant production, huge cast and all the "good stuff," I realized that the story was about a struggling frontier town whose city fathers decided that the cowboys needed feminine companionship, so they built a whorehouse and imported a lot of "ladies" to stock it! When a big musical number centered on all the girls coming in by stagecoach and all the rugged wranglers salivating to get at them, I gathered my flock, and we left.

That was years before *Best Little Whorehouse in Texas*, which astoundingly has been accepted, awarded and replayed for more than a decade. Such films are one of our increasingly standard exports to the rest of the world. But I promised you *good* news, didn't I? Well, every year the Christian Film and Television Commission (CFTC) does extensive research on the films released that year and compiles authoritative data on what works at the box office regarding paying moviegoers. And guess what? Eighty percent of the 10 most popular movies in 2005 had strong or very strong moral content and acceptability ratings. In addition, only 1 of the top 10 movies—and only 3 of the top 25—were rated R by the Motion Picture Association. Isn't that a nice surprise?

In addition, the CFTC found that movies with no or very few incidents of nudity, foul language and violence earned an average of *$45,001,733 per movie—65 percent more* than movies that contained those elements! Movies with the CFTC's low acceptability ratings earned only $27 million and change on average.

Wouldn't you think, then—doesn't it just make common sense— that anybody who wants to invest millions making a movie would want to make a profit? And that the proven best, surest way to do that is to produce something the whole family might want to buy tickets to see? Not Hollywood. At least, not the majority of the movers and shakers— the moguls who line up to get the Oscars and accolades from their peers.

That's the *bad* news. Typically, the majority of the Oscars' attention and praise are reserved for a procession of depressing, controversial, objectionable and downright decadent flicks, such as 2005's *Brokeback Mountain*, a quaint tale of two homosexual cowboys. Imagine America's families flocking to see that one!

There goes the Western—the dramatic stories in which lonely heroes fight desperate but victorious battles, the good guys always win, and the desperadoes always get what they deserve. Now, it's been dealt a possibly fatal wound.

I cringed when Clint Eastwood, the quintessential Western hero, had to give the Golden Globe for best director to Ang Lee for *Brokeback Mountain*. And I saw my friend Denzel Washington cringe as he announced that the Golden Globe for Best Film went to the same sorry tale. I probably couldn't repeat, or in this space print, what John Wayne would have to say about this. But you and I—and our fellow citizens—can have the last word about all this.

We can be encouraged by the *good news* offered by the CFTC and buy tickets to family-friendly films that some of the brave and admirable souls in Hollywood are still daring to make. We can boycott, by our absence and lack of interest, all the shameful schlock that morally challenged producers and exhibitors still think they can foist on us.

So let's hand them back their *bad news*, without profit or interest. That's the only way they'll ever get the message.

misuse a tool, most people involved in the mass media as creators, regulators and consumers are conscientious individuals who want to do the right thing, as they understand it. However, those who make up these groups often forget that their mass media choices have ethical weight and are subject to moral evaluation. Therefore, to make the right choices, they need to develop discernment and understanding.

Even many of the most astute Christians have become desensitized to cultural degradation. Many do not understand the consequences of different worldviews. They are ignorant of the persuasive power of the mass media of entertainment and do not know how to develop the discernment, knowledge, understanding and wisdom to be more than conquerors within the cultural turbulence. The good news is that there are effective ways for us and our families to learn how to be culture-wise and media-wise.

Pillars of Media Wisdom

As the director of the TV Center at City University of New York, I helped develop some of the first media literacy courses in the late 1970s. Since then, years of research have produced a very clear understanding of the best way to teach media literacy. Specifically, there are five pillars of media wisdom that will help build the culture-wise family.

1. **Pillar 1: Understand the influence of the media on your children.** In the wake of the Columbine High School massacre, CBS president Leslie Moonves put it quite bluntly: "Anyone who thinks the media has nothing to do with this is an idiot."[5] The major medical associations have concluded that there is absolutely no doubt that those who are heavy viewers of violence demonstrate increased acceptance of aggressive attitudes and aggressive behavior. Of course, media is only one part of the problem—a problem that could be summed up with the sage biblical injunction, "Do not be misled: 'Bad company corrupts good character'" (1 Cor. 15:33). As the results of thousands of studies on youth violence prove, watching media violence causes violence among children. Bad company corrupts good character—whether that bad company is gangs, peer pressure or violent television programs.

2. **Pillar 2: Ascertain your children's susceptibility at each stage of cognitive development.** Not only do children see the media differently at each stage of development, but also different children are susceptible to different stimuli. As the research of the National Institute of Mental Health revealed many years ago, some children want to copy media violence, some are susceptible to other media influences, some become afraid, and many become desensitized. Just as an alcoholic would be inordinately tempted by a beer commercial, so certain types of media may tempt or influence your child at his or her specific stage of development.

3. **Pillar 3: Teach your children how the media communicates its message.** Just as children spend the first 14 years of their lives learning grammar with respect to the written word, they also need to be taught the grammar of twenty-first-century mass media so that they can think critically about the messages being programmed for them.

4. **Pillar 4: Help your children know the fundamentals of Christian faith.** Children need to be taught the fundamentals of Christian faith so that they can apply their beliefs and moral values to the culture and to the mass media of entertainment. Of course, parents typically have an easier time than teachers with this pillar because they can freely discuss their personal beliefs. Yet even so, it is interesting to note that cultural and media literacy and values education are two of the fastest growing areas in the academic community—a trend most likely due to the fact that educators are beginning to realize that something is amiss.

5. **Pillar 5: Help your children learn how to ask the right questions.** When children know the right questions to ask, they can arrive at the right answers to the problems presented by the mass media of entertainment. For instance, if the hero in the movie your child is watching wins by murdering and mutilating his victims, will your children be able to question this hero's behavior, no matter how likable that character may be?

Educating the Heart

Theodore Roosevelt said that if we educate a man's mind but not his heart, we have an educated barbarian. Cultural and media wisdom involves educating the heart so that it will make the right decisions. So, how can you protect the eyes of innocence of your children and grandchildren? How can you redeem the culture?

In the following chapters, we will attempt to answer this question (and others) and lay the foundation for developing the wisdom necessary for you to become more than conquerors over the toxic influences of the culture and the mass media of entertainment. We will unravel the debate about popular entertainment so that you can help your family and others become culture-wise. We will examine the tools you need to use to exercise discernment and make wise choices. We will help you ask the right questions to understand that moral movies, television and entertainment focus on honor, truth, loyalty and valor. We will also help you understand the nature of the fantasy and myth genres and the various critical tools necessary to develop an informed judgment about all art and entertainment. Considering the influence that the mass media of entertainment has on our culture, we believe that this book will be an extremely important and helpful tool for you, your family and even your church.

The truth of the secure hope available only in Jesus Christ is great news that needs to be shouted from the housetops. The people of God have a wonderful opportunity to manifest His grace. However, we first need to ascertain the state of cultural affairs. The work of shaping our culture requires God's wisdom to use the right tools so that He will be glorified.

CHAPTER 2

Dare to Care

In ancient times, segments of society established their culture by customs and rituals, ethics and laws, values and institutions, language and other influences that constituted the characteristics of their society. Today, all of these elements are shaped to some degree by messages received through the mass media. In turn, our attitudes, ideals and beliefs are influenced by the culture. To update John Locke's profound insight that whoever defines the word defines the world, we say that whoever controls the media controls the culture.

Most people are caught in an intricate web that touches every aspect of their material world. It is woven of influences beyond their control, including the mass media. Above this web is God's Holy Spirit, who frees them from detrimental entanglement in every area of life. Those who have been born again see God's providence at work. Those who do not have eyes to see are subjected to the influences of the world—a world where the mass media of entertainment spins reality to conform to its preconceptions, values and desires.

Poll after poll shows that although people are concerned about the influence the culture is having on their families, they do not know how to develop the discernment, understanding and wisdom to be more than conquerors within this culture. Like the proverbial frog in the kettle, people are accepting an increasingly overheated toxic culture being brought to a boil by the mass media of entertainment.[1]

Forbidden Ideas

Once upon a time, our grandparents taught children that they could talk about anything at the dinner table except religion, sex and politics. These were topics that aroused deeply felt personal opinions. These days, however, it seems that discussions about sexual preferences and perversions or false religious notions hardly raise an eyebrow at the dinner table—or anywhere else, for that matter. What truly get people embroiled in discussion nowadays are subjects such as one's favorite song, movie or television program!

Perhaps this heightened sense of importance about entertainment and the desire to defend one's position on a particular movie, song or TV program is laudable to a degree, because it shows that people understand the power of movies, television and other mass media of entertainment. As the great bard William Shakespeare noted, "The pen is mightier than the sword." Fast forward 500 years and we see that the twenty-first-century mass media of entertainment is mightier than the sixteenth-century printed word.

It is therefore not surprising that the level of heated discussion (particularly in the Christian and conservative community) increased tremendously with the release of *The Last Temptation of Christ*, continued with the first Harry Potter movie, intensified with the release of the first episode of *The Lord of the Rings* trilogy and *The Passion of the Christ*, and then came to a boil with the release of *The Da Vinci Code*.

Should Christians Be Concerned?

To help understand the worldview issues and the influence of the media on our culture, consider the following case study of J. K. Rowling's Harry Potter series, first released in 1997.

Much of the debate about the books and movies in the Harry Potter series has centered on the issue of witchcraft. One side cringed at the thought that millions of young children would be tempted to become witches and warlocks, while the other dismissed those concerns as an archaic inquisitorial attitude. In this regard, it would be wise to apply C. S. Lewis's dictum that people can make two mistakes about the devil: (1) taking him too seriously, or (2) not taking him seriously enough. One of these extremes ignores the supernatural world while the other undervalues the victory of Jesus Christ on the cross over the devil and his demons.

We can understand why people whose worldviews are not rooted in the Bible would scoff at any concerns about witchcraft, as they do not know God's teachings on this subject. However, for Christians to scoff at these concerns is a bit more troubling, for God clearly condemns witchcraft in His Word. In Deuteronomy 18:10 we read, "There shall not be found among you *anyone* who . . . uses divination, one who practices witchcraft" (*NASB*). In 1 Samuel 15:23, we read, "For rebellion is as the sin of witchcraft" (*NKJV*).

Some Christians reject other Christians' concerns about the witchcraft in the Harry Potter films on the basis that the biblical prohibition to witchcraft and sorcery only applied to the ancient Jews in the Old Testament. But in fact, God's abhorrence and condemnation of witchcraft extends throughout the Bible. It includes the condemnation of Simon the Magician by the apostles in the book of Acts and culminates in the clear words of John in Revelation 21:8: "But the fearful, and unbelieving, and the abominable, and murderers, and whoremongers, and sorcerers, and idolaters, and all liars, shall have their part in the lake which burneth with fire and brimstone: which is the second death" (*KJV*). In Revelation 22:15, John also adds, "For without *are* dogs, and sorcerers, and whoremongers, and murderers, and idolaters, and whosoever loveth and maketh a lie" (*KJV*).

Hermeneutics Who?

One of the problems with the application of these verses today is a hermeneutic (interpretive) problem, or the lack of theological understanding about how to read Scripture. The key is to reclaim those analytical tools with which the Church was familiar for centuries. The reader needs to let the text speak for itself (*exegesis*), rather than reading his or her opinions into the text (*eisogesis*). The text should be read in context, and Scripture should be used to interpret Scripture. Furthermore, the application of a biblical principle or the analysis of an issue must proceed from Scripture. A biblical principle must act on informed reason—not the other way around. Too often in today's world, people take a desired action, make it a new tradition and assume some justification will make it acceptable.

In our postmodern age, we may need to reflect on this analytical approach in order to comprehend its value. Theology is the knowledge of God. His Word calls us to know Him so that we can make Him known. Therefore, every Christian needs to be a theologian to some degree. This happens by acquiring and developing the mental tools needed to know God and His will for our lives. This should be the goal of each of us who loves God and believes He will ultimately reward us. It is important to keep in mind that we are saved by grace and that the good news of Jesus Christ redeems us in the midst of our insufficiency.

Ontology: The Ground of Being
During the height of these debates over Harry Potter, I went to tea with a Malaysian woman who attended an evangelical Christian school. Having been raised in an area where Christianity and Hinduism compete for the attention of the people, this wonderful Malaysian lady came to an understanding of the difference between movies such as *Harry Potter* and *The Lord of the Rings* after a brief explanation of ontology.

Ontology is simply "the ground of being." It is the very essence or nature of the world in which we live. For Hindus and many occultists, the world in which we live is an imaginary one, an illusion. For Marxists, we live in a materialistic world. For Christians, we believe in a supernatural (unseen) world and also live in the physical (seen) world that has both real suffering and a real Savior.

Harry Potter's world can be manipulated through magic, as nothing is real. For a Christian, however, things are real. If you fall off a cliff—you die. Thus, actions have consequences.

What Difference Does It Make?
This makes a world of difference. Mother Teresa saw the poor and dying on the streets of Calcutta as real people, so she started taking people off the streets and caring for them. Some Hindus, however, saw them as just *Maya*—the World of Illusion—and were deeply offended when she took them in. To materialists, the poor and dying are fodder and should just be left to die.

The Creator, who made both what is seen and what is unseen, sent Christ into the world to rescue the poor and dying and give them new life. He is ready to redeem, rescue and restore people through the gospel of Jesus Christ. In a Christian world, life has meaning. It is not just conflicting ideologies; it is a matter of eternal consequence. Those who believe in Christ have hope because of His sacrificial death, atonement and resurrection as their Lord.

One of the reasons these arguments are raging is that much of the Church has become lukewarm about biblical truth and has drifted toward an eclectic adaptation of all sorts of doctrines. It has gone away from a solid understanding of hermeneutics, biblical ontology and a distinctive Christian worldview. This has led Christians to reject the deity of Christ and the atonement and the Trinity. The battle for souls and the battle between good and evil is really a battle for biblical truth.

Even those who deny the Bible is God's inerrant word, or who proclaim the Bible isn't true, are proclaiming a particular worldview and theology about the Bible, its truth and its applicability to the affairs of man. Ultimately, there is no real neutrality concerning God, the Bible, truth, Jesus Christ, the nature of being (or ontology), good and evil, and so forth. We are all responsible for the worldviews and attitudes we take. In effect, we are faced with three questions: (1) *How should we decide what to believe?* (2) *By what authority should we believe?* (3) *By what standard should we believe?*

As Paul tells Timothy in 2 Timothy 3:10-17, the Bible is a wonderful authority and a great standard that, when read and studied, can point us toward right thinking and thoroughly equip us for every good work. The Bible convinces us and convicts us. As such, it shows us beyond a shadow of a doubt that it is far better to be like Mother Teresa than a Hindu worshiping cows or an aborigine cowering in fear of offending some spirit or demon. That is the ground of difference between the Christian and the non-Christian.

Teens and Witchcraft

A study by the Barna Research Group, entitled "Harry Potter's Influence Goes Unchallenged in Most Homes and Churches" and released on May 1, 2006, showed that the same number of teenagers reared in a culture saturated with media and charmed by Harry Potter who say they believe in God have also indulged in witchcraft and psychic phenomena. The article pointed out that very few churches help their children understand why witchcraft and psychic phenomena are wrong. The study went on to report:

> Three quarters of all church-going teens (77%) and born again Christian teenagers (78%) have seen or read Potter. Despite widespread exposure to the Potter story, few teens—just 4%—say they have experienced any teaching or discussions in a church about the spiritual themes embedded in the wizard-in-training legend. Among born again teens, a minority (13%) recalls ever receiving any input from their church on the subject or spiritual themes of Harry Potter. One out of every eight teenagers (12%) said that the Potter chronicles increased their interest in witchcraft. That translates to nearly three million young people whose interest has been piqued.[2]

According to another 2006 study by the Barna Research Group, entitled "Teenagers and the Supernatural," most American teenagers aged 13 to 18 (71 percent) say they embrace the orthodox Christian view of God as the all-powerful, all-knowing and perfect Creator of the world, but 73 percent also say they have engaged in psychic or occult phenomena, including witchcraft. Here are some of the findings from the study:

Category	Percent of Teens
Believe in angels	89%
Believe in Life After Death	82%
Believe in an All-Powerful, All-Knowing, Perfect God	71%
Heaven is real	61%
Satan is a real enemy of God	58%
Have read a horoscope	80%
Have engaged in at least one type of psychic/occult activity	73%
Have encountered an angel, demon or other supernatural being	35%
Have used a Ouija board	33%
Have read a book about Wicca or witchcraft	33%
Have had my fortune told	27%

Have played a sorcery or witchcraft game	25%
Have participated in a séance	10%
Have communicated with a dead person	10%
Have visited a medium or spiritual guide	9%
Have consulted a psychic	9%
Have tried to cast a spell or mix a potion[3]	8%

Without a Plumb Line

In our culture, awash as it is in multiculturalism, tolerance and diversity, the story of the Witch of Endor in 1 Samuel 28 is very puzzling. What's wrong with Saul wanting to know the outcome of the upcoming battle? Why not go to a medium who claims to have a connection to the other side? How *dare* God disapprove of Saul consulting a witch and condemn him to die in battle, losing his kingdom in the process! Why would God get upset by a little thing such as conjuring up spirits? Why does God say throughout the Bible that He hates sorcery and witchcraft?

The answer can be clearly illustrated in *The Lion, the Witch and the Wardrobe*, the second book in C. S. Lewis's Chronicles of Narnia series. In this book, it is clear that God has already appointed the four children in the story—Peter, Susan, Edmund and Lucy Pevensie—to be the kings and queens of Narnia. But the devil, in the form of the White Witch, offers Edmund the chance to be a prince of Narnia—just as the serpent in the Garden of Eden offered Adam and Eve a chance to be like God (which, having been created in His image, they already were). Adam and Eve chose to listen to the serpent rather than trust in what God had said to them.

Rather than trusting in God, Saul chose to look elsewhere for confirmation of his victory over the Philistines. In so doing, he denied God's authority. He, like Adam and Eve, wanted to be like God by knowing the future and the outcome of his own endeavors. The interesting thing is that Samuel had already told Saul what would happen and what God had ordained concerning the outcome. But Saul did not trust God, and he opened himself to demonic deception by consulting the witch of Endor.

Christians who grow up in church often underestimate the power of the supernatural world and don't realize the very real spiritual danger they expose themselves to in these kinds of situations. Growing up in a pagan home, however, gives you a different perspective. My parents were actors who consistently indulged in mind control and séances to not only know the future but also to control it and others surreptitiously. It was a constant battle for them to play God, but it was full of disappointment, frustration and failure, because ultimately only God is God.

At the ripe old age of 28, I found the truth of the gospel—that God wanted to adopt me into His kingdom through the shed blood of His only begotten Son, Jesus Christ. I discovered that I could have a peace that passes understanding by letting God be God and becoming His servant. When I understood these truths, the horrors of witchcraft became all too clear. Witchcraft, in its self-serving perspective, denies the love, the authority and the power of God.

Witchcraft involves always wanting but never achieving. Those who practice it are constantly looking for what they can gain. Letting God be God gives us an immeasurable inheritance. It frees us from lust and want and allows us to be able to truly love, freely give and be open to sharing.

Churches and ministry leaders who deny the power of witchcraft and God's abhorrence of it could be condemning their teenagers to satanic deception, the influence of demonic spirits and the risk of eternal alienation from God. As Jesus tells us, "If anyone causes one of these little ones who believe in me to sin, it would be better for him to have a large millstone hung around his neck and to be drowned in the depths of the sea" (Matt. 18:6).

Caring Is the Only Daring

In these introductory chapters, we have laid a beginning foundation of hermeneutics, ontology and a biblical worldview. In future chapters, we will explore the psychological, sociological and political ramifications of the influence of the media of entertainment on our culture, and on the world at large.

Media, Malaise and Myopia
Pat Boone

You may have caught the Gallup poll on confidence in our nation's institutions. Most media outlets weren't eager to report that (1) Americans who rate their confidence in mainstream media as "quite a lot" hover around 30 percent; (2) the percentage that places confidence in Congress hovers near 20 percent; and (3) only HMOs and big business rated lower among institutions that solicit public confidence than Congress. (The highest rating of 73 percent honored the U.S. military—which won't be much reported, either.)[4]

Both the media and Congress earned this disgrace by ignoring things that need emphasis and emphasizing things that should be ignored. But there is hope. The Motion Picture Association of America originally gave *Facing the Giants* (a fine family film) the *R* rating for excessive content. As *Jaws* had received this rating due to violent content, the rating was considered appropriate due to *Facing the Giants'* Christian content. That should remind us that Hollywood foists secular lunacy on the public with a kind of missionary zeal. A popular outcry resulted in a correction. Fortunately, constituents of our democracy discerned that Christian values promote a healthy culture, while violence does not.

You'd think that the father of a highly publicized murder victim, speaking in Congress about what happened to his daughter, would be featured on all the "sensitive" shows, as well as in most legitimate news outlets, wouldn't you?

Not so. When Darrell Scott, father of Columbine High School shooting victim Rachel Scott, went before Congress, this very emotional moment went mostly unnoticed, both by Congress and by the mainstream media. Why? Because of *what the man said!* Yet it caused an underground buzz so great that it landed on TruthOrFiction.com: "Mr. Scott's testimony was so powerful that a lot of folks . . . doubt its authenticity. It is true, however. His remarks were before the Subcommittee on Crime of the House Judiciary Committee on May 27, 1999."[5]

I don't think that anyone who heard these words spoken will ever forget. They still echo through my personal e-mails over the years and touch deep nerves of those who subscribe to the priorities held by our Founding Fathers.

I defer further comment on the moral aspects of violence to Mr. Scott, father of Columbine High School shooting victim Rachel Scott. Here is Mr. Scott's authenticated testimony, as it was delivered to Congress in 1999:

> Since the dawn of creation there has been both good and evil in the hearts of men and women. We all contain the seeds of kindness or the seeds of violence. The death of my wonderful daughter, Rachel Joy Scott, and the deaths of that heroic teacher, and the other 11 children who died must not be in vain. Their blood cries out for answers.
>
> The first recorded act of violence was when Cain slew his brother Abel out in the field. The villain was not the club he used. Neither was it the NCA, the National Club Association. The true killer was Cain, and the reason for the murder could only be found in Cain's heart.
>
> In the days that followed the Columbine tragedy, I was amazed at how quickly fingers began to be pointed at groups such as the NRA. I am not a member of the NRA. I am not a hunter. I do not even own a gun. I am not here to represent or defend the NRA—because I don't believe that they are responsible for my daughter's death. Therefore, I do not believe that they need to be defended. If I believed they had anything to do with Rachel's murder, I would be their strongest opponent.
>
> I am here today to declare that Columbine was not just a tragedy—it was a spiritual event that should be forcing us to look at where the real blame lies! Much of the blame lies here in this room. Much of the blame lies behind the pointing fingers of the accusers, themselves.
>
> I wrote a poem just four nights ago that expresses my feelings best. This was written way before I knew I would be speaking here today:

Your laws ignore our deepest needs,
Your words are empty air.
You've stripped away our heritage,
You've outlawed simple prayer.
Now gunshots fill our classrooms,
And precious children die.
You seek for answers everywhere,
And ask the question "Why?"
You regulate restrictive laws,
Through legislative creed.
And yet you fail to understand,
That God is what we need!

Men and women are three-part beings. We all consist of body, soul and spirit. When we refuse to acknowledge a third part of our make-up, we create a void that allows evil, prejudice and hatred to rush in and wreak havoc. Spiritual presences were present within our educational systems for most of our nation's history. Many of our major colleges began as theological seminaries. This is a historical fact. What has happened to us as a nation? We have refused to honor God, and in so doing, we open the doors to hatred and violence. And when something as terrible as Columbine's tragedy occurs—politicians immediately look for a scapegoat such as the NRA. They immediately seek to pass more restrictive laws that contribute to eroding away our personal and private liberties. We do not need more restrictive laws.

Eric and Dylan would not have been stopped by metal detectors. No amount of gun laws can stop someone who spends months planning this type of massacre. The real villain lies within our own hearts.

As my son Craig lay under that table in the school library and saw his two friends murdered before his very eyes, he did not hesitate to pray in school. I defy any law or politician to deny him that right! I challenge every young person in America, and around the world, to realize that on April 20, 1999, at Columbine High School, prayer was brought back to our schools. Do not let the many prayers offered by those students be in vain. Dare to move into the new millennium with a sacred disregard for legislation that violates your God-given right to communicate with Him. To those of you who would point your finger at the NRA—I give to you a sincere challenge. Dare to examine your own heart before casting the first stone!

My daughter's death will not be in vain! The young people of this country will not allow that to happen![6]

My sympathy, admiration and gratitude are still yours, Mr. Scott. What was it President Lincoln said at Gettysburg? "The world will little note, nor long remember, what we say here. . . ." Right? Well, what Lincoln said that day was so substantive, so weighty, so *right*, that high school students memorize and recite it to this day.

CHAPTER 3

Salt and Light

God calls the Church to be salt and light. Throughout history, when the Body of Christ was responsive, the prevailing culture was marked by refined thought, good manners and artistic taste. However, when the Church failed to assert an influence that inhibited social decay, civilization coarsened into a barbarism that dismissed moral standards. As Jesus told His disciples:

> You are the salt of the earth. But if the salt loses its saltiness, how can it be made salty again? It is no longer good for anything, except to be thrown out and trampled by men. You are the light of the world. A city on a hill cannot be hidden. Neither do people light a lamp and put it under a bowl. Instead they put it on its stand, and it gives light to everyone in the house. In the same way, let your light shine before men, that they may see your good deeds and praise your Father in heaven (Matt. 5:13-15).

In a study from 2002, the Barna Research Group concluded, "Over the past 20 years we have seen the nation's theological views slowly become less aligned with the Bible. Americans still revere the Bible and like to think of themselves as Bible-believing people, but the evidence suggests otherwise. Christians have increasingly been adopting spiritual views that come from Islam, Wicca, secular humanism, the eastern religions and other sources. Because we remain a largely Bible-illiterate society, few are alarmed or even aware of the slide toward syncretism—a belief system that blindly combines beliefs from many different faith perspectives."[1]

The Barna survey also revealed that a shockingly large number of Americans believe that when Jesus Christ was on Earth, He committed sins. That would mean that His death on the cross was not a sinless offering. Most of these individuals who contended that Jesus sinned were under 38 years of age—the very generation that was impacted by the Supreme Court's decision to remove prayer and faith from public classrooms.

As we said earlier, the Church once shaped Western civilization—otherwise known as Christendom. Its aim was to heal the sick, feed the hungry, clothe the poor and create art to worship a just and loving Creator who gave form and function to reality. Now our culture is shaped by the mass media of entertainment. The results are confusion at best and vile paganism at worst. When Jesus is not perceived to be an acceptable sacrifice for our sins—or if sin is not recognized as necessitating redemption—deliverance from eternal death is left open to interpretation.

In reality, everyday relationships illustrate the biblical truth that no one is righteous. However, because every person can justify himself in his own eyes, only biblical laws reveal our sinfulness. The Bible clearly presents our hope as resting in the atonement, available only through the Messiah—Jesus Christ. Regrettably, modern evangelism offers a watered down gospel that condones unclean desires.

Today, 40 percent of all adults hold the confused belief that "the Bible, the Koran and the Book of Mormon are all different expressions of the same spiritual truths."[2] It's clear that each of these books claims a way of salvation that excludes every other way, yet a majority of both adults and teenagers contend that truth is relative to circumstances. This provides an argument that nothing is wrong, per se. The common rubric seems to be that it's just a matter of opinion.

Nice Is Not Good Enough

Moral relativism may be one reason why the antihero in recent films has become so prominent. For instance, the protagonists in *Ocean's 11* lie, cheat and steal. Yet because they are posited as the heroes, we are apparently supposed to root for them to win.

Good News Publishers noted that 50 years ago, 70 percent of children had heard the gospel and were familiar with the Bible. Today, that number is at just 4 percent.[3] As in other countries in which the influence of the Church has collapsed, there are many in the believing Evangelical Church who are grasping at straws and forming alliances with strange non-Christian bedfellows to try and slow the fall.

God does not want us to live in futility and darkness. Instead, we must lovingly make every effort to keep the unity of the Holy Spirit through peace. God has given each person His measure of divine grace as Jesus Christ has apportioned it. As the apostle Paul wrote:

> He personally gave some to be . . . pastors and teachers, for the training of the saints in the work of ministry, to build up the body of Christ, until we all reach unity in the faith and in the knowledge of God's Son, [growing] into a mature man with a stature measured by Christ's fullness. Then we will no longer be little children, tossed by the waves and blown around by every wind of teaching, by human cunning with cleverness in the techniques of deceit. But speaking the truth in love, let us grow in every way into Him who is the head—Christ. From Him the whole body, fitted and knit together by every supporting ligament, promotes the growth of the body for building up itself in love by the proper working of each individual part (Eph. 4:11-16, *CSB*).

It is not possible to function as God's children without yielding to the Holy Spirit of truth and grace. "Walk as children on light," Paul reminded the believers in Ephesus, "for the fruit of the light [results] in all goodness, righteousness, and truth—discerning what is pleasing to the Lord" (Eph. 5:8-10, *CSB*).

Should We Be Intolerant?

In a speech before the National Religious Broadcasters, the late intellectual and humorist Steve Allen once explained why tolerance is not always an option for Christians. He asked his audience, "If you came upon a burning bush where it was clear that God Himself was speaking to you, and the event was so frightening that you fell on your face before Him, and God told you that He is a jealous God who would have no other gods before him and told you exactly what judgment you faced if you refused to obey Him, what would you do?" In other words, the distinct revelations of Judaism, as well as Christianity, often compel intolerance. Not all choices are just a matter of opinion. Only absolute truth sets us free. Where the Spirit of the Lord is, there is liberty (see 2 Cor. 3:17).

Seek Wisdom, Knowledge and Understanding

In his book *Christ and the Culture*, Yale theologian H. Richard Niebuhr distinguishes between the five approaches Christians have historically taken with regard to their world. These distinctions are as follows:

- **Position 1:** The first position could be called a retreat from culture, although Niebuhr refers to it as "Christ Against Culture." He cites the Mennonite and Amish communities as the obvious examples of this tradition, which form communities of separated brethren.

- **Position 2:** The second perspective, which Niebuhr calls "The Christ of Culture," tends to equate creation and redemption. These adherents view Christ as the moral example who points us to a perfect society within the context of the existing culture.

- **Position 3:** The third approach, which Niebuhr calls "Christ Above Culture," is occupied by the centrists who live within the world but are not of the world. These centrists refuse to take either the position of the anti-cultural radicals or of the accommodators of Christ to culture.

- **Position 4:** The fourth tradition is "Christ and Culture in Paradox," which refuses either to reject culture or to confuse culture with Christianity. They see these as two different yet not antagonistic realms. In creation, God gives us work, service, pleasure, government and family. In redemption, He gives us the Church, the Word and the sacraments. The Christian who follows the Christ and Culture in Paradox tradition participates in culture as an aspect of being human.

- **Position 5:** The final tradition is "Christ the Transformer of Culture," which emphasizes God's lordship over all of creation and all aspects of life. Niebuhr appeals to John's Gospel as an example of this approach, in which Christ is depicted as "the Word made flesh"—not only the priest of redemption but also the king of creation. This tradition, which is represented by Augustine and Calvin, contends that Christians have the potential not only to exercise leadership in the culture but to present the gospel as well.[4]

God loves the world, not just the individuals in it (see Rom. 8:20-23). Those of the Christ Transforming Culture tradition view culture as a distinct, though related, part of Christ's universal reign. Redemptive activities of the kingdom of God may include any work to which Christians realize a call because they are commanded by the universal Lord in the cultural mandate of the early chapters of Genesis. Although human activity can never bring salvation, Christian men and women bring a certain transforming element as they live out their callings in distinction and honor, serving both as light that attracts non-Christians to the gospel and as salt that preserves society by bring-ing civil righteousness, justice and compassion to bear on human relationships.

During the middle of the twentieth century, the Church retreated from culture. This period was followed by one in which the people in the Church took up the battle cry of cultural warfare to resist the moral decay they saw in society. Now, the Church is beginning to move out as ambassadors for Jesus Christ to redeem the culture. Whatever cultural position a Christian adopts, faith calls for activity that shows discernment, wisdom, knowledge and understanding in the pursuit of what is right. As it is written, faith without works is dead (see Jas. 2:17). "For God has not given us a spirit of fearfulness, but one of power, love, and sound judgment" (2 Tim. 1:7, *CSB*)

Can Entertainment Be Holy?

Drama, as we know it, was invented by the Church in the Middle Ages to help the illiterate populace understand the gospel. The Miracle Plays, as these dramas were known, became suspect in the eyes of clergy, who felt that these dramas were overshadowing their sermons. Pope Innocent III outlawed drama, and the dramatists went into the alleys and the beer halls to exercise their God-given gifts in not-so-God-ordained ways.

The growth of Protestantism during the fifteenth century was, to a large degree, a result of the willingness of Protestants to embrace the technology of the printing press and print Bibles, while the Roman Catholic Church rejected the new technologies. Similarly, Edison tried to give the rights to the motion picture technology to his Christian denomination, but they rejected it. The first broadcast radio station was also located in a church in Pittsburgh, but the rector of the church demanded that his younger associate shut it down.

In his book *The Silents of God,* Terry Lindvall, former distinguished chair of visual communication and professor of film at Regent University, chronicles the other side of this relationship between the entertainment industry and the Church. His book begins with the congregation of the historic Chautauqua Tabernacle screening a motion picture on June 22, 1900, and then moves on to discuss how many movies were shown in churches. However, this practice was abandoned when theater owners told the movie companies that they would not play their movies if they were also shown in churches.[5]

From 1908 to 1925, pamphlets, magazine articles, sermons and other materials reveal that there was cooperation between the Church and the media. The dissolution of the Church's relationship with movies since that time can be attributed to the advent of Hollywood scandals, Sabbatical reform movements and alternative communication technologies. Thus, at its inception, the Church sought to appropriate the moving picture's potential for evangelism, education and social uplift. That potential has yet to be realized.

Proclaiming in the Marketplace

There are five Greek words in the New Testament that are translated into the English word "preaching." Most frequently, Jesus uses the Greek word *kerysso*, which means "to proclaim in the marketplace." The people Jesus was talking to were familiar with the Roman heralds who ran into the marketplace every morning and shouted out the news of the Emperor.

When Christians go into the marketplace of ideas to herald the good news, they're being responsive to Jesus' command to do so. In the Protestant Reformation (and again in the evangelization of South Korea), the Church grew and prospered by proclaiming the gospel. When Christians fail to go into the marketplace, the Church shrinks and suffers.

Once Upon a Time . . .

George Santayana said, "Those who do not remember the past are condemned to relive it." Christians often forget that the Church exerted a great influence on the entertainment industry from 1933 to 1966. For 33 years, every script was read by representatives of the Roman Catholic Church, the Southern Baptist Church and the Protestant Film Office. The job of these individuals was to evaluate a movie in terms of the Motion Picture Code. If the film passed the Code, it received the Motion Picture Code Seal and was distributed. If it did not pass, theaters would not screen it. The short form of the Motion Picture Code provided the following:

- The basic dignity and value of human life shall be respected and upheld. Restraint shall be exercised in portraying the taking of life.
- Evil, sin, crime and wrongdoing shall not be justified.
- Detailed and protracted acts of brutality, cruelty, physical violence, torture, and abuse shall not be presented.
- Indecent or undue exposure of the human body shall not be presented.
- Illicit sex relationships shall not be justified. Intimate sex scenes violating common standards of decency shall not be portrayed. Restraint and care shall be exercised in presentations dealing with sex aberrations.
- Obscene speech, gestures or movements shall not be presented. Undue profanity shall not be presented.

- Religion shall not be demeaned.
- Words or symbols contemptuous of racial, religious or national groups shall not be used so as to incite bigotry or hatred.
- Excessive cruelty to animals shall not be portrayed and animals shall not be treated inhumanely.[6]

During the period of the Motion Picture Code, there was no explicit sex, violence, profanity or blasphemy in movies. For the most part, movies and television programs communicated the true, the good and the beautiful. Then in 1966, the churches voluntarily withdrew from the entertainment industry. Many of the media elite bemoaned the retreat of the churches. One prophesied, "If the salt is removed from the meat, then the meat will rot." Many studio executives felt that the Church's involvement helped them to reach the large Christian audience in the United States, and they believed that Christians would avoid films that did not have the Motion Picture Code Seal.

Censorship? Or Patron Sovereignty?

Patron sovereignty has traditionally been commended by Hollywood as the right of movie patrons to determine what they want to see, or avoid, by their activity at the box office. When the churches retreated, the Motion Picture Association of America (MPAA) instituted the MPAA rating system to take the place of the Code. However, this was like letting the fox guard the hen house.

Today, scripts are read by feminist, Marxist and homosexual groups, but not by Christians. These groups reward pictures and television programs that communicate their point of view and condemn movies and television programs that disagree with them. For instance, one television network had to spend hundreds of thousands of dollars to re-shoot and re-edit a television movie so that it would not offend the Alliance of Gay and Lesbian Artists.

The Destructive Power of the Media

As a result of the influence of these anti-biblical groups, movies and television programs have become purveyors of immorality, blasphemy and rebellion. In the movie *Sweet Liberty,* Alan Alda noted that to capture an audience, a movie must include the destruction of property (as in car chases), rebellion against authority and immoral sex. The audience he had in mind was the teenagers and young adults who flock to movies. It is interesting to note how this mirrors Karl Marx's four goals in his *Communist Manifesto*: abolish property, abolish the family, abolish the nation, and abolish religion and morality.

The destructive power of the mass media was highlighted by the 1988 television remake of the famous movie *Inherit the Wind*, which dramatically retold the story of the famous Scopes "monkey" Trial. William Jennings Bryan defeated Clarence Darrow in court, but *he* was defeated by the venomous anti-Christian reporting of H. L. Mencken. As in many cases since then, Christians have found it futile to win the battle, only to lose the war to the power of the media.

In the Scopes Trial, the press communicated a strong anti-Christian bias. Society adopted that bias and moved against the Christians, even though the Christians had the law on their side. Unless the media delights in God's mercy and grace, the good news will be muffled by the anthems of immoral heroes whose glory is their shame.

Christians forget that there is a war raging inside people's minds. It is a spiritual war for the souls of those who constitute our civilization. We war against an enemy that is using every possible tactic to control our minds: materialism, humanism and all the other "isms" that conflict with Christianity. "For the weapons of our warfare are not carnal but mighty in God for pulling down strongholds, casting down arguments and every high thing that exalts itself against the knowledge of God, bringing every thought into captivity to the obedience of Christ" (2 Cor. 10:3-4, *NKJV*).

Ugly Americans

The United States is considered by many to be the most immoral country in the world. Movies are often re-edited to include more sex and violence for release in the U.S. market. For instance, in Australia, the movie *Return to Snowy River* had the hero and heroine get married, whereas when it was released in the U.S., the hero and heroine went off to live with each other without marriage.

In January 2003, researchers at Boston University released a shocking study that showed how teenagers around the world held a negative view of Americans. The study also suggested that this negative depiction was in part responsible for the outpouring of dislike for Americans that underlies the bombing of the World Trade Center towers on September 11, 2001. The study assumed the following:

> The collective condemnation expressed by a people when a negative incident occurs does not come out of nowhere. As a general principle, a negative incident can become a *cause celebre,* rallying widespread anger, only if a necessary condition is met. That condition is this: *There must already be in place a foundation of shared negative beliefs and attitudes toward the United States upon which the feelings generated by the specific incident can be based.*[7]

The study also found that negative depictions of Americans in movies and TV programs influenced the beliefs of many of the subjects. Although it can be shown that the United States has been a good world citizen overall and has provided many kinds of assistance to other nations, the finding revealed that there is no historical balance sheet of international behavior by which other nations weigh America's past contributions against their current grievances.

The study focused on teenagers because, as the researchers noted, "they are the ones who are trained and equipped to conduct terrorist acts. . . . Those who actually flew the airliners on September 11 were young adults, to be sure, but it is clear that their beliefs were shaped earlier, during their teenage years. In the final analysis, then, it is the young who are recruited to do older men's bidding."[8]

Few of those surveyed had any direct contact with Americans, but they did have access to American television programs, movies and pop music, and, based on that exposure, most of these teens considered the United States to be violent, prone to criminal activity, and sexually immoral. "These results suggest that pop culture, rather than foreign policy, is the true culprit of anti-Americanism," one of the researchers said. "Hollywood should at least be asked by our public leaders to accept responsibility for the damage it is doing."[9]

Overall Attitude Toward Americans

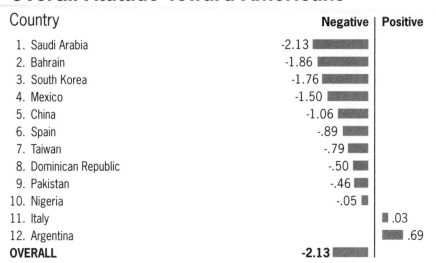

Country	Negative	Positive
1. Saudi Arabia	-2.13	
2. Bahrain	-1.86	
3. South Korea	-1.76	
4. Mexico	-1.50	
5. China	-1.06	
6. Spain	-.89	
7. Taiwan	-.79	
8. Dominican Republic	-.50	
9. Pakistan	-.46	
10. Nigeria	-.05	
11. Italy		.03
12. Argentina		.69
OVERALL	**-2.13**	

Source: Boston University, 2003

Profile of Specific Beliefs About Americans

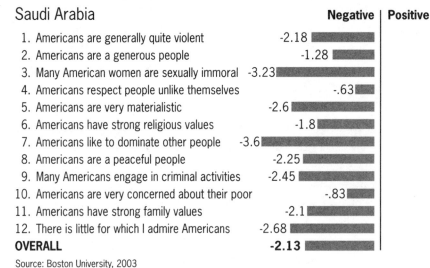

Saudi Arabia	Negative	Positive
1. Americans are generally quite violent	-2.18	
2. Americans are a generous people	-1.28	
3. Many American women are sexually immoral	-3.23	
4. Americans respect people unlike themselves	-.63	
5. Americans are very materialistic	-2.6	
6. Americans have strong religious values	-1.8	
7. Americans like to dominate other people	-3.6	
8. Americans are a peaceful people	-2.25	
9. Many Americans engage in criminal activities	-2.45	
10. Americans are very concerned about their poor	-.83	
11. Americans have strong family values	-2.1	
12. There is little for which I admire Americans	-2.68	
OVERALL	**-2.13**	

Source: Boston University, 2003

Movies Are a Communication Tool

It is important to understand that each medium has its advantages and disadvantages over other media. To communicate how something looks, a picture is worth a thousand words. However, to communicate the true nature of some event, a few words, such as "the Word was made flesh, and dwelt among us" (John 1:14, *KJV*) says more than a thousand pictures.

Each medium can be seen as a communication tool capable of accomplishing one or more functions.[10] A tool is neither good nor bad—that is determined by how we use it. When we use a tool to perform a function for which the tool is intended, it performs well. In the same way, tools of communication must be applied to our culture to deliver the right messages.

Stop "Shilling"

In days past, the "shill" was a decoy for a carnival pitchman who was hired to say negative things about some product in order to generate controversial interest. Regrettably, the Church has passed from obedience to God's Word to shilling for Hollywood. In fact, Christian groups have taken money to promote the Harry Potter movies about witchcraft, and Hollywood paid Christian groups to shill for *The Da Vinci Code*—a movie that clearly denies the resurrection and divinity of Jesus Christ.

The Church is losing its knowledge, wisdom and understanding and is selling out. It's not too late for the Church to become truly media wise. People need to know their divine Savior. Now that Hollywood has discovered the Church, we need the Church to stand up for Jesus.

Is the Church Being Corrupted?

Some time ago, almost every day for several months, someone would e-mail our organization about a study done by MarketCast that supposedly showed how Christians go to more violent, R-rated films than do liberals. Our editor, Dr. Tom Snyder, inquired what movies these studies showed Christians were viewing. He expected to hear movies such as *The Passion, Amistad, Dead Man Walking* and others with redemptive violence, but instead he found that the movies included films such as *Kill Bill* and *American Pie*, which are abhorrent.

The nature of this study can be interpreted in such a way that it may not be as dark as it appears. However, the Bible says not to give even an appearance of evil. If we go to these movies, MarketCast, which serves the major movie companies, is going to say exactly what it did say—that conservative, evangelical Christians are hypocrites who cast their vote for the worst movies. Therefore, even if it's not as bad as it seems, it underlines a very serious problem. Christians need to be involved in shaping the culture, *and* they need to be very careful that the culture doesn't corrupt their faith. They need to be the agents of change rather than the other way around.

All That Glitters Is Not Gold

More and more movies are being aimed at the faith-based audience. Some of these filmmakers are at the top of their game. Some have gone to the most prestigious film schools. But even so, after watching some of the theological errors and confusion in these movies, perhaps they (and those in the Church who are taken in by them) would also benefit from studying theology and critical thinking.

In *The Exorcism of Emily Rose,* the name of Jesus is claimed to only have power as shock treatment. Eventually, His name proves to be ineffective when confronted by modern therapeutic drugs. Regrettably, this movie has been touted by Christian marketers.

Some of the other theological gaffes in the current crop of faith-based movies are even more disappointing, such as that Jesus gave up His divinity when He was born on Earth, a sub-group of the old Arian heresy. The filmmaker and the viewer need to understand that a god who is impotent in the face of drugs, or who is only human, is no god whatsoever. He is only a confused thought.

In the massive marketing attempts to reach the Church, some of the production companies for these movies have enlisted some of the most successful evangelical associations. We must be media wise. Before we run out to see movies or go to an early premiere touted by a major evangelical association, we need to find out whether the movie is theologically sound. All that glitters is not gold.

Watchmen with Their Eyes Shut

People of faith and values who truly love the Lord are called to be forever vigilant. As God said to the prophet Ezekiel:

As for you, son of man, I have made you watchman over the house of Israel. When you hear a word from My mouth, give them a warning from Me. If I say to the wicked: Wicked one, you will surely die, but you do not speak out to warn him about his way, that person will die for his iniquity, yet I will hold you responsible for his blood. But if you warn a wicked person to turn from his way and he doesn't turn from it, he will die for his iniquity, but you will have saved your life (Ezek. 33:7-9, *CSB*).

These sound like tough words, but in fact they are not. If we could stop someone who was about to drive off a cliff and didn't do it, we would be responsible for that person's demise. God is calling us to warn others. Societies have prospered when the righteous were in positions of authority, but when those responsible neglected their calling, societies drifted into paganism, war, famine and destruction. Failure to take a stand can be overt, such as the churches that flew the Nazi flag in Germany, or covert, such as the people that Solzhenitsyn chastised in the Soviet Union for not speaking out against the evils of Stalinism and Communism.

Dan Brown, author of *The Da Vinci Code*, has specifically referenced the satanic sex ceremony in Stanley Kubrick's movie *Eyes Wide Shut* as an accurate portrayal of what he was getting at in the sexual ritual that is at the heart of the gospel (with a small "g") of his book. The only glimpse of eternity, according to Brown's repugnant story, is a brief moment of ecstasy in the sex act with a Temple prostitute. Brown also promotes neo-Gnostic, hereditary elitism as being the path to a momentary salvation. (Ancient Gnosticism made Jesus only divine, not merely human, as Brown does.) This is a pathetic diminishing of the gospel of Jesus Christ. It also extols man's baser instincts.

Meanwhile, a few leaders in Christian organizations have capitulated to Dan Brown's pagan vision. Some of these compromisers say to read the book and watch the movie, when they themselves have done neither and have no idea what *The Da Vinci Code* contains! In other words, *they don't care enough or know enough to bother trying to stop others from driving off a cliff!*

Recently, a Christian college hosted a debate between homosexuals and evangelicals. The homosexuals appealed to emotion and the heart while the evangelicals appealed to the Bible and the head. After being exposed to both sides of the argument, a student told his friend that he now supported homosexuality and that he might even be an incipient homosexual. This same lack of discernment led people to say that democracy would promote peace in the Palestinian areas of Israel, when, in fact, the majority voted for terrorism. This faulty reasoning is tantamount to sending social workers copies of child porn to prepare them for working with victims of pedophiles. Discernment and wisdom are not a quick fix but the result of careful analysis to ascertain that appropriate actions are taken.

Let me unequivocally state that I believe the message of *The Da Vinci Code* is abhorrent and no one should read the book or watch the movie. As the mass media is apt to say on politically correct issues, "Just say no." Rather, I strongly recommend that you read the gospel of Jesus Christ.

Searching for the Real Jesus

Recently, a book by a Muslim writer featured a Sufi Jesus. Although some in the Christian press touted the book, the Jesus depicted in the story was not our Savior. Rather, He was a spiritual guide who appeared in heaven talking and walking with Mohammed. He was not portrayed as the creator of the universe but merely a man in paradise. Likewise, I grew up in a non-Christian home with a mother who dabbled in Christian Science. The Jesus of Christian Science was the Divine Mind, a higher consciousness that all may attain.

So where do we find the real Jesus? Is Christ merely a cacophony of conflicting views? We find the real Jesus depicted in the pages of the Gospels. Within the accounts of Matthew, Mark, Luke and John, we find a Jesus who stood up to lawlessness and legalism. He was a real person who was fully God and fully man. This real, historical Jesus loved the world so much that He died for it and was resurrected so that all who believe in Him might be saved—not by works, nor meditation, nor secret knowledge, but by His victory over sin through death on the cross.

This is the Jesus described by the disciples who knew Him best. This is the Christ recorded truthfully and accurately in the New Testament documents included in the Holy Bible. These documents are the earliest, most reliable records we have of what Jesus did and what He taught. The teachings in these documents are clear and precise. There is no need, therefore, for any other document or teaching about Jesus, especially one that contradicts these original eyewitness testimonies of the God-Man who enlightens every man.

Instead of reading what Muslim writers, Christian Science Reading Rooms and New Age philosophers say about Jesus, it's much better to focus our time on studying the Bible so that we can take every thought captive for Christ, "so that the man of God may be thoroughly equipped for every good work" (2 Tim. 3:17).

Good, True and Beautiful

Philippians 4:8 tells us to look on what is good, true and beautiful. So we need to read the most popular book of all time: the Bible. Antipathy to the Bible proves that some people, including the ACLU, do not really believe that just because a book is popular, we should read it.

Life is short. Despite the delusions of our materialist age, each of us will die and then face God's judgment. So how can we use our time wisely? In spite of the thinking of the left, the Bible is the best place to start. And within the words of God to us, a good suggestion about how to spend our time is proclaimed in Philippians 4:8:

> Finally, whatever is true, whatever is honorable, whatever is just, whatever is pure, whatever is lovely, whatever is commendable—if there is any moral excellence and if there is any praise—dwell on these things (*CSB*).

Beside His eternal position, Jesus Christ is the central figure in history, so it's imperative that we have as accurate an understanding of who He is. With an accurate understanding in mind, we will be able to discern that He is being misrepresented to appeal to debased elements of human nature rather than being extolled as the Word of God whose manifestation reveals God's love, grace and mercy. After all, it is Jesus Christ who saves us, not we ourselves.

The Vain and God's Name
Pat Boone

The third of the Ten Commandments can be literally translated as "Do not carry the name of the Lord thy God in vain" (see Exod. 20:7). The commandment has, at most, a tangential relation to forms of cussing. It certainly is about the misuse of God's name. Yet the underlying implication is that we run the risk of defiling God's name when we claim that He sanctions our physical actions or our arguments.

What if our acts are not of God? Or even an outright sin that we nonetheless attribute to God? We may turn people away from their natural yearning for God by portraying our excesses as products of our godliness. For example, in our time, a few anti-abortionists have committed acts of murder on physicians who had performed abortions. I am fervently pro-life, but killing physicians in the name of God takes God's name in vain, and must not be tolerated any more than abortion itself should be tolerated.

The third commandment actually continues, "for the LORD will not hold him guiltless [literally, "will not cleanse"] who takes His name in vain" (*KJV*). Nothing so harsh is linked to any other commandment.

Lately, and flagrantly, we seem to see more and more secularists who would neutralize Christians while calculating not to offend, treating New Testament precepts as broadly applicable abstractions, whereas believers see them as explicit instructions in personal salvation. For example, "As you did it to one of the least of these My brethren, you did it to Me" (Matt. 25:40, *NKJV*) was given by the Master as a standard for individuals seeking the kingdom of heaven, not for governments refining policy.

The secularists who try to fuzz these Scriptures into some universal, poetic sort of applicability seem to carry the name of our Lord in vain into their advocacy of any social good they believe government should provide—anything from handouts, to favoring union labor, to forgiveness of sins!

When any of us Christians invokes the idea of God's judgment too hastily, it's usually a setback for our advancing the faith, and we do have our internal squabbles. But Christian Americans have probably become as careful as any religious population in history about talk of God being on their side of an argument. Quoting verses from Scripture selectively and then giving them broad, generalized application in support of the side one is advancing is akin to taking the name of the Lord in vain—and the two can obviously overlap.

Nowadays I cringe every time I see coveted industry award shows. Seems that, without fail, a young rapper or rock 'n' roll genius will he honored for his or her crazed, overbearing recording about pimping, supernatural sexual prowess or the like. With a straight face, the artist will stand at the podium and, before the watching world, thank God for the ability to write and perform such garbage for millions. I half expect a lightning bolt to split the stage and a voice to thunder, "I had nothing to do with that; don't attach my Name to it!"

Half-nude models and even porn stars flaunt ostentatious religious jewelry. Neo-Nazi skinhead types proclaim that the One who created us all in His image prefers that America be populated only with white Aryan "Christians," and no Jews or people of color. And one website sells a T-shirt that reads, "God Told Me to Hate You." God's name somehow gets attached to myriad dubious actions. These are just a few of the more repugnant examples, and I have to wonder if the Old Testament does not give us a cue as to what He really thinks.

Remember when Moses was still leading the Israelites through the wilderness and some rebels claimed that he should step down and let them run things? They claimed to have heard from God! What happened? "The ground under them split apart and the earth opened its mouth and swallowed them" (Num. 16:31-32)—tending to support the idea that God is impatient with . . . let's see, how's that third commandment go again?

Snapshots of Our Culture

Pat Boone

When Worst Is "Best"

I'm a singer. I hope you've noticed.

For more than 50 years now, I've made a nice living and enjoyed a wondrous life, singing. Making music. When I got my first break, made my first record, there was something new happening in music—they were calling it "rock and roll."

The fans of pop music, who made up the huge majority of listeners and buyers before rock became popular, liked well-crafted, melodic, catchy and memorable songs. A little section of New York City called "Tin Pan Alley" housed hundreds of songwriters and some performers, all turning out popular music, and the place became synonymous with American culture.

Actually, early rock was mostly rhythm and blues—R&B or "race music" (so called because it was generated almost exclusively by black musicians and known and liked mainly by a black audience). R&B was ragged and simple—too primal to be confused with "Tin Pan Alley." It wasn't subtle or cute; it was honest and direct and more than a little sensual. It was repetitive, insistent and "un-slick." It seemed to have been almost made up on the spot, spontaneous and improvisational, and it was noisier and just more exciting than what the tunesmiths were turning out in the Brill Building in New York City.

I happened along right at that time. My first records were covers, pop versions of rhythm-and-blues songs that had already become hits in the R&B market but weren't known yet to the much bigger pop audience. Elvis followed me about six months later, also doing his versions of former R&B hits such as "Hound Dog," "That's Alright Mama," "One Night with You" and a lot of others. My versions of "Ain't That a Shame," "Tutti Frutti" and "I Almost Lost My Mind" rapidly became million-sellers. And not just in the pop market—I had nine records in the R&B charts as well, indicating my acceptance as a legitimate rhythm-and-blues singer.

But while this new music phenomenon swept across the world—also creating and enlarging a whole new image of American culture—the tunesmiths were working feverishly back in Tin Pan Alley. More than anybody, they saw what was happening, and they wanted to be in the middle of it. Writers like Carole King, Neil Diamond, Neil Sedaka, Lieber and Stoller, and Ellie Greenwich caught the spirit and beat and added wonderful lyrics and very imaginative ideas to the excitement. It was still very much rock and roll but more skillful and intelligent and varied in content. "Up on the Roof," "Stand by Me," "You've Lost That Lovin' Feelin'," and "Spanish Harlem" come to mind, but there were hundreds more.

And inevitably, some of the new music found its way into the movies. But still, in America's entertainment monopoly—the world of cinema magic—good, elegant, beautiful music reigned supreme. Each year at the Oscars, the Academy of Motion Picture Arts and Sciences handed out golden trophies to the very best we were capable of in movies and music, and the world formed its opinions of who we were and what our fabled society was about.

I had the privilege of recording nominated songs and even some winners such as "Friendly Persuasion," "Exodus," "April Love," "Days of Wine and Roses," and others. And while I was first known for rock and roll, it was clear to me that the gold standard, the class and quality and excellence of America's creativity, was distilled in its popular music. Each year, while the boiling industry of rock music flourished among the masses (especially the young), the Oscars were handed out to composers like Lerner and Lowe, Burt Bachrach, Dimitri Tiomkin, Alan and Marilyn Bergman, Ernest Gold, Leonard Bernstein and others who in my estimation rank alongside Cole Porter, Sammy Cahn, Livingstone, Evans, Paul Francis Webster, Sammy Fain, Johnny Mercer and Henry Mancini.

Wonderfully, the world saw that the same culture that could produce "Tutti Frutti" could also serve up "Moon River," "Evergreen" and "The Sound of Music" and discern the difference. While rock songs earned gold records, movie songs earned gold statues. And they said something good about America.

Well, it's 2006, and today's Academy has handed out its golden Oscar to a song it declared the best our movie composers could come up with—this year's statement to the rest of the world about who and what we are. I saw some of it performed on the awards show and I turned it off, aghast that it was even nominated and considered—and appalled when it was declared the winner.

My friend Nelson Sardelli, a singer himself, one of Las Vegas's best entertainers, sent me two lyrics samples to compare: one the kind of enduring standard that reflected the best of our society, and the other a portion of this year's acclaimed winner. You tell me what this says about our culture and what the rest of the world should think about us. The first is from the Oscar-winning song "The Way You Look Tonight" from *Swing Time* (1936):

Someday when I'm awfully low
When the world is cold
I will feel a glow
Just thinking of you
And the way you look tonight[1]

Now consider this Oscar-winning song of 2006, "It's Hard Out There for a Pimp," from the movie *Hustle and Flow*:

Wait, I got a snow bunny, and a black girl too
You pay the right price and they'll both do you
That's the way the game goes, gotta keep it strictly pimpin'
Gotta have my hustle tight, makin' change off these women, yeah[2]

I'll spare you the rest—there's way too much more, and it doesn't get any better. Incredibly, "It's Hard Out There for a Pimp" will now take its place beside "Moon River," "Over the Rainbow" and "White Christmas." When the self-anointed of Hollywood decree that something of our all-time worst will now forever be enshrined as an all-time best, should it not make us sad?

Are We Still One Nation Under God?

I love the Fourth of July! Eleven times each year, Americans are asked to remember to fly the flag on days such as Armed Forces Day, Labor Day, Thanksgiving and Christmas. But I ask you: On which day do you feel more compelled to fly Old Glory than the Fourth of July? I daresay none.

But beware: We should not take this freedom for granted. There are some people who want to prevent us from reciting our glorious Pledge of Allegiance as those beautiful colors lap against our houses and to remove the words "under God" from that pledge. Only a few years ago such a notion would have been unthinkable. Not today. Now it is the subject of serious and heated debate. How have we come to this misguided moment in our nation's history?

Thankfully, not too long ago the U.S. Supreme Court overruled a liberal lower court's decree that would have given one Michael Newdow, an atheist and noncustodial parent of a nine-year-old daughter, a legal right to stop her school (and all school kids everywhere) from reciting the Pledge of Allegiance. Mr. Newdow had claimed that citing "under God" in the Pledge violated the Constitution's ban upon the establishment of a national religion.

Mind you, the girl's mother—who *does* have custodial rights and who regularly attends church—has no issues with her little girl reciting the Pledge, including "under God." For that matter, nearly 90 percent of all Americans, according to an AP poll, want "under God" to remain just as it is in our Pledge.[3] So it's clear: With the vacuous compliance of the Ninth Circuit Court, one selfish atheist is offended by two words in our Pledge of Allegiance, so he wants the rest of America to shut up! This just isn't the way democracy works.

Mr. Newdow (and some of the Ninth Circuit Court) keeps quoting the First Amendment as if Congress had somehow mandated the saying of the pledge and thereby "established religion," ignoring the fact that it is the school board and the kids themselves who *voluntarily choose* to say it the way Americans have said the Pledge since 1954. As Alan Keyes brilliantly points out, there is no law respecting the establishment of religion, because the First Amendment itself expressly forbids it! Congress can't make *any* laws about religion!

Atheism itself is a religion, a faith system built on the premise that there is no God—and one that can't be proven. Theism, of any description, is based on the premise that there is a creator God—and the evidence abounds everywhere. All our founding fathers, including Washington, Jefferson, Franklin, Adams, Monroe and Lincoln, acknowledged this. And every single one of the 50 states in America acknowledges God within the framework of their own state constitutions. Here are a few:

- **Alaska** (1956): "We, the people of Alaska, grateful to God . . ."
- **Idaho** (1899): "We, the people of the State of Idaho, grateful to Almighty God . . ."
- **Massachusetts** (1780): "We . . . the people of Massachusetts, acknowledging . . . the goodness of the Great Legislator of the Universe . . ."
- **Missouri** (1845): "We, the people of Missouri, with profound reverence for the Supreme Ruler of the Universe . . ."
- **South Carolina** (1778): "We, the people of the State of South Carolina, grateful to God . . ."

Get the picture? Our founding fathers, the ones who wrote our Constitution and maintained our liberties, were never ashamed to acknowledge our dependence on God. In fact, they fought for the right! So what are we doing? If embittered atheists like the late Madelyn Murray O'Hare and Michael Newdow have their way, we'll not only lose "under God" in our Pledge of Allegiance but school kids will also be forced to stop memorizing Lincoln's Gettysburg Address, which ends with the famous "this nation, under God, shall not perish from the earth." And that's not all; we'll have to remove "endowed by our Creator" from Jefferson's Declaration of Independence.

Will we stand for this, fellow Americans? Or shall we just meekly lie down and let a few impose their will on us? Nobody makes Mr. Newdow, or even his nine-year-old daughter, say anything they don't want to say. Shall we let him prohibit us?

"Moral Values" According to Ben and T.J.

"Only a virtuous people are capable of freedom. As nations become corrupt and vicious, they have more need of masters."

Jerry Fallwell? Nope. Pat Robertson? Nope. Louis Farrakhan? Nope. Michael Moore? Don't be ridiculous.

No, founding father Benjamin Franklin—jolly, rotund, wine sipping and woman loving but churchgoing—wrote those words in April 1787. On June 18 of the same year, he rose in a hopelessly stalled Constitutional Convention to strongly propose that each day's deliberations begin with prayer. He even stated that a local minister should be brought in to deliver a sermon while they tried to compose this document on which our whole society has been founded.

Preaching and praying, whenever and wherever, in almost any circumstance public or private, is a moral value. Not sure? Listen to T.J. (Thomas Jefferson—Mr. Separation of Church and State himself), who opined in 1798, "No power over the freedom of religion is delegated to the United States by the Constitution." That and that only is what he was referring to when he coined the famous phrase "separation of church and state" in a letter to the Danbury Baptists in 1802. Jefferson wanted to assure the congregation that the Church of England would not become an official religion, as it was in Great Britain. "I contemplate with solemn reverence," he wrote, "that act of the whole American people which declared that their legislature should make no law respecting an establishment of religion, *or prohibiting the free exercise thereof,* thus building a wall of separation between church and state" (emphasis added).

"Well," many will state, "Jefferson was talking to a church. Let them worship in their own building however they want, but keep religion out of public life and off government property!" I hate to tell you, but President Jefferson would nail proponents of this view to the wall for making this statement. In 1802, President Jefferson signed the Enabling Act, which allowed Ohio to become a state. This Act stated that the government in this new state would "not be repugnant to the Northwest Ordinance," which provided that "religion, morality, and knowledge—being necessary to good government and the happiness of mankind, schools and the means of education—shall be forever encouraged."

Still not clear? Well get this: While he was president, Thomas Jefferson also chaired the school board for the District of Columbia, authoring the first plan of education adopted by the city of Washington. Yes, I said Washington. This plan that he authored used the Bible and Isaac Watts's psalms, hymns and spiritual songs as the principle books for teaching reading to students. Assigned reading of the Bible in public schools!

But wait, there's more! President Thomas Jefferson attended Christian services on Sundays in the large Hall of Congress. And with his fellows in that body, he appropriated taxpayer funds to pay missionaries to preach the gospel to the Indians! Not only did he sign bills appropriating financial support for chaplains in Congress and the armed services, but also in the Articles of War of 1806, Jefferson "earnestly recommended to all officers and soldiers diligently to attend divine services." Clearly, Jefferson understood the Constitution and defended the liberties and rights of expression of all—even Christians.

Amazingly, moral values overrode every other consideration when our founding fathers were creating this republic.

"But hey," yell some folks, "we know about moral values, food on the table, higher minimum wage, Social Security, education, things like that. Family values, right?" No, those things are all very important to us, but they are *material values*. The subject here is *moral values*, those precepts and ideas and covenants that have guided our thinking and choices and priorities since the beginning of our nation up until now. And still, a significant majority of Americans—as evidenced by the vote count in this last election—feel that moral values are even more important than matters of security, terrorism, economy or education. After all, if people can't defend and preserve our nation's moral identity, will the rest really matter?

Let me be very clear: *Material* is what you eat and wear and drive and spend and pay taxes on; *moral* is what you feel, perceive, believe and cherish, live by—and perhaps die for.

And overwhelmingly, most Americans still feel marriage should be defined as a covenant between a man and woman and are repulsed by the statistics that document 40 millions deaths to young Americans in the womb since 1973. They still demand the right to say "under God" in the Pledge of Allegiance, and resent every mention of God and Scripture being sanded off every public facade, governmental or otherwise. They feel a militant agnostic minority is robbing the vast majority of its freedoms, and they're not going to stand for it.

The churchgoing, Bible-believing majority (including Jews, Christians and Muslims, by the way) are fed up with "accidents" such as Janet Jackson's nudity in the Super Bowl halftime show, Nicolette Sheridan dropping her towel in front of Terrell Owens in the locker room at the beginning of Monday Night Football, and Howard Stern being paid $100 million a year by Sirius to spew any kind of filth and sacrilege he chooses into the minds of our clueless young.

Enough! Millions of us still agree with old T.J., who said, "I hold the precepts of Jesus as delivered by Himself, to be the most pure, benevolent and sublime which has ever been preached to man." And we revere him for the words he had inscribed in marble on his own Jefferson Memorial: "Almighty God hath created the mind free. All attempts to influence it by temporal punishments or burdens are a departure from the plan of the Holy Author of our religion."

Likewise, we agree with old Ben Franklin when he wrote to the French Ministry in March 1778, "Whoever shall introduce into public affairs the principles of primitive Christianity will change the face of the world." And old Ben also said, "a Bible and a newspaper in every house, a good school in every district—all studied and appreciated as they merit—are the principle support of virtue, morality, and civil liberty."

Thank you, Dr. Franklin and Professor Jefferson. Class closed.

Public Servants . . . Oh, Really?

Anybody old enough to remember Jimmy Stewart in *Mr. Smith Goes to Washington*? If so, like me, you'll recall the honest small-town citizen who was appointed to fill a vacant U.S. Senate seat, and who took it very seriously. He knew that he had been selected to represent his neighbors and their interests in Washington, and so he went there to do just that.

Before long, Mr. Smith encounters the seamy, corrupt aspects of the government processes: the deals, sellouts and self-serving squandering of tax money; and the pork-barrel excesses. He hears the insistent advice, "If you go along, you'll get along." The movie climaxes with Jimmy Stewart, as the rookie senator, talking himself hoarse and exhausted in a heroic filibuster, eventually drawing cheers and hurrahs from an enthusiastic gallery of fellow citizens in the balcony of the Senate. The audience always gets goose bumps and maybe tears when they watch an earnest and dedicated young American giving his every fiber to be and do what he was elected to do. When they see someone who wants to be a genuine public servant. Isn't that what all our elected representatives do today?

Are you serious?

No, sadly, while there are still those idealistic, dedicated citizens who step forward, run arduous campaigns, win elections and go to Washington intending to be exactly what Jimmy Stewart depicted in the movie, the "game" calls for them to get in step, learn and conform to the established system, and not make waves. Before long, the promises they made their constituents are swept aside as impractical, and trades and compromises become their currency. If they're good at it, they build credits and clout and even debts from their fellows and move up the ladder to influential committees and positions. If they're not good at the game, or if they naively try to really accomplish the worthy things the voters expected of them, they generally get squeezed out and neutralized.

And those who are *really* good at it get a lot of public attention, win some favors for the folks back home, become entrenched incumbents, and keep making promises to get re-elected. Mysteriously, quite a few—though they aren't paid exorbitant salaries and have to maintain two residences just to stay in office—retire wealthy. Curious, isn't it?

I really hate to be cynical about all this, but we see it enacted over and over again, until it eventually seems just the way it is. And while all valid polls reveal the wishes of the great majority of Americans, the ones they elected don't seem to read the polls. At least not until the next election time, at which point they become *very* interested so that they can say the right things and try to convince the voters they've been fighting for their interests all along and will do even more if they're sent back to Washington.

And they usually are re-elected.

Voluntary prayer in school? Americans want it. A Flag Protection Amendment? Americans want it. Marriage protection legislation? Lower taxes? A balanced budget? Americans overwhelmingly prefer these things. Yet what do their "public servants" do? They thumb their noses at the voters, who they figure probably won't care enough to even check on who votes how in Congress. They generally vote along strict party lines, currying favor with other politicians and special-interest groups rather than the people who elected them.

We've got to wake up, folks. The Senate just failed—again—to abolish the so-called "estate tax." The House of Representatives, *our* representatives, voted 272 to 162 to kill it, obviously hearing the wishes of the people. This is, as you probably know, the confiscatory tax initiated in World War I for that immediate emergency, when taxes were almost nonexistent. This is the robbery that occurs when a dutiful taxpayer has the poor judgment to die and the government steps in to take half the dead person's assets, calling it—preposterously, conveniently and some would say erroneously—a "tax." Small family businesses and farms and homes often have to be sold just to satisfy the insatiable appetite of big-spending politicians. As Jim Martin of 60 Plus Association has said so often, "Death shouldn't be a taxable event." But it is!

Yet many Americans, including some responsible senators, have been actively campaigning to stomp this legislation of death. Just recently, a majority of the Senate voted for the people and their expressed desire. But a minority, which was large enough to defeat the effort, voted *against the people who elected them*. They think you should still have to surrender half of your already-taxed assets to the IRS when you die. I think you should find out which senators voted for you—and which didn't.

And you should remember this the next election day.

A Fowl Contagion

Well, it's here. Right in the middle of us and spreading. It's a fowl contagion and can be very dangerous. It's hard to prevent and even harder to cure. It's no respecter of persons; it can affect people of any age, economic background or culture. There's no vaccine, though there is something you can take to combat it—but I'll come to that later.

I'm not referring to the dreaded avian flu, the one we've been reading about that's transmitted from bird to bird and possibly to some humans or other creatures. No, I'm talking about another affliction. This one is a mental, emotional and verbal malady that seems to incubate most often in the young—particularly those who have already exhibited tendencies toward rebellion, rejection of authority, resentments of various types, grievances, self-righteousness, self-importance, self-indulgence and (of course) impatience.

This fever is transmitted quickly among impressionable and poorly informed young people who generally are looking for quick fixes to problems and who have often not learned yet that valuable possessions—like freedom—cost dearly. In a majority of cases, the newly affected ones have been given almost everything that's important to them with little or no expenditure of their own, and therefore they naturally assume that's to be expected all through life. They haven't developed any kind of immunity to this type of flu. In fact, they often welcome it!

Just in case you're not aware of this contagious ailment, let me describe the three main telltale symptoms. The first is usually an onset of anger and frustration, often disguised as humanitarianism, which is actually present in many cases. These emotions fester and swell, and then lead to symptom number two: spontaneous, regrettable (but apparently uncontrollable) verbal outbursts. The victim intends to shock and offend, yet is sometimes quite surprised at the negative reaction of others. This inevitably leads to the third symptom: a setting in of rigid self-defensiveness, hostility toward anyone with a differing point of view, and an unreasoning passion to be proven right and even honored for the previous offenses!

Along with these symptoms, there's usually manifest a curious blindness to reality, a myopic focus on only one set of circumstances and exclusion of other vital and pertinent factors that make up the whole picture. And finally, in the terminal and usually irreversible stage of this flu, violence erupts in one of a variety of ways.

If the victim has always been prone to a spoiled, demanding and rebellious personality, he or she will become extremely obnoxious. If the victim has tended to be more quietly cunning, seditious and manipulative in nature, he or she may actually combine with others of similar tendency and incite revolution or even violence. If, conversely, the tendency has been toward fitting in with others and conforming to established norms, the last stage may consist of a constant naïve and slavish parroting of whatever the poor victim hears and sees in the behavior of the more rabid, raving ones.

Adults, even older ones, aren't by any means immune to this flu. Curiously, though some have matured in most ways, they can exhibit a surprising regressive resonance with youthful irresponsibility and rejection of authority. For vague reasons, there seems an especial susceptibility among people in media and entertainment. There's the widespread desperate wish that war and terrorism weren't happening, and a totally unrealistic notion that wishing can make it so. Incredibly, they discount things like the destruction of the World Trade Center as one-time events and feel that if we "make nice" with our enemies, they won't attack us again. And, most astoundingly, the weepers and wishers are so intent on discrediting our leadership that they seem oblivious to the glaring fact that there has not been a major catastrophe on our soil since 9/11! Clearly, *somebody's been doing something right!*

This contagion isn't new. Far from it.

It broke out in the colonies before and during our Revolutionary War. A surprising number of wealthy and influential people liked things the way they were and weren't just British sympathizers; they openly and loudly resisted our establishing our new republic. Even after we succeeded and our Constitution was drafted, many of those people opposed and criticized George Washington the whole time he was president.

John Adams was plagued by it. So was Thomas Jefferson. A serious outbreak of this type of flu resulted in the death of Abraham Lincoln. In fact, looking back, you can discover that every president who was in office during any of our wars or conflicts had to contend with loud, strident, unreasoning resistance from some of the very people he was trying to defend.

Three pretty and talented young women, the Dixie Chicks, contracted the malady and have exhibited all the early manifestations. But so have others—too many others. Egged on by close circles of friends in entertainment and the media, groups like Green Day and Pearl Jam have loudly asserted that they know more about our national crises than our elected and experienced leaders. And individual singers like Eminem, Pink, Kanye West and, sadly, even Bruce Springsteen have assaulted the character, motives and abilities of our president.

That's what this flu leads to. Not content to employ the freedom to dissent and critique policies and administrative decisions, the afflicted ones do their utmost to *assassinate* their leader—by attacking his reputation, his authority, his ability to lead—while we're at war with forces who intend to destroy our way of life!

This flu apparently recognizes no borders. Neil Young, who composed and recorded a song soon after 9/11, "Let's Roll," exclaimed in his lyric, "You've got to turn on evil . . . you've gotta face it down and . . . go in after it and never be denied."[4] It was a call to aggressive action! But then he caught the flu. Now, Young has offered a new political screed, "Living with War," in which he repeatedly calls for the impeachment of the president, just like many rappers and rockers. Only in his case, his seditious screeching is especially odious, because he's a Canadian citizen, not an American! He's lived in our country for 40 years and has become very rich and famous and respected for his music. Yet he declares his allegiance to the Canadian flag, not our Stars and Stripes, and still he sings, "Let's impeach the president"! Did I mention this flu breeds irrationality?

There is no vaccine. But there is preventive inoculation if parents will care enough about their kids and the future of this country to employ it. It consists of teaching kids equal parts of lessons on respecting legitimate authority—history lessons that will impress on them the drastic price Americans have had to pay for our freedoms, in blood and tears and sacrifice—and serious instruction in basic manners and civility as well as citizenship.

Homegrown Heroes

I have a brother, Nick, and two sisters, Margie and Judi. In some ways, they're perfectly normal—some might say ordinary. By that, I mean they're not in the public eye, not widely known, and they've led what seem to be commonplace, non-spectacular lives.

Although Nick did have a singing career early on (with a couple of sizable chart records), his heart wasn't really in it. He married a beautiful girl named Trish, and they had four remarkable kids. Nick just retired as a sociology professor. My sister Margie is a recently retired registered nurse, having helped bring countless babies into this world and raised two outstanding kids of her own. Judi and her husband, Joe, have run a maintenance business for many years. She also works in a bank, and she and Joe created and raised a boy and a girl we all think are terrific.

Very good. Sure, there's a lot more to each story, but nothing to write about, right? Wrong. Somebody *has* just written a news story about one of Judi's kids, her son Chris. Seems he's being seen as a hero, and I'd like to share the recent story from AirTran's *Altitudes* with you:

AirTran Airways Captain Saves Student's Life

Capt. Chris Allen was only thinking about getting home on April 7, 2006, while traveling down Interstate 24, halfway between Chattanooga and Murfreesboro, where he lives. The AirTran Airways pilot of four years had just spent the past three days at recurrent training at the Pilot Training Center in Atlanta.

As Chris passed mile marker 146, he looked up and saw a Nissan Pathfinder slide across the interstate.

"It slid back and forth a few times from left to right and flipped three times," Chris said. "It bounced twice on the road, and on the third flip it went over the guardrail into a 12 to 15-foot ravine. It landed upside down."

Chris later discovered that the vehicle consisted of five students from the University of Georgia.

"It was a dramatic deal," he said. "I pulled over, and I and another guy ran down to the wreck."

Three of the students had climbed out of the truck. They were all wearing their seatbelts. Anne Taylor, a freshman who was seated in the front passenger side of the vehicle, was seriously injured. Chris found her lying on her right side, holding her left leg, and her shin bone was broken. Her fibula was also broken, and her left foot was severed right in front of the instep where the foot arches down toward the toes. Her right foot was broken in a couple of places and she had torn ligaments in her right knee.

Chris knew he had to think fast.

"When I saw her, I remembered I had an Army medical kit in my car, and I ran back down to her," Chris said. "She needed bandaging. She was mostly calm and very sweet. She was awesome. The first thing you have to do is make sure she can breathe, and she was talking to me. She was bleeding quite a bit, so I picked up her foot."

That is when Chris discovered that Anne's foot had been severed.

"I got her foot bandaged up and got the bleeding to stop," Chris said. "By the time I started to splint her leg, the ambulance came. Several other people had stopped. It took five of us to take her up the hill."

Since the accident, Chris has maintained consistent contact with Anne and her family, and he has visited Anne at the hospital. As of last week, Anne underwent her ninth surgery in which her lower left leg was amputated. Anne's family members credit Chris for saving Anne's life.

"Chris is a remarkable man, and there were a lot of things that happened to put him in that place and that time with those skills," said Ron Taylor, Anne's father.

Chris has a different philosophy: Anne saved his life.

"Just a few miles down the road, the tornadoes came through," Chris said. "If this had not happened and I had not stopped, chances are that both of us would have ended up in those tornadoes. I would have been right in the middle of that, so it worked out well for both of us. We were both meant to be there at the same time."

Now, you should know that my nephew Chris doesn't consider himself a hero. Heroes seldom do. Remember the young man who jumped into the icy, swirling waters close to the Washington, D.C., airport after the airliner went down near the 14th Street Bridge, and pulled a couple of passengers to safety at the eminent risk of his own life? Lenny Skutnik protested, "I'm no hero. These people were about to drown and somebody had to do something—so I just did what I could."

That's what heroes do.

Later, in his State of the Union address, President Reagan recognized the young man up in the balcony, and all the assembled legislators gave him a rousing, enthusiastic and deserved salute. He was a hero, and still is.

I'll bet, like Chris, he grew up in a good, "ordinary" family doing largely unspectacular things. He might never have been known to any of us if he hadn't "happened" along just when he did, at the scene of the horrific, unexpected tragedy.

But because of his upbringing, the things his parents taught him and the moral sense that he *is* his "brother's keeper," Lenny—like Chris—couldn't just do nothing. He couldn't just stand there watching people struggle in the freezing water and go under, not while he might do something, *anything*, to help. So he jumped in.

And so Chris ran back and got the medical kit, stopped the bleeding and saved the brave young girl's life. He *could* do something, so he did.

For years, every chance I've gotten I've publicly said something like "My brother and two sisters are heroes to me. Their lives are quieter than mine, but they commit themselves every day to helping others, shouldering their own responsibilities, raising their families amidst terrific challenges, paying their bills and taxes, taking active roles in their churches and community life around them, and often reaching out to help others meet their own life obstacles. They're not looking for awards or recognition, and they recognize that only God is keeping score. That's good enough for them—and that makes them heroes to me."

But every once in a while, one of my family—and likely one or more of yours—will "happen" along in a special, dramatic and crisis type of moment, and do something way "out of the ordinary" that will earn some wider recognition. There are thousands of young Americans, like Chris, serving in our military, not because they were drafted or conscripted, but because they sensed a need and responded. They're from families like yours and mine, brought up to care about our country and everybody in it. And they are *all* home-grown heroes.

Please, Leave Marriage Alone

Are we going nuts? Is the whole nation suffering from mad cow disease or becoming senile at the ripe young age of 230?

Was Chicken Little right? Is the sky falling?

Were Copernicus and all former mathematicians wrong? Is 2 and 2 actually relative and anything we want it to be?

Have we arrived at some stage in our evolution that empowers us to change the very DNA of society, of culture, the structural makeup of the human race?

Or are we just too numb—or dumb—to protest the incessant, dogged determination of some lobbying groups to corrupt and change the very fabric of humankind? I feel like I'm watching a reality version of *Gulliver's Travels*, in which a sleeping giant is gradually staked to the ground by little people and rendered helpless while he slumbers.

Or worse, I do feel we're suffering a moral trichinosis as a nation— that little-talked-about malady that occurs when *worms*, gaining entry through poorly cooked pork, infiltrate a person's muscles, gradually sapping strength and weakening the body beyond recovery. The victim doesn't realize it's happening until it's too late; all he knows is that he's losing energy and muscle tone, and he's becoming strangely and completely weak and helpless.

There are many evidences and symptoms: Some similar affliction seems to be steadily and relentlessly draining us of resolve. Most adults are aware that our founding fathers were devout believers in God; aware that the Bible, itself, was a standard *textbook* in our early colleges; aware that Thomas Jefferson in his Declaration of Independence averred our national conviction that our very liberties are conferred by our Creator; aware that even as recently as the 1950s, our Supreme Court acknowledged that America is a *Christian nation*, founded on biblical principles. Still, we have watched, apparently dumbstruck and powerless, as our kids were denied the right to pray, voluntarily, in school.

The ACLU and other left-leaning lobby groups are relentlessly suing to remove any little cross or Christian emblem from public view and demanding any mention of Scripture or God Himself be sanded or chiseled off any and every public building! This supposedly to avoid any offense to a very few who don't subscribe to Christian or biblical belief, although most of these few have *never complained*, and many keep saying they're not offended by the religious traditions of others. There is an obvious and pernicious agenda here—and we're just letting it happen, as if we have nothing to say about it!

And now, our elected representatives in the Senate have bowed to the pressure groups and voting blocs and refused to cast their votes in defense of marriage itself! The very spectacle of a proposed marriage amendment—the apparent necessity to codify in the Constitution that the institution of marriage is to be confined and defined as a contract between one man and one woman—is, to millions of stunned Americans, a very ominous sign of the times if not the last days described in the first chapter of Romans.

Anybody who hasn't read that graphic depiction of an end time society and still cares *what* the Bible says should turn there immediately and fasten his seatbelt. It reads like a Gallup poll description of life in America today.

Some lawmakers correctly state that such a complicated, difficult and sobering task as an amendment to our Constitution shouldn't be necessary. After all, they point out, 45 of the 50 states have already acted to define traditional marriage in ways that would ban same-sex unions being recognized as marriage, with 19 of those states having their own constitutional amendments and 26 having strict statutes on their books prohibiting the perversion of the institution.

And, realistically, there probably *won't* be such an amendment to our national Constitution enacted. But President Bush and the saner, more responsible members of both houses of Congress want the votes and attempts to take place so voters can find out which of our public servants really want to do the will of the majority of their constituents and which seem to merely want to stay in office by courting every little voting bloc, hoping the majority won't hold them accountable.

It's very useful, very instructive, when senators like Ted Kennedy *go on record* with statements like "the Republican leadership is asking us to spend time writing *bigotry* into the Constitution. A vote for it [the marriage amendment] is a vote against civil unions [it isn't] against domestic partnership [ridiculous], against all other efforts for states to treat gays and lesbians fairly under the law."

My friend Senator Orrin Hatch fumed, "Does he *really* want to suggest that over half of the United States Senate is a crew of bigots?"

Yes, he does. Senator Kennedy and his allies want to paint opponents of same-sex marriage as bigots—not defenders of thousands of years of moral, biological and societal reality. The positions and arrogant statements of the muddleheaded liberals will be taken into account at election time by voters who, like their more responsible servants, don't like being called bigots because they want to defend the very basic recipe for the survival of humanity.

The last time this issue came up for a vote in the Senate, I went back to Washington with only three or four other fellow entertainers who were brave enough to speak out. The outcome was the same then as now. And although each of us had pertinent things to say, I think the *most* memorable and irrefutable statement was made by a prominent black minister. He and an increasing majority of black people in this country strongly resent claims that homosexual proclivities are the same as being born with black skin and therefore a legitimate claim to deprived minority classification. In front of a surprisingly hostile press group, this minister said, "Water is comprised of two elements, two parts hydrogen and one part oxygen. You can't change that; it's just that way. If you want to combine two parts oxygen with one part hydrogen, you can—but now you have hydrogen peroxide, not water! If you want to join two people of the same sex in some kind of union, you can—but it's not *marriage*; it's something else. Call it what you want."

At that, an angry reporter intruded, "All you people are religious—you're quoting the Bible and God. What about those of us who don't believe any of that—is there any other argument against same-sex marriage?"

He thought he would stump the preacher, but he was wrong.

"Why, sure, son," responded the minister. "Look in *any dictionary in the world*. You'll see the definition of marriage as a contract, a union, between a man and a woman. Nothin' else there. If you don't believe God, at least believe *Webster's Dictionary!*"

God bless that man—and God help us to wake up and stir ourselves before the "little people" have us completely powerless.

Soul Food: We Always Need It

Are you ready for some soul food? I mean, some hearty, stick-to-your-ribs, honest-to-goodness nourishment? I'm servin' it up right here.

Good news is food for the soul. And while we're being deluged and glutted with almost every kind of depressing and troubling and anxiety-producing story imaginable, there are wonderful, encouraging things happening in our midst that we hear too little about. Well, pull your chair up closer to the table and tuck your napkin under your chin. Chef Boone has some steaming hot, delicious *good news* for you!

Anybody who watches television these days—not just the news programs, but talk shows, comedy and even current drama programs—has heard Pat Robertson, founder of the 700 Club and Christian Broadcasting Network, lambasted, criticized and lampooned as if he were a crazed nitwit. It sounds like the normally fatherly Robertson, whom I've been privileged to know well, is almost as much a cockatoo as Howard Dean, screeching inflammatory rhetoric and irresponsible indictments routinely.

True, Robertson did recently express his opinion on his own show and in a segment in which he often opines about current events in the news from a scriptural perspective, that Israel—in turning over large chunks of its land to its enemies—might be departing from God's biblically recorded will. In sort of a glancing comment, he even wondered out loud if Ariel Sharon's stroke might have been the result of moving contrary to God's will for tiny Israel. It's important to note that this wasn't a pronouncement, just a quizzical side-thought. But it got treated as a pronouncement, and it stirred up such an incredible firestorm of outrage and condemnation that Robertson felt obligated to explain and apologize for actually expressing his thoughts and musings out loud. And the Israeli government, fully aware of Pat's amazing and deeply felt allegiance and support for Israel, publicly denounced him!

Why, you'd have thought he'd published a disrespectful cartoon about Israel, for goodness sake!

Well, that kind of "news" can upset your digestive tract, so I've got some items that should cleanse your palate—not just about Pat Robertson, but about Christians in general. Among *many* other ministries, Pat Robertson and CBN created Operation Blessing, an amazing humanitarian organization. In just the last five years this organization:

- Rushed into New York immediately after 9/11 and partnered with FEMA in providing tractor-trailers, networking 81 truckloads of relief aid to victims and volunteers. Operation Blessing also brought in an additional 13 truckloads of food and relief supplies.

- Fed countless thousands of Afghan refugees in the fall of 2001, and continues to assist these war-ravaged people in rebuilding their lives through hunger relief, medical assistance and construction projects.

- Helped an estimated 261,000 survivors of Hurricanes Charlie, Frances, Ivan and Jeanne through relief and recovery efforts.

- Distributed 556.7 *million* pounds of food and relief supplies to people in need all over this world!

And while the media and Bush-whackers piled on FEMA and its apparently sluggish reactions to the Katrina crisis, Operation Blessing rushed in and took up residence, awarding $4.2 million to date in cash grants to 214 on-site faith-based organizations that in turn helped their neighbors in need. Operation Blessing also purchased an 18-ton capacity crane to remove trees and debris, literally clearing the way for nearly 22,000 FEMA trailers to be delivered to residents whose homes had been destroyed; signed a six-month lease on warehouse space to continue its relief operations; and, recognizing the urgency of medical care, teamed with International Medical Alliance to help 9,600 patients in New Orleans with an average dispensing of 650 prescriptions daily— and have to date provided over $22 million in free medicines.

Might Pat Robertson, that "wild-eyed fanatic," be cut a little slack? And what about that other Christian "bigot," Franklin Graham, who has been ceaselessly and savagely criticized for saying Islam is a violent religion based on the dictates of its own Quran and by the nature of its society wherever it holds sway?

Well, Franklin Graham is not just a preacher, not just the son and heir of evangelist Billy Graham, but is also the founder and passionate leader of Samaritan's Purse, a worldwide humanitarian relief organization. Like Operation Blessing, this extremely efficient group rushes into every crisis around the globe, dispensing medical help, food and all kinds of relief to multiplied thousands in countries all over the world.

While the floodwaters of Katrina were still swirling, Franklin flew in and set up permanent camps for Samaritan's Purse. In short order (much quicker than FEMA), Samaritan's Purse provided temporary housing for displaced victims, purchasing 100 new mobile homes for a network of 20 local churches to distribute to the most needy, and worked with those and other churches to equip their gymnasiums as shelters. And in addition to the important spiritual counseling and encouragement the organization offers continually, it networks with many local agencies to help the whole devastated area get back on its feet.

Franklin Graham and Samaritan's Purse didn't wait for a FEMA call; they heard one from a higher source and responded immediately. They do what they do in Jesus' name. Like them, let's give credit where it's due. Franklin and his associates are thinking, caring, giving Christians, and they practice what they preach.

Now, for your good news dessert, let Chef Boone introduce you to Mercy Corps, out of Portland and Seattle. Like the two organizations mentioned above, Mercy Corps is a Christian humanitarian relief organization, some 25 years old now. While most of its efforts have been focused in the worst famine-racked, drought-ravaged, earthquake-devastated areas around the world, when Katrina struck our shores, Mercy Corps was on the scene in hours.

Its chairman, Dan O'Neill, has been too busy to attract media attention with provocative statement, and has thus been free to direct the organization's incisive programs. These programs include:

1. Leveraging generous private funding and child help efforts to over 70,000 hurricane-displaced children of all ages

2. Launching a $400,000 grant initiative in New Orleans to help effective, proven social-service groups get back on their feet and back to the business of helping their neighbors, eventually reaching as many as 100 recipient organizations

3. Investing in high-return areas that need capital to rebuild the retail services needed to sustain the returning population—an initial allotment of $350,000 will provide $10,000 to $20,000 chunks of capital to get established-but-damaged businesses back to work

While giant government agencies and Congress allot billions of our tax dollars (and hours and hours of finger-pointing and blame and excuses), these *privately funded* faith organizations are diligently and effectively helping thousands in the Gulf Coast and millions around the world in concrete and extremely effective ways. That's what churches are supposed to do, to "look after orphans and widows in their distress" (Jas. 1:27)—and so many are doing it!

If once in a while one of our Christian leaders says something that others don't understand or applaud, can't he or she be spared the need to gear up a prolonged apology campaign? After any great meal, the cook usually gets to have his say, and each of these leaders and their organizations have literally been feeding the hungry by the tens of thousands. And I dare say none of the critics of what some consider the leadership's ill-chosen words has done a fraction of their well-chosen deeds.

PART II

THE SUSCEPTIBILITY OF CHILDREN AT EACH STAGE OF DEVELOPMENT

CHAPTER 5

The Eyes of Innocence

The innocent eyes of children need protection from exposure to the immoral, perverse, and grotesquely violent images that pervade the mass media of entertainment. The Bible warns us against having a conscience that is defiled and worthless (see Titus 1:15), yet children are left to witness the worst of our culture while their parents are unaware or absent.

Many parents assume that Christian elementary schools are a safe haven. I have opportunities to speak at these schools, and I find that even the first-graders have seen many of the worst sexual and violent movies. While videotaping the *Media-Wise Family* DVD course at a conservative Christian school in Texas, I asked the young children in a first-grade class if they had seen one of the most violent and sexual movies of that year: *Scream*. Forty percent raised their hands and said yes. When I asked one little boy to describe the movie, he described a scene in which a buxom blond was killed. This is just one example of how movies can corrupt our youth.

Would You Hire This Babysitter?

A few years back, the evening news broadcasted a story about a babysitter in Dallas, Texas, who had molested the baby she was supposed to protect. The parents, who had become suspicious, installed a hidden camera. The evening news showed the babysitter starting to undress in front of the baby. Millions were horrified and wondered how the parents had failed to check this sitter's credentials. The news team closed by remarking that this type of abuse probably occurred more often than anyone knew.

They were right. There is one babysitter who is constantly abusing millions of our children: a television set. No one fires this babysitter or brings criminal charges against it, nor do many people try to rehabilitate it. The same could be said about computers, iPods and other mass media of entertainment.

No matter how much we condemn the mass media for influencing the behavior of our children, we must admit that there are several accomplices in this tragedy. These accomplices include churches that don't instruct parents how to teach their children discernment and parents who allow their children to watch television, go to movies or surf the Internet without adequate supervision.

Child Abuse via the Silver Screen

Even the secular press understands the problem of exposing children to violent and improper television and movies. In an article in the *Los Angeles Times*, James Scott Bell, a writer and novelist in Los Angeles, noted:

> The country was rightly repulsed at the videotape of Madelyne Toogood beating her four-year-old child in an Indiana parking lot. We know such mistreatment can have a terrible effect on a child's mental health. But how many Americans indulge in a worse form of abuse without a second thought? I'm talking about taking kids to the movies. The wrong movies.
>
> The other night I saw *Red Dragon*, the third installment in the Hannibal Lecter series starring Anthony Hopkins. When the bad guy (Ralph Fiennes) bites off the tongue of a screaming reporter, then stands up, mouth bloody, and spits out the offending organ, I squirmed in my seat. What I couldn't stop thinking about, however, was the little girl in the seat in front of me.
>
> She looked about six years old . . . Two hours of mayhem ensued. People stabbed, set on fire, tortured. Your average day at the office for serial killers. Every now and then I'd lean over and see the little girl with her eyes fixed to the screen.[1]

For many children throughout the world, the culture czars have shut out the light of the good news of the Bible while adding sexual perversion, avarice and political correctness to their curriculums. For many children, the mass media has become their primary caregiver and teacher. The average child in the United States only gets about 21 minutes a day of primary attention with their parents, but, according to the

Motion Picture Association, spends up to 10.25 hours per day with the Internet and TV. Therefore, by the time the average American child is 17 years old, he or she has watched 63,000 hours of mass media, spent 11,000 hours in school and gone to church for only 800 hours (assuming he or she has gone every Sunday for one hour since birth).

Because of this, most children do not know the important liberating lessons of the Ten Commandments that it is wrong to lie, cheat and steal, but they do recognize the top 10 celebrities or the top 10 tunes that they can download on their iPods.

Children Want to Be Media Wise

Still, studies show that most children want their parents involved in their lives and want to be media wise. A survey conducted in 2001 of 1,014 high school students across the United States showed that almost half of respondents would pick a family member—not a pop icon or a sports star—as a role model. In addition, the majority of respondents said that they could confide in someone in their family. Furthermore, 84

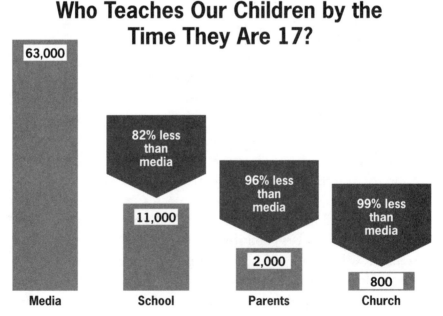

Who Teaches Our Children by the Time They Are 17?

63,000 — Media

82% less than media — 11,000 — School

96% less than media — 2,000 — Parents

99% less than media — 800 — Church

Source: *MovieGuide*® 2003

percent said that their future success would be defined by whether they had close family relationships. More than a quarter said that a major cause of school violence was parents spending too little time with their children, second only to bullying by other students.[2]

When I talk to these teenagers and younger children, the majority of them say that they want to make media and culture-wise decisions. However, their schools, churches and parents must help. Many media-awareness training courses have proved effective over recent years, yet the most basic media and culture-wise course involves parents reading to their children—especially if the book is the Bible.

In a recent survey conducted by the American Bible Society, 70 percent of the 12- to 15-year-olds surveyed said that the messages of the Bible applied to their lives. African-American teenagers were significantly more likely to agree with this statement than teenagers of all other races and ethnic groups. Another major finding in the survey was that teenagers are likely to turn to the Bible in times of crisis. About 58.9 percent of girls—as compared to 52 percent of boys—said they were more likely to read the Bible when a family member or friend was sick or dying.[3]

Seek Understanding

Scientists argue that such significant evidence exists to connect the content of the mass media and social behavior—especially aggressive behavior—that it's time for researchers to move on and focus on the processes

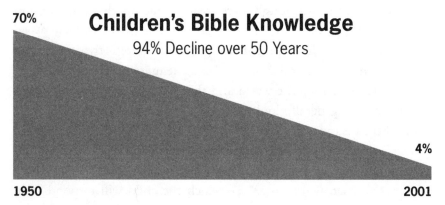

70%

Children's Bible Knowledge
94% Decline over 50 Years

4%

1950   2001

Source: *MovieGuide®* 2005

that are responsible for this relationship. Dr. Victor Strasburger, chief of the American Academy of Pediatrics' section on adolescents, stated, "We are basically saying the controversy is over. There is clearly a relationship between media violence and violence in society."[4]

The media research team of Robert Lichter, Linda Lichter, Stanley Rothman and Daniel Amundson conducted a report on four decades of entertainment TV and found that there were about 50 crimes, including a dozen murders, during every hour of prime time television. This indicates that our children may see from 800,000 to 1.5 million acts of violence and witness 192,000 to 360,000 murders on television by the time they are 17 years old.[5]

The next generation must maintain a real world that will not correlate to their virtual reality. Lichter and his fellow authors note, "Since 1955, TV characters have been murdered at a rate 1,000 times higher than real-world victims." If the same murder rate was applied to the general population, everyone in the United States would be killed in just 50 days![6]

If you are over 40 years old, you probably watch only six movies a year in theaters, most of which are family films. In contrast, teenagers watch an average of 50 movies, 80 percent of which are R-rated or rated PG-13. They watch another 50 movies a year on video.[7]

Cognitive Development in Children

Many of the theories regarding the influence of culture on children that have developed over the years involve the stages of cognitive development of children. Although there are many factors that are common to all ages of development, there are also unique distinctions between each stage of child development that requires different treatment with regard to exposure to and training about the mass media.

Children often see the world and the media quite differently than adults. Parents generally look at television programs semantically in terms of the meaning of what is said or what is happening. Children see syntactically in terms of the action and special effects in the program. Thus, with regard to music, a mother will say to her child, "Did you hear the lyrics in that awful song?" To which the child will respond, "Ah, Mom, I don't listen to the words. Did you hear the rhythm and the beat?"

An episode of *Mr. Roger's Neighborhood* highlighted this generation gap. As Mr. Rogers was visiting a class of little children, a girl asked him how he got out of the television set to be with them that day. Mr. Rogers said that he was never in the television set, and then carefully explained how TV worked. He then asked the girl if she understood him. She said, "Yes, but how are you going to get back into the TV so I can watch you this afternoon?"

Growing Pains

Cognitive development is often directly impacted by the mass media, especially television. It is important to understand that while thinking is part of cognition, cognition is the process of knowing (something philosophers and theologians call "epistemology"). Cognitive development is similar to building a house step by step from a blueprint or installing an operating system on a computer so that it can do all of the tasks it is directed to do. Each step must be taken in the right order, or the result will be disastrous. In the same way, each stage of human development has unique characteristics that must be processed in order.

As I was teaching at an Ivy League graduate school, a woman in the audience shrieked because her toddler took a sharp object and was about to do what every toddler does with whatever they pick up: put it in his mouth. After quickly taking the dangerous object away, the mother started to lecture him. When the wave of concern in the room died down, I noted this child was in the sensation stage of cognitive development, which meant that his learning came through his senses. Thus, his mother's lecture had no effect on him, because the toddler could not understand the logic of her arguments. Toddlers need parents to make wise decisions for them.

When one stage of cognitive development passes to another, the previous stage is forgotten. When my six-year-old boy, Robby, was frightened by a thunderstorm, my 11-year-old, Peirce, tried to get his younger brother to be quiet by telling him to shut up. When this method didn't work, Peirce told Robby that the reason for the thunderstorm was that God was angry with him. Of course, this only aggravated Robby's fears. So I pointed out to Peirce that Robby was affected by the storm differently because he was trying to sort out the difference between fact and fiction. Robby was in the imagination stage of cognitive development.

Peirce was reminded of an incident that occurred when he was in the imagination stage. He had a sleepover with his nine-year-old friend, who had nightmares all night long. When I asked Peirce's friend the next morning what was bothering him, the friend said that his father had taken him to see the R-rated movie *Total Recall*. The boy said that he didn't like the scene where Arnold Schwarzenegger shoots Sharon Stone, who was posing as his wife, and says, "Consider that a divorce."

When I called his father to tell him of the fears expressed by his son, the father replied that his son was a man and that they went to a lot of R-rated movies. I explained that taking him to see these films was putting him on the front line of psychological and spiritual warfare. It was just like sending him into a battle before he was old enough to be trained to carry a weapon. A few months later, the father called to admit that he could see that his son was disturbed by the movies.

Personality Affects Susceptibility

As we investigate the stages of development of children, it is important to remember that each child has a unique personality and will thus be susceptible to different media and cultural influences. Thus, some will be susceptible to violence, some to sex, some to drugs, some to gambling, some to acquiring things, and so forth.

The key word is "susceptible." It appears that the majority of people who view a violent or sexual television program or film seem to be unaffected or desensitized by what they see. A minority of 20 to 30 percent see themselves as the victim. Seven to 11 percent want to mimic the actions of the protagonist, whether viewing an advertisement selling beer, a minister seeking conversions, or a violent program depicting rape. A significant percentage will mimic the protagonist only if they are susceptible to his or her specific desire.[8]

Five Seasons

Psychology, including cognitive development, can help us understand why children are affected by the messages of the culture and the mass media. In the late 1970s, the research of the renowned child psychologist Jean Piaget was used by television researcher Robert Morse to correlate the stages of cognitive growth to research the affect of the mass media.[9] The research suggests that every child goes through the following five stages:

1. **Sensation stage** (approximately ages 0 to 2 years).[10] During this stage, children's sole means of processing reality is through their senses. They will think that they are the center of the universe, that something exists only if they can see it, and that everything around them serves them.

2. **Imagination stage** (approximately ages 2 to 7).[11] During this stage, children's cognition is dedicated to the acquisition of representational skills such as language, mental imagery, drawing and symbolic play and is limited by being one dimensional. Children will have very active imaginations, often confusing fact and fiction, which makes them uniquely susceptible to what they see in television and movies. As an example, a four-year-old girl was critically injured when she apparently tried to fly after watching *Harry Potter and the Sorcerer's Stone*. Authorities in Shelby, North Carolina, said that the girl watched the movie and then crawled onto a kitchen counter, straddled a broom and jumped off.

3. **Concrete operational stage** (approximately ages 7 to 11): During this stage, children acquire the ability to simultaneously perceive two points of view, enabling them to master quantities, relations and classes of objects. At this stage, there is a strong correspondence between children's thoughts and reality. They assume that their thoughts about reality are accurate, and they distort the facts to fit what they believe to be true. While younger children react more to direct violence than suspense, children in the concrete stage of cognitive development will be more affected by suspense. Thus, little children may get bored by *Jaws,* which is mostly suspense, while older children may be traumatized by it.

4. **Reflection or formal operations stage** (approximately ages 12 to 15): It is during this stage that adolescents' abstract thoughts gain strength. They will still have incomplete differentiation as a result of their inability to conceptualize the thoughts of others—as exemplified by the assumption that other people are as obsessed with their behavior and appearance as they are—and they are also more likely to take risks during this stage because they will have difficulty conceptualizing the consequences of their actions. For example, when the movie *The Program* was released, several teenagers were killed or seriously injured when they mimicked the main characters by lying down in the middle of the road to prove their courage. One national radio personality said that these teenagers were really stupid; however, one of the teenagers who died was at the top of his class. What the radio personality did not understand was that these teenagers were at a stage of development in which they were the most impulsive and the least able to consider the consequences of their actions. Like most adults, the radio personality didn't remember what it was like to be in a previous stage of cognitive development.

5. **Relationship stage:** This stage occurs when the adolescent grows into a mature adult and there is complete differentiation. The adult understands that others are different and accepts those differences by learning to relate to others. Furthermore, the adult is able to conceptualize the consequences of his or her actions and take the necessary steps to reduce risks.

Babes in Toyland

A Tufts University study released in January 2003 showed that TV carries messages that influence the behavior of children as young as 12 months old. In the study, 10-month-old and 12-month-old infants watched a videotape of an actress reacting to a toy with a positive or negative emotion. When the actress appeared to be afraid of the toy, the babies avoided playing with it and appeared worried or even cried. When the actress enthusiastically played with the toy, the infants were more likely to play with the toy.

Tufts child behavioral expert Dr. Donna Mumme noted, "It was quite striking to us that one-year-olds were able to gather that much information from a 20-second television clip." Dr. Mumme concluded that parents may want to "think twice before they let an infant see television programs meant for an older person."[12]

The Effects of Graphic Horror on Children

In another study, researchers Barbara J. Wilson, Daniel Lynn and Barbara Randall examined the harmful effects of graphic horror on children and discovered some important distinctions:[13]

- **Visual versus non-visual threat:** The principle of perceptual dependence suggests that younger children are likely to be frightened by movies and television programs with visually frightening creatures such as witches and monsters. Older children will focus more on conceptual qualities, such as the motives of a character, and are likely to be more upset by an evil, normal-looking character or by an unseen threat than by a benign but grotesque character.[14] Younger children tend to be more frightened by *The Wizard of Oz* than older children, while older children tend to be more frightened by movies such as *Poltergeist* and *Jaws*, which rely more on non-visual threats.

- **Reality versus fantasy:** Younger children are unable to fully distinguish between reality and fantasy.[15] Although the terms "real" and "make-believe" may be used in conversation, younger children do not understand the implications of these terms. The notion that a character or an event is not real has little impact on a younger child's emotions. Because of this, movies with fantasy offerings involving events that could not possibly happen, such as Harry Potter, are more frightening to younger children, whereas fictional programs involving events that could happen, such as *Jaws*, are more frightening to older children and adults.[16]

• **Abstract versus concrete events:** A concrete threat is explicit and tangible, while an abstract threat must be inferred from information in the plot. Thus, an evil character that attacks a victim is an explicit threat, while movies about evil conspiracies or disasters such as poisonous gases incorporate an abstract threat. Younger children have difficulty drawing inferences from entertainment and are more likely to focus on explicit rather than implicit cues in the plot, so they will be more frightened by a movie depicting a concrete threat than one involving an intangible or obscure hazard.[17]

• **Threat versus victim focus:** Movies that require viewer involvement and that focus primarily on the victims' emotional reactions are less upsetting for younger than for older children. The movie *Jaws* is a good example of this, because the viewer often only sees the upper bodies of the victims as they are being attacked by the unseen shark.

Contextual Features of Violence

More important than the sheer amount of mass media horror and violence children watch is the way in which even small amounts of violence are portrayed.[18] Therefore, "a number of contextual features of violence are critical determinants of whether such depictions will facilitate aggressive behavior."[19] According to Wilson, Lynn and Randall, these contextual features are:

• **Reward versus punishment associated with violence:** Violent depictions in which the aggressor is rewarded are most likely to produce imitation effects or foster attitudes supportive of aggression.[20] In fact, characters need not be explicitly rewarded—as long as there is no punishment associated with a violent act, young viewers will often imitate such depictions.[21] Furthermore, when the characters' self-assertion succeeds over their self-controlled social behavior, children may construe this as a type of reward—especially if the violence is portrayed without negative consequences, neither the perpetrators nor victims suffer much, and the aggressor is rewarded for antisocial actions (which is the case in the Harry Potter films).[22]

- **Timing of the reward:** The timing of the reward or punishment has important implications as well.[23] In many movies, the perpetrator receives material rewards immediately after performing an aggressive act. Punishment, however, is delivered toward the end. Since young children are not able to coherently link scenes together and to draw inferences from them, younger children are more likely than older children to see the violence as acceptable.[24]

- **Degree of reality of violence:** Violence perceived to be realistic is more likely to be imitated and used as a guide for behavior. Older children are better able to distinguish reality from fantasy and are more emotionally responsive to programs that depict realistic events, such as the movie *Scream*. Younger children are responsive to both realistic and unrealistic violent acts that are concrete and visual.[25]

- **The nature of the perpetrator:** Children are more likely to imitate models that are perceived as attractive or interesting.[26] Children who strongly identify with violent media characters are more likely to be aggressive themselves than are those who do not identify with such characters.[27] Younger children are more likely to focus on the consequences of their behavior to determine whether the character is "good" or "bad," whereas older children tend to focus more on the character's motives.[28]

· **Justified violence:** Violence that is portrayed as justified is
more likely to be imitated by children.[29] A common theme in
many movies is the portrayal of a hero who is forced to be violent because his job demands it (such as in the Dirty Harry
movies) or because he must retaliate against an enemy (as in
the Harry Potter films). Although the message may be ultimately prosocial (e.g., "don't be a criminal"), the moral is conveyed in a violent context. In one experiment examining the
mixed messages children receive in media, researchers found
that kindergartners were more likely to hurt a peer after
watching a cartoon depicting justified violence.[30] Both
younger and older children showed less understanding of a
moral lesson when it was conveyed in the context of justified
violence versus no violence. Therefore, a hero who commits
violence for some good cause is likely to be a confusing role
model for children.

· **Similarity of movie situations and characters to viewer:**
Viewers are more likely to imitate media violence if cues in the
program are similar to those in real life.[31] Also, children are
likely to imitate models that are similar to themselves.[32] Thus,
movies depicting children as violent are more problematic
than those involving violent adults. Preschool and early elementary school children focus on younger characters that are
violent, whereas preteens and teenagers attend more to
aggressive teenage characters.

· **Amount of violence:** Although the way in which violence is
portrayed is critical, the sheer amount and explicitness of
violent content is also important with regard to the viewer's
emotions. Excessive exposure to violence may produce a psychological blunting of emotional responses. Children who are
heavy viewers of violence show less arousal to violence than
light viewers. In one experiment, children who watched a violent film or television program were found to be subsequent-

ly less likely to seek help when the other children became disruptive and violent. Thus, exposure to media violence leads to a lack of responsiveness to real-life aggression.[33]

Dangerous Minds

Part of the problem with television and movies is the lack of time for the viewer to reflect, react or review the information he or she is receiving—processes that are absolutely necessary for cognitive development. The very act of watching television and movies can be harmful to the cognitive development of children and, as a consequence, may adversely influence their moral, social, emotional and religious development. Videos and television also "debilitates an important cognitive function in adults, the one that permits abstract reasoning and hence related capacities for moral decision making, learning, religious growth, and psychological individualization."[34]

The Twilight Zone

Children who are heavy users of mass media entertainment demonstrate a decreased capacity for creative imagination, concentration and delayed gratification. They are less able to form mental pictures and engage in less imaginative play. Children who are heavy users of mass media entertainment also have greatly decreased attention spans. Their capacity for delayed gratification translates to less tolerance for reading a book or other activities.

The child's symbolic function, perception and abstract reasoning are damaged in a manner that resembles dyslexia. In fact, the rapid increase in reading disabilities (or dyslexia) in the United States may be, in part, attributed to heavy television viewing. Television inhibits eye movement and thereby the acquisition of reading skills. Researcher Robert Morse believes that television saps the cognitive strength, analogous to the situation in nursing homes where inactivity leads to cognitive impairment. After an hour or two of television watching, people come away cranky, irritable, tired and ready to explode.[35] In an article in *The Atlanta Constitution*, John Rosemond notes:

The next time your child watches television, look at him instead of the screen. Ask yourself, "What is he doing?" Better yet, ask yourself, "What is he not doing?"

In answer, he is not . . . Practicing motor skills, gross or fine. Practicing eye-hand coordination. Using more than two senses. Asking questions. Exploring. Exercising initiative or imagination. Being challenged. Solving problems. Thinking analytically. Exercising imagination. Practicing communication skills. Being either creative or constructive.

Also, because of television's insidious "flicker," (every four seconds, on the average, the picture changes) television does not promote long-term attention.

Lastly, because the action shifts constantly and capriciously backward, forward and laterally in time. . . . television does not promote logical sequential thinking.

So what? Well, interestingly enough, the deficiencies noted above are characteristic of learning-disabled children, children who don't seem able to "get it all together" when it comes to learning how to read and write.[36]

Honey, I Shrunk the Kids

By contributing to cognitive impairment, mass media of entertainment has a deleterious effect on a child's moral, social, emotional, and religious development.[37]

With regard to social and emotional development, a child needs dramatic play to develop in these areas, but dramatic play, as we have noticed, is inhibited by watching television or movies. Watching social interaction on television is not enough, because a child must do or act. He or she must be more than just an observer, or his or her social and emotional development will be impaired.

In the case of psychological maturation, the necessary function of suppressing detrimental functions of the libido is impaired because television and the other mass media indulge these detrimental functions. With regard to religious development, impairment of the symbolic function results in the "clogging of the filters of religious perception" so that the child's doorway to experience of the transcendent is blocked.[38] Television watching causes the viewer to see reality or the nature of being (ontology) as illusory, whereas Christianity is posited on a real ontology or nature of being. God created a real world in which events are independent of our consciousness or our imaginations. Television inhibits a Christian ontology and worldview.

Children Imitate Modeled Behavior

The observational learning theory suggests that children imitate modeled behavior.[39] Researchers have found that when a young viewer watches a violent television episode, he or she stores that behavior in his brain. When a similar situation arises in reality, the viewer may retrieve and mimic the violent act once viewed. One mother stated to me that her young son loved the Harry Potter movies, but he frustrated her by not obeying anything she commanded him to do. The boy had learned from Harry Potter that disregard for explicit orders and rules brought rewards.

Dr. Victor Cline reports that more intelligent and imaginative viewers are more susceptible to mimicking and becoming addicted to the viewed behavior. Cline found that the vast majority of criminals behind bars for sexual crimes are intelligent.[40] In the last interview before his execution, serial killer Ted Bundy described to Dr. James Dobson the stages of addiction that he experienced to become a killer, starting with 1950s' soft-core pornography, which was much milder than what is being shown in most movies and television programs today.

Attitude change theory suggests that when some children watch a great deal of violent television, they develop a favorable attitude toward aggressive behavior and see violent behavior as normal and acceptable.[41] Other children are anesthetized or desensitized by the same overloading process.

Virtual Sociopaths

Another area of research on the influence of the mass media on children and adults is false memory syndrome, unchained memories, memory therapy and associated psychological insights that have captured the national imagination. Scientists have discovered that the more intense and realistic the exposure is to over-stimulating messages, the more likely the memory is to be encoded, stored in the memory, and retrieved later, unless resolved.

One factor that probably contributes to the false memory syndrome is the tremendous amount of movie and television sex, violence and occultism that has filled the minds of youth over the years. Other mass media have planted images that are misconstrued due to improper processing along with other routine activities. However, unlike the many daily events that are repetitive and dull, these entertaining programs are a potent and often dissonant, if not traumatic, brew of emotive messages that lodge in the nooks and crannies of the child's memory waiting to pop into their dreams or consciousness.

Research indicates that the minds of our youth are confused regarding reality and history. Everyday examples abound, from the woman who saw the movie *Independence Day* and afterwards told a reporter that the government is hiding a flying saucer, to those who saw the movie *The Wind and the Lion* and assume that this historical incident involved a beautiful woman and a dashing desert chieftain rather than the real characters—an old Greek immigrant and a Moroccan thief.

Memory therapists have been able to induce adults to fabricate a childhood history from disjointed memories. Regrettably, some of these adults acted on these false memories. Whether they are from a therapist or the mass media, false memories interfere with development, reasoning and common sense. Individuals who are confused by false memories may develop psychoses and neurosis. Regrettably, these individuals could become tomorrow's deviants. How people confuse their memories of fact and fantasy is open to question, but almost everyone has a story of some young person whose view of history was based on a television or movie revision of facts. In his article "The Monster in the Mists," Walter Reich points out:

> The institution of memory deserves all the respect and protection it can get. One indication of how vulnerable to manipulation it already is can be appreciated from the fact that Holocaust deniers have managed to receive, in recent years, a respectful

hearing on college campuses and elsewhere, despite the existence of mountains of first-hand and traumatic memories of the Holocaust provided by many thousands of survivors—memories that don't have to be recovered because they are all too vividly, and all too persistently, remembered.[42]

Perhaps we have moved from George Santayana's insight that "those who do not remember the past are condemned to relive it" to a more terrifying realization that "those who confuse the past are condemned to lose touch with reality." In the end, a person's memory is all that stands in the way of chaos.

Adrenaline and Brain Development

When the mind believes that it is about to engage in a life-threatening activity, the body releases adrenal epinephrine into the bloodstream that results in an adrenal rush. Likewise, viewing sexual activity and nudity can trick the body to release raging hormones without the burdens attendant to human relationships. These *physiological phenomena* engage the viewer, often causing him or her to want more exposure to the stimuli that cause artificial physical elation.

Another study showed that boys who watch a great deal of violent programming exhibit less arousal when shown new violent programs than boys who watch less violent fare.[43] This study seems to explain why consumers of mass media sex and violence need more prurient or violent fare for equal stimulation. Of course, all of this can add up to addiction, because most of the offerings of the mass media are emotive rather than intellectual.

Teenagers are subject to tremendous peer pressure. They have a predisposition to seek out movies and programs that arouse them. They then become so aroused that they desire the emotive situations portrayed in the movie or television program in their own lives.

Neuroscientists have also found that the adolescent brain will not mature until the person is in his or her twenties. A National Institute of Health study suggests that the region of the brain that inhibits risky behavior is not fully formed until age 25. In fact, one of the last parts of the brain to mature is in charge of making wise decisions and controlling emotions. [44]

Changes in brain neurology are paralleled by hormone changes that confuse the teenager about sex, self and safety. Some bipolar teenagers are more apt to see hostility where none exists. This may explain why children with bipolar disorder tend to be more aggressive and irritable and have poorer social skills than healthy children. In fact, the study conducted at the National Institute of Mental Health shows that bipolar youths misinterpret facial expressions to be hostile more often than their healthy counterparts. [45]

Truth or Consequences

Since 1966 (the year the Church abandoned Hollywood), violent crime has increased in the United States by 560 percent, illegitimate births have increased 419 percent, divorce rates have quadrupled, the percentage of children living in single-parent homes has tripled, the teenage suicide rate has increased more than 300 percent, and SAT scores have dropped almost 80 points. Rapes, murders and gang violence have become common occurrences. While there are many factors that have contributed to this cultural decline, it is clear that the mass media has had a significant influence on people's behavior. [46]

Researchers affiliated with the National Bureau of Economic Research at Stanford University found that children in America are fatter, more suicidal and score lower on standardized tests in recent years than they did during the 1960s. [47] After years of denial, even 87 percent of the top media executives admit that the violence in the mass media contributes to the violence in society. [48] Even children are aware that entertainment media can influence their behavior.

Yet in spite of the clear correlation between violence in the mass media and violence on the street, very few people are yelling, "Stop!" The growing American tolerance for brutal sex and violence in the mass media suggests the proverbial frog that is oblivious to his demise as he is slowly brought to a boil. If we understand the consequences of the research, then before our children are brought to a boil by the mass media of entertainment, we will intercede to protect their eyes of innocence.

CHAPTER 6

Child's Play

Children are on the frontline of the culture war. Throughout history, religions and worldviews have been at war with each other, but, in the last century, many of the warring ideologies have refocused their attacks on children as the means to winning the war and remaking society.

For instance, in the past, both the Communists (International Socialists) and the National Socialists vigorously targeted children for reeducation in schools and in various youth organizations such as Hitler Youth so that they would become the new Communist or Socialist man or woman who would oppose all things Christian. Today, other ideologies and religions are doing the same thing. Some are doing it consciously for ideological reasons, and some to make money or manipulate the masses.

Why would these groups oppose all things Christian as the Marxists of the Frankfurt School demanded in the 1930s? Christianity is antithetical to tyranny, and for tyranny to triumph, people must be separated from God. Christianity liberates people from the control of the internal forces of lust and pride, as well as the fear of oppressive external controls, setting people free to build a civilization based on love for God and for their fellow men and women—a love that emphasizes respect and responsibility.

In his 1983 Templeton Prize Address in London, England, Alexander Solzhenitzyn cut right to the essence of why the Soviet Socialist system in Russia killed, tortured and suppressed millions in the name of perfecting the new Communist society:

> Over a half century ago, while I was still a child, I recall hearing a number of old people offer the following explanation for the great disasters that had befallen Russia: "Men have forgotten God; that's why all this has happened." Since then I have spent

well-nigh 50 years working on the history of our revolution; in
the process I have read hundreds of books, collected hundreds
of personal testimonies, and have already contributed eight
volumes of my own toward the effort of clearing away the rubble left by that upheaval. But if I were asked today to formulate
as concisely as possible the main cause of the ruinous revolution that swallowed up some 60 million of our people, I could
not put it more accurately than to repeat: "Men have forgotten
God; that's why all this has happened."[1]

Lulled by Abundance

The roots of civilization are only one generation deep, and if one generation fails to understand the lessons of history, the results can be an
enhanced barbarism embellished by the technological marvels of the
age. So it was with Germany when it went from being the most cultured
and civilized society to National Socialism. So it was with Russia when
it went from being Holy Mother Russia to International Socialism.

Today we are lulled by entertainment and abundance. "What difference does it make if a little girl is gunned down by her classmates?" one
student asked me at an Ivy League college, as I lectured just after the
tragedy at Columbine. We face a precarious situation when this type of
thinking invades our most revered institutions of higher learning.

More TV Equals More Violence

A study led by Jeffrey G. Johnson of Columbia University and the New
York State Psychiatric Institute, published in the journal *Science*, found
that teenagers and young adults who watch more than one hour of television daily are more likely to commit violent crimes and other forms
of aggressive behavior.

The study found a link between violence and viewing *any* television,
not just violent programming. Adolescents and young adults who
watched television for more than seven hours per week had an increased
likelihood of between 16 and 200 percent of committing an aggressive
act in later years. "The evidence has gotten to the point where it's overwhelming," Johnson said.[2]

Glorifying Gangs

Closely related to the riots are gang movies that have left a trail of tears and death. Police have called some of these films "irresponsible" and "exploitive." Several people have been killed and wounded at the openings of films that exploit gang violence. At the opening of filmmaker John Singleton's movie *Boyz in the Hood*, 33 people were injured and two people died from gunshot wounds. When *Boyz in the Hood* was shown in one California prison, 14 people in the prison died in one night of race rioting.

Violence broke out in at least eight states after the premiere of *Juice*. Some time later, a teenager named Hicks pleaded guilty to malice and armed robbery in what a prosecutor called a totally pointless murder. "One of the co-defendants [Mr. Clegg] said he and Mr. Hicks [the killer] had seen the movie *Juice* the weekend before this particular incident, and there was a sequence in it where a totally pointless murder was committed," Clegg said. "I'm told the words Mr. Hicks spoke at the time he fired the shot came from that movie: 'Oh, by the way, *bam!*'"[3]

On the positive side of the influence of the entertainment media equation: The epic movie *The Passion of the Christ* introduced people throughout the world to Jesus Christ; *A Man Called Peter*, about the preacher Peter Marshall, brought a flood of many young men into the pulpit; and *Chariots of Fire* brought friends of mine to Jesus and gave many more a sense of God's purpose in their life.

Slasher Movies and Stephen King Novels

It is clear to any parent that children learn to a large degree by mimicking the behavior of the adults around them, including those on television and in movies.

One of the most famous copycat crimes was the connection that a judge in Liverpool, England, made between the horror movie *Child's Play 3* and the murder of two-year-old James Bulger by two 11-year-old boys, Robert Thompson and Jon Venables. According to the judge, *Child's Play 3* presents some horrifying parallels to the actual murder of little James Bulger, and the movie was viewed repeatedly by one of the killers just before the murder took place. The judge noted:

- The horror movie depicts a baby doll that comes to life and gets blue paint splashed in its face. There was blue paint on the dead child's face.

- The movie depicts a kidnapping. James was abducted by the two older boys before they killed him.

- The climax of the movie comes as two young boys murder the doll on a train, mutilating the doll's face. James was first mutilated and bludgeoned by the two older boys and then left on a railroad track to be run over.[4]

This story was widely publicized around the world, but the link to *Child's Play 3* was overlooked or withheld by the mainstream media. If the media had been asked why, their answer might have been enlightening.

In 1993, 13-year-old Eric Smith lured four-year-old Derrick Robie into the woods, bludgeoned his head with rocks and sodomized his body. According to press reports about the crime, Eric loved reading Stephen King novels and watching gruesome slasher movies—the more pornographic the better. Jurors found Eric Smith guilty of second-degree murder.

In Houston, Texas, Scott Edward May, a 17-year-old obsessed with slasher movies, the occult and heavy metal music, attacked a girl during their first date, stabbing her when she closed her eyes for a good-night kiss. "I love knives," May's statement read. "I like to go to the movies a lot. A lot of people get stabbed in the movies. I really liked the *Texas Chainsaw Massacre*. A lot of people got stabbed in that."[5]

Hannibal the Cannibal

Over the years, there have been innumerable reports of grisly crimes that were inspired by and mimicked the fictional product of the entertainment media. It is important to take note of the powerful influence of the mass media. One of the most notorious movies spawning copycat murders is *The Silence of the Lambs*, a movie about a serial killer known as "Hannibal the Cannibal." The same week that *The Silence of the*

Lambs won the 1992 Academy Award for "Best Picture of the Year," a young man decapitated his handicapped mother and yelled, "I'm Hannibal the Cannibal!" as he was led away by police.[6]

In a related case, Brian Allender told a psychiatrist that he had watched *The Silence of the Lambs* shortly before murdering and mutilating a Vancouver prostitute in January 1992.[7] Dr. Shabehram Lohrasbe interviewed Allender eight times following the murder and said he displayed no clinical signs of a major mental disorder or sexual deviancy. He concluded that Allender's conduct was caused by three factors: (1) an unnatural relationship with his mother, (2) a preoccupation with pornography and voyeurism, and (3) viewing *The Silence of the Lambs* prior to picking up the prostitute.

Desensitized and Confused

It is strange that our society has become so desensitized and confused that even prisoners are fed a mass media diet of movies like *The Silence of the Lambs.* I recently received the following incisive analysis of the effects of sex and violence on captive minds from a prisoner's perspective:

> In many (perhaps most) prisons, . . . the movies are selected by an inmate advisory council. . . . Would it surprise you to learn that the favored genres are those containing the most naked flesh engaging in fornication, the most horrific gore and the most gratuitous violence?
>
> Men are highly aroused sexually through what they see. . . . Incarcerated men are already in a sexually frustrating situation, and arousal of sexual thoughts and feelings only aggravates the problem.
>
> There is not a man in here, . . . who can watch sex on the screen without being affected by it in a manner that is emotionally and spiritually detrimental.
>
> Allow me to be blunt: *it is an absurdity to believe that the effect of sex and violence in movies is any different upon you and your children than it is upon me and my fellow inmates.* A short while ago many of us stood in the same ticket lines as you. We've sat in

the same movie theaters, watching the same movies. We've rented videos from the same video stores as you. The world system touches every life, and every person is led into sin in the same ways, through the lust of the eyes, lust of the flesh and the sinful pride of life (1 John 2:15-16).

How many minds out there are being programmed right now to do the things that could result in their joining us in prison? How many people are being desensitized, emotionally manipulated to follow harmful role models and conditioned to accept aberrant sexual behavior as normal? How many hearts are being turned to stone?[8]

An article in the *Los Angeles Times* asked, "Why Do Critics Love These Repellent Movies?" Stephen Farber responded that moviegoers looking for guidance are alienated by the reviewers' penchant for grotesque violence. He said it has become chic to praise a movie for being nihilistic, macabre and unsentimental. He concludes that "in contemporary . . . criticism, there's no perspective, no sense of what is truly valuable."[9]

Lethal Weapons of Mass Media

Michael Medved notes that more than half of the children in our society watch TV without supervision, and 40 percent have a TV set in their room. Further, television is only part of their entertainment diet. Radio, CDs, videos, video games, computer games, magazines, comics and the Internet are included in the regular diet of most American children.[10] A 1992 report from the American Psychological Association states, "Television can cause aggressive behavior and can cultivate values favoring the use of aggression."[11]

Cigarette companies are no longer allowed to advertise on television because of the threat to human life and health that such advertisements pose. Yet television and movies advertise sex and violence day after day to the detriment of thousands of people who are maimed, raped or robbed by the deluded Ted Bundys of this world. To reiterate the words of Dr. Victor Strasburger, "There is clearly a relationship between media violence and violence in society."[12]

In an interview with Bill Moyers on PBS, David Puttnam, former president of Columbia Pictures and the producer of *Chariots of Fire*, explained that once people are exposed to the spectacle of blood and sex, they become hardened to the titillation of the last violent or sexual act that they see. Just as a drug addict keeps looking for the initial "ideal" rush, so those who are addicted to the sex and violence in films seek increasing doses of sex and violence to appease their lust.[13]

Reel World Values Versus Real Values

Many aspects of Hollywood's virtual reality skewer our children's attitudes and prompt them to imitate self-destructive or uncivil behavior. Confusing the reel world with the real world can create fears and anxieties that are abnormal.

The entertainment media, including entertainment television and movies, does not portray reality but a particular and intentionally emotive perspective on reality. Even reality programs and television news programs concentrate on the exploitable and the emotive. Hollywood often recycles the same plots, ideas and characters. In an analytical examination of the messages of the reel world, Dr. Robert Kubey pinpointed the primary messages of the media:

- For everything there is a quick fix.
- Young is better.
- Open and unfilled time cannot be tolerated.
- Violence is acceptable.
- Religion is unacceptable.
- Sex is only good outside of marriage.[14]

Is this the way we want our children to view the world? Is this the way we want the rest of the world to view us? These messages eat away at the fabric of our civilization.

No Place to Hide

We cannot hide the fact that mass media is an integral part of contemporary society. The larger-than-life images, the emotive beat of pop music and the virtual reality of the Internet reflect and shape our culture. We can hear the call to appreciate our talents and take a stand for biblical principles or risk the affect of these influences to seduce audiences into perversion and senseless violence.

According to studies by the Annenberg School of Communications, substantiated by the National Institute of Mental Health, television programs and films:

- Directly affect a small percentage of the viewers who are suscep- tible to the message of the movie and will emulate that message in their own lives by copying the sexual, violent or immoral act modeled in the movie

- Adversely affect a larger proportion of the audience, causing them to fear the act in question

- Have no apparent effect on the largest portion of the audience, although there may be long-term consequences of watching anti-social material[15]

The point of this litany of problems is that the media and the arts are pervasive in our society. Either denial or license will allow the problems to continue to grow out of control, but the weapons of our warfare are mighty in God for pulling down strongholds (see 2 Cor. 10:4).

TV and Teen Sex

A study of American children ages 12 to 17 has found that those who watch a lot of television with sexual content are about twice as likely to start having intercourse during the subsequent year as those with little such exposure. "Exposure to TV that included only talk about sex was associated with the same risks as exposure to TV depicting sexual behavior," said Rand Corporation behavioral scientists Rebecca Collins and her colleagues who conducted the study. "[TV] sends the message that everybody's having sex and nobody's thinking about responsibili- ty and nothing bad ever happens," Collins added.[16]

The study further confirms research by education professor Diane Levin, author of *Remote Control Childhood? Combating the Hazards of Media Culture*, and psychologists Dr. Victor Cline, Dr. Stanley Rachman and Dr. W. Marshall, who found that viewing sexual images has led to increased sexual activity and deviant behavior, including rape, among children and teenagers.

In addition, a study by the Henry J. Kaiser Family Foundation revealed that the amount of sex on television has nearly doubled since 1998. Seven of 10 episodes in sitcoms, dramas and reality shows contained some racy content, but overt sexual activity was less common. Only 10 percent of the shows depicted or implied sexual intercourse.

Kaiser found 3,780 scenes with sexual activity on today's TV, but only 1,930 seven years ago. In 1998, 56 percent of the shows contained sexual content, compared to 70 percent today. Kaiser hopes that the study will focus attention on whether TV has influenced casual attitudes toward sex by teens, who the study estimates watch 20 hours of TV per week.[17]

American Teenagers in Danger!

Teenagers are disproportionately affected by the epidemic of sexually transmitted diseases, or STDs, including the deadly AIDS virus. By age 25, one of two sexually active young people will acquire an STD, according to the American Medical News and the World Congress of Families.[18]

A recent Kaiser Family Foundation survey of 500 teenagers ages 15 to 17 found that the majority knew about birth control pills, but more than 25 percent of that majority didn't know that the pills offer no protection against STDs, including AIDS.[19]

As recent studies have shown, depictions and references to sex in movies, videos, television programs, music, and video games have greatly exacerbated this dangerous epidemic among America's youth. Parents can no longer afford to let the mass media dictate what their children see and hear.

Nearly half of all new cases of sexually transmitted diseases in the United States occur in people ages 15 to 24, according to a February 2004 report by the nonprofit group Advocates for Youth. The group also found that the rate of gonorrhea and Chlamydia among people ages 15 to 24 has risen more than 50 percent (53.5 percent) since 1998! Dr. Margaret

Polaneczky, an obstetrician-gynecologist in Manhattan, blames the STD outbreaks on the surge of casual sex. "It's the whole 'Sex and the City' thing," she said.[20]

No Fig Leaf for the Ivy League

The sexual degradation of our young people has been so comprehensive that the Ivy League founded to propagate the gospel of Jesus Christ now publishes pornography. On May 4, 2006, Kelsey Blodget wrote in *The Dartmouth* that pornography is becoming more socially accepted:

> Campus-specific pornographic magazines, like Yale University's "Sex Week at Yale: The Magazine," especially can create a significant stir among college students, garnering both negative and positive feedback. Students at the University of Chicago published the controversial "Vita Exolatur," featuring naked female undergraduates from the school; Boston University published "Boink," "the campus guide to carnal knowledge"; Vassar put out "Squirm"; and Harvard printed "H Bomb," which showed perhaps the most nudity of all the publications.[21]

Hollywood Idols

In her book *Soft Porn Plays Hardball*, Dr. Judith A. Reisman wrote that in 1948 there was an "incident of impotence of only 0.4% of the males under 25, and less than 1% of the males under 35 years of age." By 1970, almost all "of the male population experienced impotence at some time, and chronic or repeated impotence probably affects about 30 to 40% of men at any given time."[23]

The research of Dr. Reisman and others demonstrates that much of this impotence is due to the increase in pornography in the mainstream mass media that makes males dependent on visualizing pornographic images in order to make love to their wives.

The Rules of Evidence

Four major medical associations in 2001 concluded that violence in entertainment influenced children to become more aggressive, and the

Teens on MySpace
Katharine DeBrecht

Browse through the profiles on MySpace.com, a top Internet hangout for teens and a magnet for predators, and you'll see from many of the provocative poses by young girls that the message they are receiving is "Sexual Makes Special."

The teen years are often marked by the need to feel accepted and fit in. Is soft porn the way we show our youth how to be accepted? Are parents, by allowing Hollywood and advertisers to saturate our youth with visual and verbal sexual messages, leaving our children as bait for predators?

In a CBS news report, technology analyst Larry Magid was asked to view a profile of a 15-year-old girl with a profile that included the phrase "Drink a 40, smoke a bowl, sex is good, life is great." When asked what he'd do if he was a predator, Magid said, "I'd target her."

Unfortunately, many parents do not realize or they ignore what is really going on in MySpace.com, a virtual everything-goes spring break for kids. . . . Couple the Hollywood sexualization of our youth with the explosion in Internet porn and you have a match made from hell. By feeding an addiction after being glued to Internet porn, what does the predator do to get his fix? Hop on over to MySpace.com and hunt for prey. According to the Center for Missing and Exploited Children, last year there were more than 2,600 cases of adults luring children via the Internet.

John Maltby, who lectures in psychology at Leicester University and coauthored a study on youth attitudes toward celebrities, says, "Celebrity worship now provides an important reference point for growing up. It's part of the transfer of attachment from parents to peer group. Also, whereas in past times family, friends and teachers were influential role models, celebrities now fulfill that role."

Consider one of the largest "tween" stars Ashlee Simpson and her soft porn stint as one of the latest Candies Girls. Posed on a bed, with a sideward look to the camera framed by dangling locks of hair, Simpson dons a low cut tee revealing a lacy bra, bare thighs and Candies high heels. There's a teddy bear in the background.

How does the CEO of Candies, Neil Cole, see this ad? "She's a little promiscuous, but everything's covered, and she just looks fun. She looks a little bit sexy." Cole says the ad shows "a young girl who's growing up. And it's a combination, I think in a lot of young girl's rooms you see teddy bears, and they probably have high heels."

Candies has established a foundation to use celebrities to speak out about teen pregnancy and offers T-shirts with the phrase, "Be sexy, it doesn't mean you have to have sex." In a world that sees a plague of sexual predators after our children, do we really want our tweens dressing like twenty-somethings?

By the mere poses of these children emulating celebrities on MySpace.com, it is evident that celebrities do influence our children. . . . Celebrity out-of-wedlock births, divorce and infidelity are glamorized, yet these same behaviors cause disastrous results for mainstream American families, such as poverty, teen pregnancy, STDs, depression and suicide. . . .

Teens themselves do not have the maturity to be able to see through the trance of "idolatry," making sex look good to them. At their young age, they do not have the ability to see the dire consequences of early sexual experiences. Because of the images they see on a constant basis, subliminally programming them towards sex instead of innocence, they skip the innocence of their youth and are deprived of a safe and clean environment in which to mature and flourish.

It is common for parents to claim that when children emulate sexy celebrities, it is either a phase or the sign of the times; yet look at the times we live in: excessive Internet porn, sexual predators in the home via a computer screen, teachers charged with statutory rape, etc. Is the molestation, abduction, rape or murder of our children a "phase" or "sign of the times" we are going to accept?

According to advertising agency WPP, one in four advertisements contains a celebrity, compared to one in eight just 10 years ago. Top designer Del Rosario's director of sales and marketing, Brian Sullivan, who believes having celebrities don their products is "absolutely imperative," says, "the whole world has never been more obsessed with celebrity lifestyles than it is right now."

Parents themselves are allowing their teens to line the scantily clad pockets of these celebrities who are gyrating all the way to the bank, while our children, eagerly emulating these celebrities, are increasingly at risk to sexual predators. . . .

I feel that I have to be perfectly candid to wake Hollywood and parents up. Please know what is at stake here. The predator is constantly in a state of sexual arousal. The animalistic nature of the predator is such that there is no conscience. There is only an insatiable drive to consummate the act of his/her desire. There is no regard for the "personhood" of his/her victims. Will you ignore the reality of your responsibility to our innocent children, or will Hollywood continue to use sex to make billions, and will parents just go on with the flow and hope for the best?

I call both Hollywood and parents in to accountability by knowing that if you do not protect children from these images and messages, *you are responsible* for the consequences of childhood early sexuality, rape, pregnancy, STDs, and becoming prey to sexual predators.

Here's the thing: You have a sex-charged culture. On one side you have predators that are in a constant state of the hunt. On the other side you have vulnerable children mimicking celebrity models of promiscuity. The first lines of defense for these children are parents.[22]

Federal Trade Commission found that the entertainment industry was marketing violent movies, music and games to children. Therefore, parents have no excuse for not teaching their children to be media wise.

In a joint statement, the American Medical Association, the American Academy of Pediatrics, the American Psychological Association, and the American Academy of Child and Adolescent Psychiatry warned that violence in movies, video games, TV, and rap music contributes to violent behavior among children. "The conclusion of the public health community," the statement reads, "based on over 30 years of research, is that viewing entertainment violence can lead to increases in aggressive attitudes, values, and behaviors, particularly in children."[24]

When violence is glorified or at least given a glossy, glitzy treatment, it is no wonder that actual violence results.

The Dumbing Down of America

In its first international assessment of educational progress, students from six countries were tested on the effects of television by the Educational Testing Service of Princeton, New Jersey. The results were shocking. The more students watched television, the lower their academic performance. Thirteen-year-olds in the U.S. watched TV the most and ranked last in mathematics and near the bottom in science. South Korean students outperformed all others academically and by wide margins in mathematics. They watched television less and did more homework than their counterparts.[25]

A 10-year study of more than 1,000 children showed that infants who were exposed to too much television experienced severe speech and language difficulties. These children were unable to understand their own names or the names of their family members. At age 3, they spoke like two-year-olds. Dr. Sally Ward, author of the study, warned that parents who let the television babysit their children may be damaging their infants' communication skills.[26]

Excessive exposure to television affects a child's ability to focus. The skill of "mapping," which is pointing at an object while the child pronounces its name, is crucial for teaching speech. Children accustomed to the visual effects of television find it hard to focus on anything else. Ward cautioned that infants less than 12 months old should not be exposed to television, while preschoolers should be limited to one hour a day.[27] Hollywood is rewriting how the next generation views God, the devil and ourselves.

Where Love and Peace Must Begin

The late Mother Teresa of Calcutta, noted humanitarian and 1971 winner of the Nobel Peace Prize, spoke about how precious life is at the National Prayer Breakfast Speech Against Abortion in 1994. Some of her poignant words apply:

> Our children depend on us for everything: their health, their nutrition, their security, their coming to know and love God. For all of

this, they look to us with trust, hope and expectation. But often father and mother are so busy that they have no time for their children, or perhaps they are not even married, or have given up on their marriage. So the children go to the streets, and get involved in drugs, or other things.

We are talking of love of the child, which is where love and peace must begin.

But I feel that the greatest destroyer of peace today is abortion, because it is a war against the child—a direct killing of the innocent child—murder by the mother herself. And if we accept that a mother can kill her own child, how can we tell other people not to kill one another?

How do we persuade a woman not to have an abortion? As always, we must persuade her with love. The father of that child, whoever he is, must also give until it hurts. By abortion, the mother does not learn to love, but kills even her own child to solve her problems. And by abortion, the father is told that he does not have to take any responsibility at all for the child he has brought into the world.

Any country that accepts abortion is not teaching the people to love, but to use any violence to get what they want. That is why the greatest destroyer of love and peace is abortion. . . .

If we remember that God loves us, and that we can love others as He loves us, then America can become a sign of peace for the world. From here, a sign of care for the weakest of the weak— the unborn child—must go out to the world. If you become a burning light of justice and peace in the world, then really you will be true to what the founders of this country stood for. God bless you![28]

PART III

THE MEDIUM

AND THE MESSAGE

CHAPTER 7

Behind the Scenes of Hollywood

The entertainment industry is much like the Wizard of Oz, where the people believe that the Wizard is omnipresent and omnipotent, but when Toto pulls back the curtain, he turns out to be nothing but a little old man whom Dorothy chides for bullying and scaring everyone. This chapter explores the true nature of the mass media of entertainment and examines who are the puppet masters of cultural influence.

Although the entertainment industry accounts for one-sixth of our gross national product in the United States of America, experts contend there are less than 100 people who make the final decision to green light an entertainment project for production and distribution. These individuals work for one of eight major companies that control approximately 98 percent of the box office, television programs and major media in America.

In effect, there is a very tight concentration of power in the hands of a few executives, producers and agents who make it very difficult for a producer with no track record to break into the movie business. With regard to television, the major networks have to fill 20,000 hours of programming time every year and need new ideas to capture and hold their audience.

Don't Give Me That Old-Time Religion

In spite of their need for programs, the television gatekeepers have very little contact with religion, and so they make it very difficult for a producer who wants to produce a program with Christian content for the network program schedule. For 40 years—from the 1934 Communications Act until the 1970s—a religious program producer had reasonable, though difficult, access to the networks because they scheduled a certain amount of religious programming as part of their obligation to operate in the public interest, convenience and necessity. However, since the late 1970s, the Federal Communications Commission has relaxed the public interest obligations of broadcasters, and so the networks have cut back on (or cut out) public service programming or religious programming.

The Culture of the Mass Media of Entertainment

During the Golden Age of Hollywood, the movie industry was influenced by immigrants who loved their new home, America, and who made movies reflecting that love, such as *Yankee Doodle Dandy, Mr. Smith Goes to Washington* and *The Ten Commandments*. During the 1960s, the entertainment industry started to change dramatically. Now the major entertainment companies are controlled by Japanese corporations (such as Sony), professing Christians such as Rupert Murdoch, and a wide range of other ethnic, religious and gender-defined individuals who (like in other industries) have one common goal: to make money. The key to their position and survival in the entertainment industry is their desire to be part of the team representing their particular entertainment industry studio.

It is important to understand the rules that govern the mass media of entertainment culture to develop media wisdom in this area. What follows are brief snapshots of key aspects of the entertainment industry that will help you develop discernment.

1. Hollywood controls the entertainment industry marketplace.
Once upon a time, I brought together a group of wealthy investors who desired to make movies in order to help them understand the industry. Each month, they were introduced to a top executive or a top talent in the entertainment industry.

One investor asked the president of a major movie studio if he would want to distribute his movie if it could be produced for one-tenth of the cost by the investor. The president asked, "Why would we want that?" Then he added, "If you want to make movies, we will set you up with an office on the studio lot, which costs ten times more to rent per foot than it would across the street. And we will sell you supplies from the studio store for ten times more than you could buy them outside the studio store. Then we will assign you movies that we agree to produce and use your money to produce them."

I helped the investors understand that a movie studio is, in part, a production company. If the investor produces the movie outside of the studio, the studio cannot write off its sound stages, shops, personnel and utilities, so that the costs of the production covers its unfair share of the overhead of the studio. The studio is interested in movies being made within the system.

Producers with movie studios resemble sharecroppers on a plantation or employees in a company town. After the Civil War, many plantations rented to sharecroppers their shacks and all the equipment the sharecroppers needed to farm the plantation. When the harvest was brought for sale to the plantation warehouse, the price for the harvest was paid after deducting all that was owed for the equipment and supplies. Often this meant that the sharecropper got practically nothing. Likewise, when the box office returns arrive, all these costs are deducted, often leaving the producer in debt.

2. Hollywood uses and abuses wealthy outsiders.
The major studios not only produce movies but also place the financing for them with banks and institutional investors—at an average cost of $100 million to produce and distribute one movie. The history of Hollywood is filled with brilliant, wealthy outsiders who lost a lot of money and left in disgrace. In a 2004 article from the *Los Angeles Times*, Patrick J. Kiger exposed this treatment of wealthy outsiders:

> "We don't go for strangers," spoke one of F. Scott Fitzgerald's characters in the writer's final, unfinished Hollywood novel. But he didn't get it completely right. The industry likes interlopers just fine—as long as they empty their wallets and don't overstay their welcome. That scenario has been repeated in Hollywood almost as often as the two-unlikely-cops-become-wisecracking-crime-fightin'-buddies action thriller. An outsider, flush with success in some other industry or bankrolled by a family fortune bursts onto the scene with dreams of becoming the next Louis

B. Mayer, only to slink away a year or three later in ignominious defeat. The most recent, high-profile examples—Messier and Edgar Bronfman Jr., the Seagram heirs whose Hollywood ambitions were intertwined with Vivendi's—are only the latest in a series that goes back to the early days of Hollywood, when sharpies such as William Randolph Hearst and Joe Kennedy came west to get their pockets picked . . .

Why do all these powerful, wealthy alpha males venture out of their comfy enclaves and plunge into an utterly unfamiliar, notoriously Byzantine business that they often approach with distain and condescension? What sort of mass-induced hypnotic state convinces a German investor, for example, that it's a sensible idea to sink millions into a film homage to L. Ron Hubbard's *Battlefield Earth*? Or an otherwise adroit telecommunications mogul into putting his name in the credits of an unnecessary remake of *Around the World in Eighty Days*? Is there some sort of semiotic explanation for why otherwise astute people from another culture—whether it's Amsterdam or Peoria—get hopelessly tangled up in movie industry lingo and end up mumbling about "synergy" after that disastrous first-cut screening? . . .

"They don't do the same sort of traditional business analysis that they would if they were entering, say, the machine-tool business," says Dartmouth College business school professor Sydney Finkelstein, author of the book *Why Smart Executives Fail*. "Then again, when you're making machine tools, you're not seduced by the idea of sitting in the audience with a bunch of movie stars at the Academy Awards. Instead, you get seduced by the glamour and it screws you up." From an empirical point of view, though, an outsider would have to be totally insane to try the movie industry in particular, because the economic model is bizarrely different from just about any other business. The movie industry actually earns only a 3% to 4% return on investment, which is lousy when compared with steel-making or book publishing.

To make it worse, the statistical curve for movie profits isn't much of a curve at all. . . . Instead, it's shaped more like a playground slide—6% of the product earns 90% of the money, and 70% to 80% of the product sinks into oblivion. This results in what economist De Vany calls an industry of "extreme uncertainty." That is, successes are aberrantly rare and outlandishly enormous. The movie *Titanic*, for example, grossed $600 million domestically in 1997, in a year when the average film grossed $23 million. Results like that are impossible to predict. . . .

Another added complication: Most industries don't have Hollywood's peculiar distribution system, in which a would-be blockbuster suddenly covers most of the nation's movie screens like kudzu and competitors get what's left. That's the equivalent of one brand of microwave oven getting all the shelf space at Best Buy, Target and WalMart for a week, but then disappearing instantly if it doesn't sell. . . .

Language also can be a problem for outsiders. . . . "The language of Hollywood is so filled with hyperbole that you have to be able to decode it," behavior expert Kramer explains. "Otherwise, you don't pick up that when a guy tells you that your project is fantastic and it'll be exciting to work with you, he really means that he's going to tell his assistant not to put through any more of your calls."[1]

On the other hand, if you don't have money, you are not a player. Once upon a time, several of the investors whom I had assembled to learn about the entertainment industry decided to go to the Cannes Film Festival. I had lunch with some of them when they came back. They were derisive of the others who went to Cannes because they did not have a yacht and stayed in hotels. Thus, the studios pay attention to your financial status, although they do not need your money.

3. *Hollywood is a club.*

If you have ever belonged to a club, you know that you can bring your friends and treat them to dinner, but they can't come back to eat the next day if they are not members. Whatever race or creed, they must be members of the club to use the club. Clubs recognize their members. Hollywood is just such a place.

4. Hollywood is a poker game.

Literally, the top studio executives have weekly poker games where they share information and discuss the entertainment industry. If you are not in the game, well . . . you are an outsider.

5. Hollywood is the lawless Wild West.

Once, while a millionaire was buying a famous movie studio, his lawyer was selling the studio's assets to a competing studio that the lawyer in question also represented. The lawyer would be disbarred in any other area of the country for doing this, but no one tackles the ethics of Hollywood because the mass media shapes the culture and elects the politicians.

6. Hollywood is a family.

For years, Hollywood executives have hired their family and friends to fill the key roles at the studios. The non-family members are the exception.

7. Hollywood is a dream factory.

For the last 100 years, the Hollywood dream has been replacing the foundational Christian precepts of the American vision of freedom and justice for all. The assumption is that the media can prescribe what should be considered acceptable. However, as Isaiah 55:9 tells us, God's ways and thoughts are higher than our ways and thoughts. Perhaps we should ensure our culture perceives the right vision as stipulated in Proverbs 29:18: "Where there is no vision, the people perish" (KJV).

The entertainment industry executives are always concerned that the next big dream will pass them by or that they will back a dud. Yet who can evaluate what dream will sell? To avoid making a tough decision on a project that could go either way, the executives will often say that they will look at the project—and then let it languish in development hell. As long as they have the project, the person who brought it to the executive cannot go anywhere else with it and will be trapped unless he or she can figure out a way to push it forward.

8. *Hollywood doesn't respond well to those who try to play it for a fool.*

One studio head said that his company was seriously considering picking an independent movie up for distribution from a person of faith. However, when the executive asked the young independent how much the movie cost to make, the independent inflated the budget. The executive walked, telling the man that he made movies everyday and knew exactly what the independent's movie cost. Who was he trying to fool?

Likewise, one studio executive said that he was talking with a person who obviously came from the faith community who had pitched a movie with sex and violence. Evidently, the young producer thought that he needed to put in sex and violence to sell his project. The executive walked, telling the young person to be true to himself.

9. *Hollywood looks for films that are consistent to their premise.*

Every story has its own logic. A movie about faith triumphing over adversity must show that faith triumphs. The other side of the directive is that the story must be consistent to its premise. One movie about a missionary gave no indication why the missionary would give his life to save the pagan natives who killed him. The neophyte Christian producer avoided the message of faith so well that no one could make any sense of the movie.

10. *Hollywood takes pleasure in the misfortunes of others.*

Often, people are happier about someone else's misfortune than about their own success. This is certainly true in Hollywood, as the following article from the *Los Angeles Times* reports:

> The Germans have a word for it—*schadenfreud*: the pleasure one takes from the misfortune of others—and in Hollywood it's a way of life. If show business were a religion, its first commandment would be: Instead of enjoying your own success, take pleasure in others' failure. One producer I know used to go around his office

chanting "O-P-M-F." Translation: Other people must fail. As Ned Tanen, a former studio chief at Paramount and Universal, once put it: "The only words you need to know about Hollywood are 'negativity' and 'illusion.' Especially 'negativity.'"

Why do so many people in Hollywood root for everyone else to fail? You could chalk it up to jealousy and insecurity. You could say it's a telling example of Hollywood's spiritual emptiness. You could blame it on an insular culture that encourages cutthroat competition. Whatever the reason, *schadenfreude* is deeply imbedded in Hollywood culture. "This is a town filled with envy and jealousy," says *Tomb Raider* producer Larry Gordon, who's been a high-profile force in Hollywood for years. "You've got two kinds of people—the people who've made it who are angry that they're not more successful and the people who haven't made it who are angry because they think the other guy is a lucky [expletive]."

The equation is simple: Power + Success = Envy.[2]

11. *Hollywood is vulnerable.*

Even with all the negatives of the Hollywood culture, it must be noted that the entertainment industry is vulnerable. Mel Gibson proved this with *The Passion of the Christ*—a film many in Hollywood dismissed, but which eventually earned $611 million at the box office.[3] Likewise, Pixar proved this by avoiding the typical Hollywood model and producing a number of films with great animation. "Pixar has become the envy of Hollywood because it never went Hollywood," stated William C. Taylor and Polly LaBarre, cofounders of *Fast Company* magazine.[4] Quality, perseverance and faithfulness will overcome.

12. *Hollywood is nothing to fear.*

As Romans 8:37 tells us, "In all these things we are more than conquerors through him that loved us." Therefore, we do not need to be afraid of Hollywood or the lion's den. In fact, the only phrase that is repeated in every book of the Bible is "Do not be afraid." So pursue the vision God has given you to transform the culture with confidence in His Grace. As 2 Corinthians 2:14 tells us, God always leads us in His triumphal procession.

Hollywood—Back to the Future
Tom Flannery

Back in the 1960s, Warren Beatty was trying to sell Warner Brothers' head Jack Warner on the idea of distributing *Bonnie and Clyde*. It wasn't going very well, so Beatty, who has a reputation for being able to talk a turtle out of his shell, tried flattering the crusty old studio boss into giving his film the green light.

"It's an homage to all those great gangster movies you made in the 1930s," he told him.

Warner was unimpressed.

"What the [bleep] is an homage?" he asked.

In the end, Beatty got his distribution deal and *Bonnie and Clyde* ushered in a "new wave" of American motion pictures, much more heavily influenced by French *auteurs* like Godard than they were by anything ever made in America.

The movies themselves were often extremely well done, helmed by gifted directors and performed by the best crop of young actors since Brando and Monty Clift (arguably the two best ever) rose to stardom a couple decades earlier along with a group of others, most of whom came out of The Actors Studio and were practitioners of "The Method" under legendary Lee Strasberg.

But these movies were missing something profoundly important that had always been part of American films: a grounding in moral truth.

To that end, Beatty's adaptation of the Bonnie Parker/Clyde Barrow story is a very glamorized version of the duo, who in real life were cowardly, cold-blooded killers but are portrayed in the film as kind and lovable (at least as kind and lovable as those who rob banks and kill people can be made to look). Their criminal behavior is trivialized, if not celebrated.

With the success of early new wave hits like *Bonnie and Clyde* and *Easy Rider*, gratuitous sex and violence became rampant in major mainstream pictures, along with, in many cases, the virtual nonstop use of profanity and blasphemy. All in the name of "keeping it real."

Recreational drug use became commonplace and religious faith came under fierce attack—at first in declarations of atheism by hip and attractive young couples (*Love Story*) or angry denunciations of God by heroic lead figures (*The Poseidon Adventure*), but eventually to the most vile, obscene and unspeakably blasphemous assaults against Christianity, and Christ Himself, imaginable (*Dogma, Saved!* and of course *The Last Temptation of Christ*, among many others).

What was once considered shockingly inappropriate was now par for the course. Truth was nonexistent, and the last thing we should ever do is judge anyone or anything on the basis of any moral standard. Situational ethics replaced eternal truth and new wave films venerated the anti-hero. The artists of the new wave weren't interested in the black and white of right and wrong (which they found boring at best, offensive at worst), but rather the gray area of moral equivalence—but those who love the Lord hate evil (see Ps. 97:10).

To be sure, there were anti-heroes in the old days—Humphrey Bogart, most notably—but the difference is that they usually made the right moral choices. Bogie deeply loved Bergman in *Casablanca*, but he gave her up in the end, for the good not only of Bergman, but of the world itself at a time when Nazism was on the march.

The modern anti-hero is perhaps best reflected in Travis Bickle, the character DeNiro plays in *Taxi Driver*. At one point in the film, he is on the verge of assassinating a politician for no particular reason, but then he turns his fury upon a violent pimp, rescuing a young girl in the process and becoming a hero. The message is that our heroes could just as easily be deranged killers as not, determined not by right or wrong, good or evil, but just by the outcomes of random acts (Social Darwinism, in effect).

The new wave movement had essentially transformed the film industry into a vehicle for political activism and social change. Hollywood certainly made plenty of propaganda pictures during World War II, but these were pro-American movies designed to boost the morale of a war-weary country. Many of the biggest stars of the era, like Gable and Jimmy Stewart, were patriots who enlisted and served in the war. Conversely, the propaganda pictures that began in the late 1960s/early 1970s were anything but pro-American, and they celebrated the very worst elements of society.

Most disturbingly of all, for the first time ever, our nation's most prominent filmmakers set out to systematically undermine the Judeo-Christian values that made America great in the first place. The film business was no longer about entertainment; it was about engineering radical social change through a downgrading of culture (profuse violence, nudity, profanity and blasphemy) combined with a prodigious dose of politically correct thought.[5]

A Second New Wave?

In his book *Easy Riders, Raging Bulls,* author Peter Biskind argues that the young-turk filmmakers of the new wave saved the movie business but eventually lost the battle of artistic control to the big studios. In fact, it was these young turks who were primarily responsible for ruining the film business—a business that has never recovered from the damage they inflicted.

This is not to say there have not been any films with a solid moral core made since the new wave, because there surely have been. Still, the anti-traditionalist trend continues to this day. During the past few years, in particular, there has been an unsettling uptake in morally twisted political/social commentary in the movies. There have been films promoting everything from abortion (*Vera Drake, The Cider House Rules*) to the occult (*Little Witches, Harry Potter and the Sorcerer's Stone*) while consistently attacking the traditional family as a warped and outdated institution (*American Beauty, Pleasantville.*)

In addition, after years of promoting the gay agenda through films such as *Philadelphia, Far from Heaven* and *If These Walls Could Talk 2,* Hollywood has now moved on to redefining the transgender lifestyle as normal (and thus deserving of individual rights) in such films as *Flawless, The Birdcage* and *Transamerica.*

As Biskind documents in his book, the revolution that the new wave filmmakers tried to carry out was undercut by another group of young turks—filmmakers such as Spielberg and George Lucas. These filmmakers were just as liberal in their political thinking, but they were more interested in entertaining the masses with traditional good-versus-evil stories (with good ultimately prevailing) than bombarding them with left-wing agitprop.

With that, Hollywood experienced a boom unprecedented in history. At the same time, though, a substantial segment of the industry, unwilling to abandon their new wave roots, continued pumping out "socially conscious" films (as liberals have described them) in the mode of those produced in the early 1970s. Most of these films were released to critical acclaim and Oscar honors but usually meager returns at the box office.

In his 1992 book *Hollywood vs. America*, Michael Medved showed how Hollywood's war on traditional values from the time of the new wave created a major backlash among moviegoers, who stayed away in droves from these politically correct offerings. Many of them, fed up with such fodder over so many years, simply stopped going to the movies altogether. Still, Hollywood continued producing more of the hard *R* variety despite the fact that many of them bombed or underperformed.

This all reached a crescendo with the release of the gay-themed *Brokeback Mountain* and *Capote;* the aforementioned *Transamerica* (which promoted trans-genderism); the terrorist-sympathizing tracts *Syriana*, *Munich* and the best documentary nominee *Paradise Now;* the racially charged *Crash;* the pharmaceutical-industry bashing *The Constant Gardener;* the feminist labor drama *North Country;* and *Good Night, and Good Luck*, George Clooney's answer to Ann Coulter's book *Treason,* in which she offers up a spirited defense of the anticommunist movement of the1950s.

While the makers of these films were saluting their works as something of a motion picture renaissance and hailing 2005 as a return to the new wave values of the 1970s, audiences had a decidedly different reaction. The combined box office grosses of the year's five best picture nominees were the lowest in the previous 20 years. Not only that, but overall box office returns dropped by a stunning 6 percent—a fact that was picked up as a major story in the industry trade papers.

The Rest of the Story

The good news is that—as is happening throughout all of society—things are changing for the better in the film industry—slowly, perhaps, but changing all the same.

First, there's a change taking place within the industry itself. In recent years, many stars—including Stephen Baldwin, Patricia Heaton, Kirk Cameron, and others—have become Christians and are now committed to producing Bible-based or family-friendly entertainment. Many stars are also taking risks to back their own faith-based projects. For instance, when Mel Gibson (for *The Passion of the Christ*) and Robert Duvall (for *The Apostle*) were refused financing and distribution by all of the power players in Hollywood, they sank their own money into these faith-based labors of love to bring them to the big screen. Duvall saw a modest return on his $3 million investment for what was essentially a small indie film. Gibson, as we have mentioned, made hundreds of millions of dollars when *The Passion* became something of a cultural phenomenon.

Research conducted by the Christian Film and Television Commission indicates that some unmistakable trends are taking place in the industry. Film festivals are sprouting up that honor traditionally themed movies and documentaries. Christian ministry ventures have entered the marketplace, producing movies such as the Left Behind and Omega Code series. And there has been an increase in the use of websites (such as *Movieguide*®) that allow people to view ratings and recommendations of films based on how family-oriented and biblically correct (as opposed to politically correct) they are. (For a sample *Movieguide*® review, see the appendix for a review of *Amazing Grace*, the story of William Wilberforce.)

It's been a long time coming, but more and more of Hollywood's movers and shakers are finally realizing the benefits of releasing family-oriented films. With the enormous box office successes of family offerings such as *Pirates of the Caribbean 2* and *Cars* and the rise of family-oriented films overall (up from just 6 percent in 1985 to 45 percent by 2002), new wave filmmakers—who have now become the entrenched old guard—are hanging on to power for dear life. But the pendulum is swinging against them. It may only be a matter of time before we'll again be able to say, with the utmost enthusiasm, "Hooray for Hollywood!"

Hollywood's New Enlightenment

In recent years, Hollywood has championed films with explicit and lewd themes that most Americans would be embarrassed to watch with their mother. Yet for all the hype, box office receipts have continued to decline over the last three years. Hollywood executives have seemed confounded to understand why Americans are no longer turning out for movies in the same force as they used to.

The low box office numbers in recent years would seem to indicate that Americans are not interested in films full of violent, sexual and anti-American content. Perhaps this is because 41 percent of Americans state that they attend church weekly,[6] while up to 92 percent say they are Christians.[7] Even non-Christian moviegoers respond favorably to inspiring and redemptive stories with morally outstanding heroes and heroines. This family-friendly demographic is flexing its influence in more than just box office receipts.

In July 2006, Walt Disney Company's new president of production, Oren Aviv, announced in a major company-restructuring plan that Disney intends to change its focus toward more family-oriented films— a policy change that reflects the desires of many of our friends at Disney at the highest levels.

Other studios have also started to explore the faith and values market, including Fox Faith (which released *End of the Spear*), Sony Provident-Integrity (which released *The Gospel* and *The Second Chance*) and Paramount (which released *World Trade Center*, starring Nicolas Cage, a patriotic movie full of positive faith and values). Like Disney, these studios are beginning to understand that movies containing explicit material earn much less money than family-friendly movies with morally uplifting, redemptive content reflecting Judeo-Christian values.

Since the bottom line is the main concern of studio executives and their financiers on Wall Street and overseas, Hollywood's decision makers can no longer choose to ignore these facts. They simply cannot afford it.

The Coming Earthquake in Hollywood
David Outten

Hollywood and the entire entertainment industry are beginning to feel the earth move under their feet. Today the tremors are small, but anyone with the least sense of anticipation can see that the relationship between entertainment producers and their audience is about to go through a radical transformation.

It's not the first such earthquake. The introduction of television shook the movie industry and the introduction of the videocassette recorder (and DVD) further reshaped the landscape, but the next revolution may be the most profound.

Like the others, this revolution is technology driven. Unlike the others, this one threatens the dominance of the studio system. It is *very* expensive to get thousands of 35mm prints made and distributed to theatres. Few filmmakers have the resources, so a relatively small group of executives have the power to green light, or approve, a project.

Today, it's possible to produce a movie and sell it directly to audiences on the Internet. The quality is lacking and the trend is in a very early stage, so Internet movie sales are not a major threat to this year's box office. However, as the technology improves, the major studios will no longer be the only ones who have a distribution system, and the cost of quality productions will be reduced.

Even more profound will be the convergence of the Internet with the living room television. This process has already begun but is still cumbersome and expensive. In a short while, it will be as simple as using an iPod and even more popular. It could spell the end for television networks, cable services and video stores (at least in their present form). The concept of "on demand" will expand to thousands of Internet film stores and libraries. Virtually any movie or program made will be available for some competitive price. Many programs will be free. Many churches already offer their sermons online in small videos. This will expand to full screen.

The important thing is that the program director—more than ever—will be the viewer. Hopefully, as viewers gain more power, the winner will be quality family entertainment. *Movieguide*® has been reporting for years that quality family entertainment makes more money than sex, violence and immorality. There will be more independent family movie producers. Like Pixar, they may even become the popular, profitable studios of the future. And, like Mel Gibson, someone will produce a movie that hits a home run with the millions of Americans who attend church every Sunday.

More than ever before, the major studios and media conglomerates will have to ask themselves if the movie they're making really needs foul language, ultra violence, explicit sex, nudity, crude jokes, and other offensive material.[8]

CHAPTER 8

The Power of Parables

Given all of the research that points to the malignant effects of the entertainment media on our children and on our society, what's the bottom line? What spiritual approach should Christians take when considering films such as *Harry Potter*, *The Lord of the Rings* and *The Chronicles of Narnia*—not to mention all of the other media artifacts that daily bombard our homes and communities?

Jesus Christ knew the power of stories and told parables to teach, influence and inspire His disciples. Parables are short fictitious stories illustrating a moral principle or a religious doctrine. Books and movies are like parables in that they also can illustrate moral principles and religious doctrines, including beliefs about God and Jesus Christ. Even an atheist has a theology—a belief about God—in that he or she doesn't believe that God exists.

Of course, Jesus Christ told parables that, in the Christian worldview, taught moral principles and religious doctrines that are good, true and beautiful. Therefore, Christians believe that all stories should teach the good, the true and the beautiful. They also believe that stories should not contradict the things that the Bible teaches, including the moral principles given to Moses by God in God's Law and the moral principles given by Jesus and His disciples in the New Testament documents.

Christians furthermore believe that all stories should not contradict what the New Testament teaches about Jesus Christ, moral truth and spiritual truth. They also recognize that except for the human writers of the New Testament documents—who were perfectly inspired by God and enlightened by His Holy Spirit—all stories are made by fallible human beings and thus reflect the sinful, error-prone nature of humanity.

In taking this approach, it is good to note what Paul says in 1 Timothy 4:7: "Have nothing to do with godless myths and old wives' tales; rather, train yourself to be godly." Notice here that this biblical passage does not say to reject all stories or all traditional folktales—only those that are godless, those that are completely false, and those that are evil.

However, many self-described Christians (including major denominations and churches) have strayed from this biblical, Christ-centered worldview. They don't accept many of the teachings of the Bible and the New Testament. Their beliefs may contradict an essential teaching necessary for their salvation, but often they try to rationalize their beliefs by making rationalizations about the biblical text, such as saying that the Bible's understanding of a particular issue is historically or scientifically flawed. Thus, although they may hold on to some, and even many or most, essential teachings of the Bible, their understanding seems cloudy at best, or heretical at worst.

This is similar to the situation regarding the Harry Potter books and movies. Some Christians who like the books (or who at least are not concerned about their possible effects on their children) are telling people that the witchcraft in *Harry Potter* either is not the same kind of occult magic practiced by modern-day witches and self-described neopagans or is not the same kind of witchcraft and sorcery condemned by the Bible. Other Christians condemn Tolkien's books and *The Lord of the Rings* movies because they contain a fantasy mythology independent of the Bible's creation story and its depiction of human history. Still other Christians unnecessarily try to terrify parents by insisting that children who read *Harry Potter* or watch the movies are in tremendous danger of becoming ensnared into satanic witchcraft rituals or satanic pagan cults. All of these positions are terribly flawed.

Misperceptions on *Harry Potter* and *The Lord of the Rings*

The first point that many Christians often raise is that the witchcraft in *Harry Potter* is not the same as that used in the Bible. Yet although *Harry Potter* is a series of fantasy stories for children that exaggerate the idea of witchcraft in a whimsical, frequently humorous and adventurous way, there is no substantial or material difference between the witchcraft and sorcery in *Harry Potter* and the witchcraft and sorcery condemned in Scripture.

The Bible clearly condemns sorcery, divination, witchcraft and the casting of spells, and it condemns people, mediums and spiritualists who consult dead people. Contrary to what *Harry Potter*'s defenders say, all of these evil things are part and parcel of the occult sorcery that occurs in *Harry Potter*. Furthermore, all of these things actually do indeed occur within many versions of modern-day forms of witchcraft, neo-paganism and/or spiritism. In fact, if you go to the Scholastic Books website on the Internet, one of the *Harry Potter* pages will refer you to the Scholastic Books website for its T*Witch books and products based on a series involving two twins who practice witchcraft and neo-paganism. One of the T*Witch pages encourages children to send in their own spells, including protection spells, love spells and homework spells.

When we looked at that page on June 10, 2003, we found an 11-year-old girl named Kiki from Illinois who wrote, "Sun and moon, sea and fire, let me have my desire." We also found a 12-year-old from Texas, named Liz, who wrote another spell that said, in part, "O goddess of night" and "Mighty sun god."[1] Another Scholastic Books page on the Internet encourages school children in grades three and above to "Write your own magic spell."[2] Also, the Warner Brothers *Harry Potter* website offers a CD-ROM for *Harry Potter and the Sorcerer's Stone*, where children can attend classes at Hogwarts School of Witchcraft and Wizardry and learn spells.

Given these facts, why is it beyond the pale of foresight to believe that some children and teenagers who get involved in the fantasy world of Harry Potter might not, at some point, get swept up into the practices and beliefs of modern-day witchcraft and paganism? What guarantees can Warner Brothers, Scholastic Books, your local school board or J. K. Rowling give to us that many children and teenagers will not be tempted to do such a thing?

Now, I can imagine someone saying, "Kids play cops and robbers, but that doesn't make them turn to a life of crime." However, in the game of cops and robbers, the robbers are supposed to be the bad guys, but in the game of *Harry Potter*, the witches and sorcerers are the good guys and the people who can't use occult magic, who don't use occult magic or who refuse to use occult magic are seen as being the bad guys.

In effect, *Harry Potter* seems to turn good into evil and evil into good! This is thoroughly abhorrent.

But what about J.R.R. Tolkien and *The Lord of the Rings*? If the witchcraft in *Harry Potter* cannot be separated from the witchcraft that is prohibited in the Bible, should not *The Lord of the Rings*—in which characters also wield magic—also be condemned?

In fact, Tolkien (and also Lewis to some degree) did create some confusion in Christians' minds about magic. However, there is an important distinction. Tolkien's mythology and his *Lord of the Rings* novel take place in a fantasy realm in a mythical past where the honorable and humble hobbits, elves, dwarves and men are helped by supernatural powers derived from God to defeat supernatural powers that have turned evil and demonic in rebellion against God. Also, in Tolkien's world—which is a real physical world that cannot be manipulated by sheer mental or occult power—sin has real consequences. The worlds that Tolkien created have *real* consequences and *real* hope.

Tolkien's fantasy is not meant to take the place of biblical history but is intended to point toward the Bible, toward God and toward Christianity, in an allegorical fashion. Thus, in *The Silmarillion* and *The Lord of the Rings*, there is Christian symbolism referring to the creation and providence of God the Father, as well as symbolic metaphors to the Holy Spirit and to Jesus Christ. Tolkien created his fantasy stories in the spirit of the heroic myths, legends and romances of the past but imbued them with strong Christian meanings. Because of this, he infuses his heroes with a grace and civility that are truly inspirational.

A third position that Christians often erroneously take is that children who read *Harry Potter* or watch the movies are in danger of becoming ensnared into witchcraft or pagan cults. In the rush to condemn all forms of witchcraft, including divination, the casting of spells, spiritism and magical curses, some Christians have carelessly classified all forms of witchcraft and all forms of neo-paganism as satanic. To be sure, Satan is behind all forms of non-Christian belief systems, but so is willful human sin and rebellion against God. We should also note that the apostle Paul says in 2 Corinthians 11:14-15 that "Satan himself masquerades as an angel of light" and Satan's servants "masquerade as servants of righteousness."

Many self-proclaimed witches and neo-pagans laugh at depictions of their beliefs that claim they advocate Satanism and demonism. They correctly protest that very few, if any, of them consciously worship Satan. In fact, even most Satanists do not actually and consciously worship the devil or Satan but are just licentious hedonists who use these negative, demonic personas to mock and snub their noses at Bible-believing Christians. Some modern-day witches and neo-pagans also point out that many modern-day witches or pagans may refer to such things as the Mother Goddess and her consort the Horned God or talk about other gods and goddesses, including the Moon God or the Sun God, but they do not really believe in the existence of these deities and spirits. They also note that those witches and neo-pagans who do not believe in the existence of these deities and spirits are, instead, using symbolic references and fantasies in order to honor, love and commune with nature.

In reality, modern-day witchcraft and paganism is a diverse, amorphous collection of pagan cults, heathen religions, New Age cults, practitioners of witchcraft, Wiccan pagans, Wiccan witches or sorcerers, feminist cults, self-proclaimed Satanists, and solitary practitioners. The techniques practiced and taught by this diverse collection include a host of things such as divination, clairvoyance, spell casting, spirit channeling, herbal healing, astral projection and spiritism. Their actual beliefs can be diverse and include such beliefs as animism (attributing conscious life to objects in nature, phenomena in nature, or inanimate objects), polytheism (the worship of many gods), henotheism (the worship of one god among many), pantheism (the belief that everything is god), some form of deism (the belief that a god has become removed from his subjects), or a combination thereof.

Many witches and neo-pagans do seem to accept the notion of human reincarnation and karma (the belief that the things we do in this life will affect us in our reincarnated life). This Americanized belief in reincarnation and karma seems to have its sources in the occultism and spiritism that gained popularity in the late 1800s and early 1900s, in particular with the Theosophy movement and the teachings of such people as Edgar Cayce. Radical feminism, especially the kind that falsely (and often viciously) attacks the alleged patriarchal doctrines in the Bible and Christianity, also has influenced the neo-pagan movement. So has the modern ecological movement. In this regard, syncretism or the combination of different and even totally separate philosophical and religious beliefs and practices appears to be one of the primary qualities of the neo-pagan movement. Sometimes it seems, in fact, that the only belief system that neo-pagans exclude from this contradictory pagan and occult morass is Christianity, especially any Christianity that takes the Bible seriously.

Even so, Christians must be careful in making rash comparisons between *Harry Potter*, modern-day witchcraft, neo-pagan cults and a demonized, inordinately powerful Satanism. We must avoid a conspiratorial view of this matter, even though we know that modern-day witchcraft, neo-pagan cults and Satanists tend to share some things in common: They hate God, and they hate the children of God.

Despite this cautionary note, Christian and Jewish parents should continue to object vociferously to such things as *Harry Potter*, modern-day witchcraft and neo-paganism, especially when it is being shoved down children's throats by millions of dollars in marketing from some of the biggest corporations in the whole world and by a government bureaucracy of well-meaning, but misguided, teachers and librarians. Ironically, many of these same teachers and librarians, and many neo-pagans, scream to high heaven when a Christian wants to put any of the Ten Commandments on a school bulletin board or a Christian student wants to mention God or Jesus Christ in an academic paper or at a graduation ceremony, but they have no problem with letting schoolchildren fantasize about becoming Harry Potter at Hogwarts or using witchcraft like him. We must thoroughly reject such self-righteous double standards.

Instead of behaving like these hypocrites, Christians should be willing to objectively point out the very real dangers of *Harry Potter* while at the same time avoiding hysteria and emotional arguments. We do not have to raise the terrifying specter of satanic rituals, bloody human sacrifices and satanic demons, or distort the beliefs of modern-day witches and pagan cults, to take a firm stand against the witchcraft and occult paganism taught in *Harry Potter*. In fact, that's the kind of thing that many of the witches and neo-pagans do in their hysterical rants against Christianity, the Church and Bible-believing Christians.

For example, years ago, Tom Snyder, one of our editors at *Movieguide*®, went with some friends to witness a New Age environmentalist fair in San Francisco. Tom and the others passed out some tracts and articles about Christianity and the nature of truth at a booth they had rented. One day, a scruffy-looking individual in a T-shirt stormed the booth screaming about the evils of the Roman Catholic Church during the Middle Ages.

"But we're not Catholic; we're Protestants," Tom and his friends kept trying to tell the young man as they tried to engage him in a calm discussion. Yet the man wouldn't listen. He kept ranting and raving incoherently about Roman Catholicism until he quickly got tired and stomped away.

Of course, very few Christians get this irate when talking to, witnessing to or debating somebody who has a different worldview. Many Christians have, however, told falsehoods and rumors (often unknowingly) about non-Christians. For example, many Christians have spread the false rumor about an atheist group that is allegedly petitioning the federal government to censor the mentioning of God or Jesus Christ on the public television airwaves. On the other hand, there was, in fact, a recently proposed regulation in Great Britain that would have outlawed Christian ownership of television stations, and some governments are writing "hate speech" laws and regulations that would censor certain religious viewpoints, such as God's firm, total command in the Bible against homosexual behavior.

The price of liberty is eternal vigilance, but so is the price of our freedom of speech. If we abuse our freedom of speech by spreading untruths, false rumors and slanders against groups and beliefs we oppose, we may encourage our enemies to deprive us of free speech altogether.

A Difference That Makes a Difference

As we have shown, there seems to be only minor differences between the exaggerated witchcraft of *Harry Potter* and the witchcraft condemned by God and Jesus Christ and His disciples in the Bible. There also seems to be little difference between the exaggerated witchcraft in *Harry Potter* and most of the kinds of witchcraft in the neo-pagan movement.

There is a great deal of difference, however, between *Harry Potter* and the movies that Peter Jackson and his team of filmmakers have crafted from Christian author J.R.R. Tolkien's *Lord of the Rings*. These movies are a wonderful epic fantasy about good and evil with top-notch actors, storyline and special effects. Happily, the filmmakers have left in plenty of Tolkien's biblical, allegorical Christian references, not to mention his strong, positive moral worldview. In doing this, they have fashioned a masterful blend of fantasy and adventure that has positive Christological implications.

In contrast to *The Lord of the Rings*, as we have mentioned, the Harry Potter movies have a strong pagan worldview with very strong occult content. They encourage children to dabble in witchcraft, sorcery, divination and talking with dead people and other "spirits." Without proper parental supervision, children may succumb to these anti-Christian, anti-biblical beliefs and drift toward a hedonistic or pagan lifestyle that denies the power of God and that denies the truth of the Bible. *Harry Potter* and the advertising, media hype surrounding the series also may inspire children or teenagers into investigating the many pagan, witchcraft websites on the Internet that attempt to repackage the very real dangers of witchcraft and paganism in order to inculcate young minds with tales of other gods and goddesses, sorcery, sexual hedonism and worse.

Although he has many good qualities, Harry Potter's disobedience, lying and propensity to break the rules set him against the biblical model of a righteous hero. Furthermore, Harry has supernatural powers, which, contrary to the strained analogies made by some commentators, is not the case for any human child aside from Jesus Christ. Nor is it the case of any of the human characters in *The Lord of the Rings*, nor of Frodo and Sam, the humble Hobbit heroes in Tolkien's tale. That said, every human child is created by God with unique, sometimes brilliant, talents and gifts, and every child who comes to know Jesus Christ as Lord and Savior is filled with His Holy Spirit and the gifts that the Holy Spirit bestows on him or her. These gifts are not the same as the supernatural, paranormal powers of Harry and his friends.

In contrast to Harry, Frodo is a humble, loyal, honest and real hobbit who succeeds by grace and mercy. In *Harry Potter*, Harry triumphs because he is superior. He was born special, although for many years he did not know it. This time of unknowing gives Harry a tendency to be secretive, to disobey and even to lie. Frodo, on the other hand, is a humble everyman who triumphs because of a higher grace, which is manifest in the supernatural beings, such as Gandalf and Arwen, who help him.

Gandalf, by the way, is not a human wizard but an angelic being with supernatural powers given to him by the Creator. Arwen is an elf, a member of a race of special creatures created by God. In *The Silmarillion*, Tolkien says that the elves are similar to angels, though they are less in power and stature. Guided by Gandalf, Frodo understands that he is not gifted in some special way, but undertakes his quest because it is the right thing to do. His commitment to do the right thing, plus his mercy, his compassion and his faith in the greater good give him the ability to triumph.

In the first two Harry Potter books and movies, the initial villains are Harry's muggle (non-magic) relatives and guardians, who are very cruel to Harry. Regarding Harry's muggle relatives, the books and movies do not say that they are Christians, but they are a middle-class family living in England. Regrettably, they often act in an unloving and repulsive manner, even to the point of locking Harry away in his room for no good reason. Also, Harry's aunt and uncle spoil their own mean little boy and let him get away with things that they wouldn't let Harry do. Harry thus finds a home away from his family at Hogwarts School of Witchcraft and Wizardry, with people who are like him in their special powers of witchcraft and wizardry.

In both *The Lord of the Rings* movies, the family is portrayed in a positive way. For example, one character named Faramir expresses concern for his brother Boromir; the aforementioned elf Arwen has great respect for her father, Elrond; and a king named Theoden expresses great pangs of regret that he let Saruman and Wormtongue (Saruman's human compatriot) poison his mind, resulting in his son's death.

Faith, hope and love are positive forces in the three *The Lord of the Rings* movies, as is the guiding of a divine providence. Christian virtues, such as abstaining from witchcraft and going to benevolent authorities for help, are portrayed negatively in the Harry Potter movies. Also, Harry and his friends too often escape adult supervision, which sends a bad example for children to follow. Contrast this with the images of the children in Helm's Deep in *The Two Towers*, where the parents of the children protect them and help them.

In every narrative-style movie, video, television program and play, the premise can be found by analyzing the story. In *The Lord of the Rings* trilogy, Frodo, a friendly, likeable, humble hobbit, must destroy an ancient evil ring that has the power to unleash a hellish nightmare on relatively peaceful Middle Earth. "Good triumphs over evil" is clearly the premise in the trilogy, in which the good is represented by grace, mercy, honor, loyalty and love, and evil is represented by the magical ring that tempts all creatures to sin or rebel against God.

In the Harry Potter movies, however, Harry is a supernaturally empowered wizard who breaks the rules of Hogwarts School of Witchcraft and Wizardry in order to temporarily defeat the evil wizard Voldemort. Thus, the premise in *Harry Potter* is that the more powerful and more attractive wizard defeats the less powerful less attractive one. As such, *Harry Potter*'s premise reflects a false gnostic worldview—an evil worldview that clearly contradicts Scripture, the Word of God. This gnostic occult worldview of *Harry Potter* also portrays evil as having tremendous power and states that the hero can only succeed by participating in occult power. *The Lord of the Rings,* on the other hand, portrays evil as something that no one would want to imitate. It also shows that rebellion, disobedience and sin have negative consequences.

Besides having a premise that drives the story to its logical conclusion, many media products make one or more moral statements. *The Lord of the Rings* has the biblically sound moral statements that humility, loyalty, mercy and commitment are to be valued; that there are some good things worth fighting for; and that there is a divine plan. In contrast, *Harry Potter* teaches that disobeying rules is praiseworthy if successful, families and school rules are restrictive, and playing tricks and practical jokes on others is justified if it is funny.

Christians and Jews believe in a real epistemology, which means that they have knowledge because God tells them and enlightens them and because God has given everyone's spirit the ability to use logic and understand spiritual truths essential to their salvation. He has told us that His laws, which stem from His character, govern all creation, so we know that everything that occurs in nature and in this world are subject to His laws and His character. *The Lord of the Rings* has this real epistemology.

Many media products, including *Harry Potter*, posit that you cannot know truth or goodness and therefore are trapped in an unpredictable and frightening world. Other media products, such as Sartre's famous play *No Exit*, take an existentialist perspective that you cannot know anything, so you must believe that life is essentially meaningless. For Christians and Jews, however, the biblical view of reality is that we live in a real world, created by the real God, where there are real problems, real pain and real suffering that we cannot ignore or wish away. For those of us who are Christians, the creator God has saved us from real evil, sin and death through the real death and resurrection of His Son, Jesus the Christ, who was wholly God and wholly man. Any other ontology, or view of the nature of being, denies this gospel.

Thus, although *The Lord of the Rings* certainly is not a perfect work, there is a real difference between it and the Harry Potter stories. It's a real difference that makes a difference.

Farther Up and Farther In

In the same way, C. S. Lewis's *Chronicles of Narnia* also represents a story with a biblical ontology and worldview. Almost 100 million people have read *The Lion, the Witch and the Wardrobe* alone—a fact that is staggering considering that most books sell less than 10,000 copies. Although many readers have said that they missed the book's clear Christological allusions, the book has been credited over the years with leading many people to Jesus Christ, and it continues to be a favorite among Christians.

In this regard, C. S. Lewis wanted the story to get past the "watchful dragons" of young minds trained by an increasingly secular British culture so that his readers would understand the good news of Jesus Christ. He revealed his method in a March 1961 letter to a young girl named Anne:

I think you will probably see that there is a deeper meaning behind it. The whole Narnian story is about Christ. That is to say, I asked myself "Supposing that there really was a world like Narnia and supposing it had (like our world) gone wrong and supposing Christ wanted to go into that world and save it (as He did ours) what might have happened?" The stories are my answers. Since Narnia is a world of Talking Beasts, I thought He would become a Talking Beast there, as He became a man here. I pictured Him becoming a lion there because (a) the lion is supposed to be the king of beasts; (b) Christ is called "The Lion of Judah" in the Bible; (c) I'd been having strange dreams about lions when I began writing the work. The whole series works out like this.

The Magician's Nephew tells the Creation and how evil entered Narnia. The Lion etc. the Crucifixion and Resurrection. Prince Caspian restoration of the true religion after corruption. The Horse and His Boy the calling and conversion of a heathen. The Voyage of the "Dawn Treader" the spiritual life (especially in Reepicheep). The Silver Chair the continuing war with the powers of darkness. The Last Battle the coming of the Antichrist (the Ape). The end of the world and the Last Judgement.[3]

Thus, The Chronicles of Narnia delivers a detailed Christian allegory that chronicles the major biblical events in our world—from the Fall to the death and resurrection of Christ to the Last Judgment.

A Christian Allegory

In 1950, C. S. Lewis constructed the first book in his Narnia series: The Lion, the Witch and the Wardrobe. The tale, which is set during World War II, begins with the evacuation of four children (Peter, Susan, Edmund and Lucy Pevensie) from London to the countryside in order to escape the bombings. The children are sent out of the city for their protection and soon arrive at the home of the eclectic Professor Kirke.

As the children settle into their new surroundings, they decide to play a game of Hide and Seek. Lucy, seeking an appropriate hiding place, soon stumbles on an old wardrobe. The wardrobe leads her to Narnia, a world with talking animals and mythical creatures. Unknown to Lucy, the world is controlled by the evil White Witch, who has turned Narnia into a state of forever winter, but never Christmas.

A prophecy in the land says that four sons and daughters of Adam and Eve will be brought to Narnia to assist Aslan, the son of the Emperor-Beyond-the-Sea, free Narnia from the White Witch. To thwart the prophecy, the White Witch has told the creatures of Narnia that if they see a son or daughter of Adam and Eve, they should kidnap and bring them to her. When Lucy meets a faun named Mr. Tumnus, he at first considers kidnapping her and delivering her to the White Witch. However, he eventually decides to put his life in jeopardy by letting Lucy return to the world of men.

When Lucy returns to the world of human beings, her brothers Edmund and Peter and her sister, Susan, do not believe that she was in Narnia—until Lucy goes to Narnia through the wardrobe a second time. This time, Edmund follows her, and eventually he becomes a pawn of the White Witch.

Like Satan, the White Witch in Lewis's parable offers Edmund something that he already has—the authority to rule Narnia—and traps him with a counterfeit sacrament of Turkish delight. It falls to Edmund's sisters and brother to find the great Emperor, Aslan, to try to set him free. When they do, Aslan speaks with the White Witch and tells her that—as Christ did for all the sins of humankind—he will die to pay the penalty for Edmund's treachery.

In the end, Aslan is sacrificed by the witch and dies on the Great Stone Table. Yet he possesses knowledge of "The Deep Magic Before the Dawn of Time"—an allusion to the Old Testament—that states that when a willing, innocent victim is killed by a traitor, the Stone Table will crack and death itself will be reversed. Aslan returns to life, and in a final battle defeats the tyrannical rule of the White Witch, forever breaking her control over Narnia.

In December 2005, the Disney Corporation, in conjunction with Walden Media, released a live-action film version of *The Lion, the Witch and the Wardrobe*. Fortunately, like the film adaptation of *The Lord of the*

Rings, the executives at Disney and Walden chose to release a film that was not only entertaining but that also clearly retained the deeper truth and essence of the author's original work. In fact, very few people will see the slight divergences that the movie takes from C. S. Lewis's novel, and even fewer will see the very subtle theological shifts in the new movie. Thus, the good news about the movie is that it works well and can serve as a great tool for Christians and the Church to help people understand the truth of the gospel of Jesus Christ.

C. S. Lewis never wanted a movie made of his books, but one imagines that he would be proud of this production. The movie also seems to fit his overall goal: to create a "supposal" of Christianity to lead people to the gospel. "*Narnia* is already capturing attention in Christian circles," noted one reviewer, "and many church leaders are noting its potential as an evangelism tool."[4]

Yet even though the movie has retained its theological foundation, some of the theology present in the book has been toned down in the movie version. These changes are subtle, with a little more emphasis on the creation rather than the Creator. There are no direct references to the Emperor-Beyond-the-Sea, for example. Also, the sacramental communion banquet with the coming of Father Christmas and the gifts of the Spirit has been truncated into a very brief scene with Father Christmas. Furthermore, the resurrection romp with Aslan, Lucy and Susan has been eliminated, and the movie focuses more on the children being the solution to the evil in Narnia—when in fact the children, just like the people in our world, are more than conquerors only because they are heirs to the victory that Aslan wins on the Stone Table (the victory that Jesus Christ won for all of us in the real world on the cross!).

Andrew Adamson said that when he directed the movie, he started from his memory. He felt that the book was too thin, so the movie reflects his memory of the book, not the actual book. He understands the element of sacrifice and redemption, but his concern was for the empowering of the children. Clearly, his perspective helped produce the subtle shift from the great clarity of the book itself, but his love for the original source ultimately keeps the movie on target.

Therefore, you have to be very close to the book and very theologically astute to notice the changes. In fact, the movie is a very clear Christological allusion, or imagining, of the story of Jesus Christ. The minor changes do not take away from the fundamental meaning of Lewis's great story, which lifts up the Son of God, Jesus Christ, as our deliverer from the eternal winter of sin and damnation.

The Cosmic Battle

C. S. Lewis's story reflects the real cosmic battles that take place every day in our world. The Bible clearly teaches us that we are in a cosmic battle for the souls of our children and the souls of our nations. It is a cosmic battle for the true, the good and the beautiful. It is also a cosmic battle for justice, virtue and honor.

The players in this cosmic battle are God, the ultimate source of all truth, justice, goodness and beauty; Jesus Christ, who sacrificed Himself for our sins and crushed the head of Satan; and humanity, which is torn between its sinful nature and the call of God to turn away from sin and return to Him. Thus, each one of us, in our own individual way, shares the ordeal of Jesus Christ when He was tempted by Satan in the wilderness.

In the description of that historical conflict in Matthew 4, the Spirit leads Jesus into the desert. Jesus eats nothing for 40 days and becomes very hungry. The devil comes to Jesus in the desert and tells Him to turn a stone into bread to assuage His hunger. Jesus refuses and quotes Deuteronomy 8:3, saying, "Man does not live on bread alone, but on every word that comes from the mouth of God."

Then the devil takes Jesus to the highest point of the Temple in Jerusalem and tells Him to throw himself over the edge and command His angels to save Him. Jesus refuses and quotes Deuteronomy 6:16: "Do not put the Lord your God to the test."

Finally, the devil shows Jesus all the splendor of the kingdoms of the world. "All this I will give you," the devil says, "if you will bow down and worship me." Jesus replies, quoting Deuteronomy 6:13: "Away from me, Satan! For it is written: 'Worship the Lord your God, and serve him only.'" Faced with this strong biblical opposition, the devil leaves Jesus, and angels come and attend Him (see Matt. 4:11).

This narrative passage may be one of the most important ones in all of Holy Scripture. Whenever the devil tempts Jesus to sin, Jesus, who is filled with the Holy Spirit, puts the focus back on God and back on God's Word. Furthermore, when the devil finally leaves empty-handed, God's angels come and minister to Jesus. Thus, there is real power in God and in God's Word, and Jesus relies on that power.

In the same way, as we ourselves go about our daily struggles, from the greatest struggles to the smallest struggles, we too can be ministered to by God's angels if we are filled with the Holy Spirit and if we focus on God and on God's Word, through Jesus Christ. That is the best way we can have victory over the devil and over our sinful nature, which is emblematic of the devil's power. Here we have, then, a sacred story, full of the power of God, that can teach, influence and inspire us throughout our whole lives. It is a perfect example of the power of the storytelling gift that God has placed in our hands.

Storytelling can be a powerful tool used by God to lead us toward the purity, righteousness, nobility and love that Paul mentions in Philippians 4:8 in the New Testament. However, it can also be a powerful tool used by satanic powers, including sinful human beings who have rebelled against God and who have rejected the Word of God and the Gospel of Jesus Christ, pointing us toward evil and falsehood.

Ultimately, it is God as He has revealed Himself through the Holy Bible that is the final standard by which we should live. God is the Rock that lifts us high and protects us from the foes without and the foes within. As Psalm 62:1-2 and 11-12 tell us, "My soul finds rest in God alone; my salvation comes from him. He alone is my rock and my salvation; he is my fortress, I will never be shaken. . . . You, O God, are strong, and that you, O Lord, are loving. Surely you will reward each person according to what he has done."

Therefore, we should put our trust in God at all times and pour out our hearts to Him (see Ps. 62:8). And we should follow His Word, the Bible, because all the words in it are God-breathed and are "useful for teaching, rebuking, correcting and training in righteousness" (2 Tim. 3:16).

This, then, is the spiritual approach we should take while we protect our homes and communities from the negative influences of the entertainment media and while we continue working diligently to encourage the entertainment industry to adopt higher standards based on the Word of God.

In taking this approach, we should recognize that even the most innocuous and lightweight movie, video program or musical performance (or parable) will teach some kind of message that may influence the thinking and behavior of millions, and even billions, of people, including children and teenagers. We must be really wise, therefore, in what kinds of entertainment products that we and our families consume. As Paul writes to the Church in Philippians 4:8, "Whatever is true, whatever is noble, whatever is right, whatever is pure, whatever is lovely, whatever is admirable—if anything is excellent or praiseworthy—think about such things."

Jesus, who sits at the right hand of our Father in Heaven and sees all, is watching us, and God is taking down our names.

PART IV

VALUES, PRINCIPLES AND

WORLDVIEWS

CHAPTER 9

Worldviews and Beyond

The greatest issue facing our culture involves understanding the Christian worldview.[1] It is a more important issue than poverty, racism, AIDS, immoral entertainment, low SAT scores, the budget deficit, divorce, illegitimate births, domestic violence and even abortion. While each of these is a serious problem, they are simply the fruit of bad worldview thinking. To the degree that we understand and embrace biblical thinking in all areas of life, to that degree the social ills of our nation will subside.

The increase of America's social problems coincide with departing from a clear perception of the guidance of God's Word, and the remedy for these serious social illnesses is to embrace biblical precepts that once impacted our nation as a healing balm. As the overall positive influence of God's grace and mercy once caused our culture to flourish, the lack of that influence is causing prosperity to subside. The milestone of removal of prayer from school clearly marks this degeneration.

Dr. Ronald Nash, a professor at the Reformed Theological Seminary, said the following about the importance of teaching a Christian worldview:

> America's mainline denominations were lost to liberalism and unbelief because in the century following the American Civil War the Christian church lost the battle in the world of ideas. The most important step for Christians is to become informed about the Christian worldview, a comprehensive systematic view of the life and of the world as a whole. No believer today can be really effective in the arena of ideas until he or she has been trained to think in worldview terms.[2]

Yes, the truth sets people free, but this truth, the Word of God, must be understood and applied by the Body of Christ. Jesus said, "You are the salt of the earth. But if the salt loses its saltiness, how can it be made salty again? It is no longer good for anything, except to be thrown out and trampled by men. You are the light of the world. A city on a hill cannot be hidden" (Matt. 5:13-14). Even more serious, when the Church stops being true biblically, as commissioned throughout the Old and New Testaments, the Church, unknowingly, offers a counterfeit Gospel with "another Jesus" to lost sinners.

How can the Church better approach these front lines—education, economics, crime, family, marriage, and others—to win the cultural battle? First, the army of the Lord needs to add recruits on the church rosters. The consensus-seeking church is not attracting new members, while more hard line "new" religions grow in numbers. Second, even those who enter Christ's army in devout repentance from sin are not entering into disciplined Bible studies to acquire an arsenal for victorious soldiers. Their eternal home is secure, but their daily temporal lives are spent in defeat. We must put on the "full armor" of God (Eph. 6:10-18).

For the most part, today's Church is simply not delivering the goods.

Powerless Christianity

In his book *No Place for the Truth*, David Wells stated, "The vast growth in evangelically minded people in the 1960s, 1970s and 1980s should by now have revolutionized American culture. With a third of American adults now claiming to have experienced spiritual rebirth, a powerful countercurrent of morality growing out of a powerful and alternative worldview should have been unleashed in factories, offices and board rooms, in the media, universities and professions, from one end of the country to the other. The results should by now be unmistakable. Secular values should be reeling, and those who are their proponents should be very troubled."[3]

The Bible says, "But you will chase your enemies and they will fall before you by the sword; five of you will chase a hundred, and a hundred of you will chase ten thousand, and your enemies will fall before you by the word" (Lev. 26: 7-8, *NASB*). With the odds 100 to 1 against them,

God's people defeated the enemy. So with today's ratio of only 2 to 1 (unbelievers to believers, supposedly), why isn't the Church winning?

Wells continued, "This surely is an odd circumstance. Here is a corner of the religious world that has learned from the social scientists how to grow itself, that is sprouting huge mega churches that look like shopping malls for the religious, that can count in its own society, the moneyed and powerful, and yet it causes not so much as a ripple. And, its disappearance, judged in moral and spiritual terms, is happening at the very moment when American culture is more vulnerable to the uprooting of some of its cherished enlightenment beliefs than ever before, because it knows itself to be empty. Thus, it is that both American culture and American evangelicalism have come to share the same fate, both basking in the same stunning, outward success while stricken by a painful vacuity and emptiness in their respective centers."[4]

What the Church is serving is a shallow and unsalted gospel. Although the message is being delivered with deep compassion for lost sinners and with a burden for a hurting culture, it lacks comprehensive truth to shape the minds of believers and redirect their behavior. Without biblical principles for all areas of life—especially in critical areas such as the structure and role of civil government, economic policy, education curriculum, Church/state relationships, health care, entertainment, arts, foreign affairs, and crime—new believers stay off the battlefield.

Without the transforming power of the cross, the Church carries a white flag against the forces of deception. In this mode of operation, "winter" holidays make Christ only conspicuous by His absence, while educational curriculums include virtually any reading material except the Bible. Rather than lifting Jesus for the world to see, the battlefields of our culture are quieted by a false peace that denies the hope of freedom from sin, redemption through His blood and grace to abide with our heavenly Father as we yield to the Holy Spirit.

Ransacking the Camp

A gospel that only encourages converts to realize Christ's victory in death is not the dynamic model presented in the New Testament. This is a "What's in it for me?" message, of which the Church's martyrs had no part. Early Church converts were not martyred for believing in Jesus in their private thoughts but for challenging the secular anti-Christian authorities of their day.

Jesus said, "Not everyone who says to me, 'Lord, Lord,' will enter the kingdom of heaven, but only he who does the will of my Father who is in heaven. Many will say to me on that day, 'Lord, Lord, did we not prophesy in your name, and in your name drive out demons and perform many miracles?' Then I will tell them plainly, 'I never knew you. Away from me, you evildoers!'" (Matt. 7:21-23). The chief reason why most Christians don't think in worldview terms is because of the self-centered mentality of how one becomes a member of the kingdom of God.

Man's redemption comes by grace: "By grace you have been saved, through faith—and this not from yourselves, it is the gift of God" (Eph. 2:8). Even so, Jesus identified the redeemed: "For whoever does the will of My Father who is in heaven, that person is My brother and sister and mother" (Matt. 12:50, *CSB*).

The Church must be recognized by fruit being produced as witnesses of His love, joy and peace—not only declarations of faith. Each week, tens of thousands are acknowledged as converts into the Kingdom, yet instead of having any impact on society, one would think the Church is on an extended retreat. Meanwhile, the enemy is ransacking the camp. Anti-biblical philosophy abounds at all levels of government, schools are failing everywhere, marriages and families are coming apart faster than new ones are being formed, immorality of the worst kind is being flaunted openly and, horror of horrors, this immorality is being sanctioned from certain segments of the Body of Christ.[5]

With the high-growth "accept Jesus" evangelism, the church is transforming itself into a civic religion based on community needs, a place of weekly fellowship that provides day care, youth activities, mom's-day-out, and 20- to 30-minute nonconfrontational messages, all designed to fit the climate of our day. What they are not looking for is sacramental worship, theological Bible study or pastoral confrontation over sin or commitment. Apart from a return to solid Christian worldview, a new day in Christendom is arising.

A Lost Generation

Christian educators and parents are painfully aware that a high percentage of young people stop attending church after leaving home. Many live in a manner highly displeasing to the Lord. One study of more than 3,500 incoming freshman who identified themselves as born-again Christians found that between one-third and one-half said they no longer considered themselves as such by their senior year (decisions that defected!).[6]

The Church was once the dominant force in our universities, producing scholarly statesmen who drafted state constitutions and created organizations to care for the less fortunate. Contrary to the Christian worldview at work 200 years ago, the agenda for today's public square is being shaped by secular and anti-Christian forces. The Church's job is mostly viewed as getting people ready for heaven. Our youth, who are thinking more about living than dying, perceive the Church as lacking a desire to influence culture-shaping institutions such as the legislative assemblies and courts. They see a Church without a Christian worldview.

Believers Turned the World Upside Down

When the Church held answered questions regarding spiritual matters such as creation, God's relationship to man and man's purpose with biblical answers, it held a position of respectability and wielded substantial influence. This was certainly the case with the first-century Church, whereby in Acts believers were said to have "turned the world upside down." The Church's influence was dynamic until the fall of the Roman Empire in A.D. 476.

Further, the Christian Church wielded influence politically and economically, as well as spiritually, during the Reformation period under Luther's and Calvin's leaderships, and (primarily through the teachings of Calvin) significantly impacted and shaped most of the Northern European countries, England and eventually America. Also, early in this century, saloons and gambling halls closed for lack of business as a result of American evangelist Billy Sunday's proclamation of the gospel.

During the Dark Ages from A.D. 700 to 1200, the Church gave way to gross immorality, until the gospel was once again held up as the standard of righteousness. A modern day example is the moral decline of young people beginning with the Supreme Court's disallowing prayer in public schools in 1962.[7] This trend continued in 1980 when the Supreme Court pulled the Ten Commandments from a school bulletin board in Kentucky and thus from bulletin boards in public schools throughout the nation.

Without a comprehensive view of life, the Church focuses only on spiritual and eternal matters while social life deteriorates. As Francis Schaeffer noted so clearly:

> The basic problem of the Christians in this country in the last 80 years or so, in regard to society and in regard to government, is that they have seen things in bits and pieces instead of totals. They have very gradually become disturbed over permissiveness, pornography, the public schools, the breakdown of the family, and finally abortion. But, they have not seen this as a totality—each thing being a part, a symptom, of a much larger problem. They have failed to see that all of this has come about due to a shift in worldview—that is, through a fundamental change in the overall way people think and view the world and life as a whole.[8]

Do We Worship Ourselves?

In his book *The American Religion*, Yale scholar Harold Bloom analyzed the emergence of a post-Christian America in his book and noted that the god we worship is ourselves. Bloom states the real religion of America is Gnosticism, an elitist Christian heresy that combines mystical Greek and oriental philosophies and claims that a person needed special knowledge to get to the highest heaven. Christianity posits that you need only faith to believe in the factual knowledge that Jesus rose from the dead to receive salvation, which is the gift from God.

A plethora of worldviews is presented in the mass media, which differ from biblical Christian beliefs. An overview follows, to recognize a

variety of perceptions regarding the nature of reality and how to perceive what is real. How many worldviews are there? In a strict biblical
sense, there are only two—Christian and anti-Christian, otherwise
known as paganism. This would be the meaning of Jesus' words, "He
who is not with me is against me, and he who does not gather with me
scatters" (Matt. 12:30).

Christian Worldview Uncovered

Creedal Christians believe God made the world and "so loved the world,
that he gave His only begotten Son" (John 3:16, *KJV*). All faithful Christian
churches want to impact the world as much as possible to glorify God. To
apply biblical principles to all areas of life, and Christ's authority over all
things, even as He has given the Church the keys to make disciples of all
nations, is to say, "Our goal is nothing less than a Christian civilization."
Is there any other appropriate worldview than that the Bride of Christ will
be glorious and victorious for the return of her King?

This means that God is to be acknowledged in all aspects of society, particularly in government, commerce, entertainment, education
and the arts. Impossible? Not for the God who created the universe
simply by speaking it into existence, and not for the Church called by
Christ. "You are from God, little children, and have overcome them;
because greater is he who is in you than he who is in the world" (1 John
4:4, *NASB*). With God's power and with clear, comprehensive instructions in His Word, the Church can and will bring Christian thought
and behavior to all aspects of world civilization. We need to know
this and work accordingly. By the empowering of the Holy Spirit,
we will overcome.

How are Jesus' enemies defeated? Paul gives the answer: "The God of
peace will soon crush Satan under your feet. The grace of our Lord Jesus
be with you" (Rom. 16:20). This is the Church destroying anti-Christian
thinking day by day, mile by mile.

What Is a Worldview?

According to Norman Geisler and William D. Watkins in *Worlds Apart:
A Handbook of World Views*, a worldview is "a way of viewing or interpreting

all of reality."[9] Later, they add that a worldview provides "an interpretive framework through which or by which one makes sense out of the data of life and the world."[10] As such, all comprehensive worldviews seem to share at least five things:

1. **Cosmology:** a view of the physical, or material, universe
2. **Metaphysics:** a view of what might or might not exist beyond the universe
3. **Anthropology:** a view of human beings and their environment and culture
4. **Psychology:** a view of the human soul and the mental, emotional, spiritual and interior life of human beings
5. **Axiology:** a philosophy of values

In general, a good worldview must have at least three components: internal consistency, explanatory power and empirical adequacy or sufficiency. Thus, it must be logical, it must be able to explain many different kinds of phenomenon, and it must fit the facts.

How a Person's Theology Shapes Worldview
Here are some key doctrinal questions for you to use to evaluate different worldviews.[12]

The Doctrine of God
- Does God have all power and authority over the universe, or is history a battle between good and evil forces (dualism)?
- Is this world rational and ordered? What is justice, goodness, truth, beauty? How are these reflections of God's character?
- What is the significance of the affirmation that "the Word became flesh" for our view of our humanness and the importance of this world?
- Is God the separate, sovereign creator of the universe as in theism? Or is God part of the universe as in pantheism, polytheism and monism?

Going Even Deeper to Understand Other Worldviews
Dr. Peter Hammond

We are living in a world war of worldviews. The Bible warns us: "See to it that no one takes you captive through hollow and deceptive philosophy, which depends on human tradition and the basic principles of this world rather than on Christ" (Col. 2:8).

Whether consciously or unconsciously, consistently or inconsistently, everyone is influenced by a worldview—a set of presuppositions and assumptions that may be true, partially true or false. Our worldview consists of those sets of beliefs and presuppositions, which we hold about basic realities of our world. Our worldview determines our values, influences how we think and therefore guides how we live.

The Basic Questions of Life
Our worldview requires us to answer the basic questions of life:

1. *What is reality?* Materialism maintains that there is no reality beyond the physical.

2. *What is our basis of knowledge?* Rationalism seeks to discover the structure of reality guided by human reason alone. Empiricism declares that reason alone is not sufficient, all our knowledge must be based on information provided by our senses.

3. *How can we know what is right or wrong?* Existentialism evaluates everything from subjective personal experience. Agnosticism maintains that it is impossible to settle the primary questions in life because of the limitations of human knowledge.

4. *What is man?* The evolutionist maintains that we are matter in motion, evolved slime, monkeys who mutated from goo to the zoo to you. From mud to monkeys to man. A cosmic accident. The result of random chance.

5. *What happens to a person after death?* According to Hinduism, we are reincarnated in a kind of cosmic recycling of souls, either moving up the ladder to become holy cows, or sliding down, because of bad karma, to possibly become insects.

6. *What is the meaning of history?* Marxism maintains that history is driven by economic determinism. The post-modernist maintains that there is absolutely no meaning to history.

7. *Why is there suffering and evil?* The Polytheist, who believes in many gods, maintains that it is because of conflict between the various gods.

8. *What is the purpose for our existence?* The Hedonist maintains that we should live for our own personal pleasure. The materialist proclaims that *"He who dies with the most toys wins!"* Humanism ultimately destroys all purpose for one's existence. You came from nothing; you are going nowhere; life is meaningless.

9. *How should we live?* The Muslim claims that we should live in obedience to Sharia law—based upon the Quran and the Hadith—the teachings and practices of Muhammad.

The Biblical Worldview

The biblical worldview, however, provides us with different answers to our basic questions of life:

1. *The Bible makes clear that God is ultimate reality.* "In the beginning was the Word, and the Word was with God, and the Word was God" (John 1:1).

2. *Our basis for knowledge is God's Revelation.* "In the past God spoke . . . through the prophets . . . but in these last days he has spoken to us by his Son" (Heb. 1:1-2).

3. *We can know what is right and what is wrong from the Word of God.* "All Scripture is God-breathed and is useful for teaching, rebuking, correcting and training in righteousness" (2 Tim. 3:16).

4. *Man was created by God, but human nature is sinful.* Because we have been created by God, there is some good even in the worst of us. However, because we are fallen, there is bad even in the best of us. "For we are God's workmanship, created in Christ Jesus to do good works" (Eph. 2:10).

5. *After death, each one of us shall face eternal judgment.* We will either enjoy God's gracious rewards in Heaven or endure just punishment in hell. "Man is destined to die once, and after that to face judgment" (Heb. 9:27).

6. *God is sovereign over history.* "The Most High is sovereign over the kingdoms of men and gives them to anyone He wishes" (Dan. 4:25).

7. *Suffering and evil are a result of man's rebellion against God since the Fall.* "Do not be deceived: God cannot be mocked. A man reaps what he sows" (Gal. 6:7).

8. *The purpose of our existence is to glorify God and to worship Him forever.* "Whatever you do, do it all for the glory of God" (1 Cor. 10:31).

9. *We should therefore live in obedience to the Bible.* "The LORD your God commands you this day to follow these decrees and laws; carefully observe them with all your heart and with all your soul" (Deut. 26:16).

The following are some religious worldviews we need to understand.

Humanism

By way of contrast, humanism is a religion that deifies man—and dethrones God. Francis Schaefer defined humanism as "the placing of man at the centre of all things and making him the measure of all things." Alexander Solzhenitzyn described humanism as "the proclaimed and practiced autonomy of man from any higher force above him."

- The theology of Humanism is *atheism*—the belief that there is no God.
- The biology of Humanism is *evolution*. Man is a product of evolutionary chance.
- The ethics of Humanism is *amorality*, or relativism. There are no moral absolutes.
- The psychology of Humanism is *self-actualization* or existentialism. Everything revolves around self.
- The sociology of Humanism is *a classless world society*—the abolition of the traditional family.
- The economics of Humanism is *socialism*—the redistribution of wealth through government interference.
- The politics of Humanism is *globalism*—a one-world government.

One can recognize the humanist agenda in many films, articles and books:

- Man is a product of evolutionary chance, and this theory must be taught as a fact of science in schools.
- Education must be controlled by the state.
- Education must be secular, free of moral absolutes, and non-Christian.
- Sex education must be compulsory in the schools.
- Pornography should be allowed as free speech.
- Abortion is a woman's right.
- Homosexuality is an acceptable alternative lifestyle.
- Criminals are victims of society requiring treatment and rehabilitation. Rather than punish criminals, it is society as a whole that should be punished.

- The right of citizens to obtain, own and use firearms for self defense must be limited and eventually eliminated.
- All power and authority must be gradually and progressively centralized in big government.

The results of humanism are written all over the pages of recent history: the revolutions, the massacres and totalitarianism of the Communist East, and the permissiveness and decadence of the democratic West, including the pornography plague, the drug epidemic, the crime explosion, the escalating inflation, the abortion holocaust and the AIDS and STDs pandemics—these are just some of the inevitable results of the moral anarchy of humanism.

Animism

Animism is *spirit worship*. It has been heavily promoted by some Hollywood films such as *Pocahontas* and *Brother Bear*. Animism is the primary religion of millions of tribal people scattered throughout Africa, New Guinea, the Pacific Islands, North and South America, Australia, New Zealand, India and Japan. Elements of basic animism are also adhered to by many nominal Muslims, Buddhists and Christians.

Animism involves *necrolatry*, the worship of the souls of the dead. Tribal people tend to regard the departed ancestors as part of the clan and fear the harm that the departed can do to the living. They especially fear that those who died unnaturally will come back to haunt them. Animism involves spirit worship, believing in the existence of personal spirits or demons, as well as impersonal spiritual forces in nature, which inhabit the earth, the air, fire, water, trees, mountains and animal life. Life for the Animist is dominated by a host of taboos and rituals to placate the spirits.

Animism involves *naturism*, the personification and worship of the forces of nature. For example, the worship of the sun in ancient Egypt, the sacred cow of the Hindus in India and the sacred mountain of Shintoism in Japan. Naturism normally involves *polytheism* (the worship of many gods) and *idolatry*. In nature worship, rituals and sacrifices are intended to guarantee fertility. Human sacrifices are an extreme example of this.

Animism involves *totemism* ("Brother–Sister–Kin"), emphasizing the unity of the clan with some sacred plant or animal. Animism involves *fetishism* (the superstitious belief that there is some spiritual energy or force in charms, amulets or fetishes). Normally witchdoctors are involved as Shamans, "expert mediators" who know the proper incantations and sacrifices at times of sickness and disasters to placate the spirits. The witch doctors use imitative magic to bring harm to an enemy by attacking a representation of him (such as a voodoo doll!) or contagious magic, which utilizes some hair clipping, nail paring, sweat, spit or feces to bring a curse on an individual. The blood of an animal (or a person) may be drunk in order to gain the strength of that animal or (in the case of cannibalism) person.

Animism is characterized by the absence of real love and hope. There are *no moral absolutes* (sin is seen as the violation of culture, custom and spirit forces rather than any personal ethical transgression). The whole of life is pervaded with, and governed by, fear. Animism is pervaded by *fatalism* and a sense of helplessness in the face of external forces.

Animism does not deny God as much as ignore Him by worshiping natural forces and mysterious demon powers through magical ceremonies and sacrifices.

Hinduism

Hinduism is actually a collection of religions incorporating Animism and philosophy, one god and many gods, vegetarianism and sacrifices. Hinduism is a pluralistic network of religious beliefs and systems ranging from the philosophical (self-realization) to *Vedic* (rituals and good works) to village Hinduism (idolatry, occultism and animism).

Hinduism is syncretistic; it absorbs elements of any religion it encounters. Widely perceived as a religion of tolerance, its global influence is significant through the New Age movement and the Hare-Krishna movement. Many concepts of Hinduism have become part of the twenty-first-century postmodern culture, including yoga, gurus, karma, reincarnation and transcendental meditation.

The Hindu concept of god is *pantheistic*. Hinduism, as a conglomeration of ideas, beliefs, convictions and practices, varies from people to people and from region to region. However, Hinduism can be understood under six broad categories:

1. *Philosophic Hinduism* is dominated by the authority of the *Vedas* and the *Upanishads*. Philosophic Hinduism teaches that there is a spark of divinity in man, hence to call man a sinner is blasphemous. Therefore, there is no need for a savior.

2. *Religious Hinduism* places strong belief in *Avatars* (incarnations of gods). Hindus are at liberty to choose their own god from amongst a pantheon of over 330 million gods. They teach that salvation can be obtained in one of three ways: the way of knowledge, the way of devotion, or the way of good deeds.

3. *Popular Hinduism* is influenced by ancestral tradition, worship of animals, temple cults, magic and exorcism. Popular Hinduism is primarily concerned with receiving blessings and prosperity from a god who protects its adherents.

4. *Mystic Hinduism* follows those who claim to have supernatural gifts of healing, the ability to perform miracles, to read the inner thoughts of people, and to prophesy the future. These mysterious and apparently spiritual gurus are seen as *Avatars* (incarnations of gods).

5. *Tribal Hinduism* is much influenced by animism, spiritism, the occult, necromancy and animal worship. The fear of the unknown produces instinctive dread over these followers' minds.

6. *Secular Hinduism* is increasing as more and more Hindus become nominal in their beliefs and indifferent to religious practices. They follow only those customs that fulfill their materialistic tendencies.

Underlying all Hindu behavior, religious activity and thought is the doctrine of karma. According to Hindu thought, all of life is controlled by this law, the law of works. Your behavior in a past life determines your fate in the present life, and your deeds in the present life determine your future reincarnation. The endless cycle of birth and rebirth is called *Samsara*—reincarnation. When you build up bad karma, you move down the ladder. If you have developed good karma, you move up the ladder. A Hindu works for the day when, having completed his karma, he will finally be able to break out of this cycle of reincarnation to escape into freedom called *moksha*.

Hinduism is a religion of polytheism, pantheism and syncretism. Hindus believe that all religions lead to god. They, therefore, reject the need to change from one religion to another. Hindus also reject the concept of sin. Vivekananda said, "It is a sin to call anyone a sinner."

Although the concept of salvation exists within Hinduism, it is understood as liberation from the cycle of rebirth, not forgiveness for one's own personal guilt. The Hindu doctrine of salvation is radically different from the Christian doctrine. Similarly, when a Christian speaks of being born again, a Hindu would generally think of reincarnation.

It is not necessary to defend the existence of God to Hindus, although, with their pantheistic concept of God, it is essential that we clarify and define who we mean by God. The Hindus have great respect for sacred writings, including the Bible. Hindus will listen attentively to an exposition of Scripture.

Hindus also have great respect for the person of Christ; the quality of His relationship with people, His teachings (particularly the Sermon on the Mount), His suffering and His unique and vicarious sacrifice of Himself, all have a strong appeal to the Hindu. As Christian communicators, we need to build on this basic respect for Christ with an understanding of what Christ taught and who He is—the Word made flesh.

The Hindu doctrine of karma is a barrier to their understanding of salvation. However, it can be used as a bridge to communicate the gospel to Hindus. The Bible does teach that what we sow is what we reap. What we do now effects our eternity. However, "It is appointed unto men once to die, but after this the judgment" (Heb. 9:27, *KJV*).

The Hindus must be told of our Lord and Savior, Jesus Christ who, by His suffering and death upon the cross, triumphed over sin and has taken upon Himself the penalty for all our sins. Hindus need to understand the atonement.

Islam

Islam, being a monotheistic religion that claims to build upon the foundations laid by Judaism and Christianity, has numerous points of agreement with Christianity. Christians and Muslims agree that:

- God created the world and all that is in it, as well as Heaven and hell.
- God is all powerful, He knows everything and He is everywhere, all the time.
- God has revealed His will to mankind through the prophets.
- God has given us laws, which should govern our lives and prevent us from doing wrong.
- God will judge all people: Some go to Heaven, while all others are doomed to hell.

Muslims are often allies of Christians in opposing evolution, atheism, pornography, gambling and abortion. However, Muslims deny the deity of Christ. To the Muslim, Jesus was a good man but not the Son of God. Islam denies the Trinity and the atonement of Christ on the cross. In fact, there is no atonement or reconciliation of the sinner to God. Neither the sacrifice of Jesus Christ nor by any other sacrifice in Islam can sin be forgiven.

Much of the Quran is made up from Bible stories; however, they are often misunderstood. For example, Adam and Eve sinned, not in an earthly garden, but in paradise. They were cast down to Earth after they had sinned. Noah had only one son, and he drowned in the flood. Moses, in the Quran, was adopted by Pharaoh's wife, not his daughter. Although the Quran recites Moses' confrontation with Pharaoh 27 times, the most integral part of the story, the Passover, is omitted!

The Tower of Babel, according to the Quran, was built by Pharaoh in Egypt! The Quran teaches that Mary, the mother of our Lord Jesus Christ, was the sister of Aaron, and the daughter of Imran, who lived 1,500 years before the birth of Christ! The Five Fundamentals, which all Muslims must believe in, include:

1. One god, Allah
2. The existence of angels
3. The revealed books (*Taurat*—the Old Testament, particularly the books of Moses; the *Zabur* – the Psalms of David; the *Injil*— the New Testament, particularly the Gospels; and the *Quran*)
4. The prophets sent by Allah
5. Life after death

The Six Pillars of Islam are:

1. The open confession of that there is no god but Allah and that Muhammed is his prophet
2. The five daily prayers toward Mecca
3. The keeping of the fast each night during the full month of Ramadaan
4. The giving of alms
5. The pilgrimage to Mecca
6. Holy war (*jihad*)

Despite the history of Muslims persecuting Christians, the Quran teaches that Jesus was born of a virgin, was holy and faultless, that He is the Messiah, the Word of God, a spirit from God, that He created life, that He healed the sick, that He raised the dead, that He came with clear signs and miraculous wonders as a sign to all mankind, that He is illustrious in this world and in the hereafter, that He was raised to heaven from where He will come back for judgment (Surah 4:171; 5:113; 19:19-21,91; 43:61).

What the Quran teaches about the Lord Jesus is a good place to start when witnessing to Muslims. Of which other prophet could it be said that He was holy and faultless, that He healed the sick and raised the dead, and that He is coming again to judge?

Evaluating a Person's Worldview

To evaluate the worldview of any film producer, scriptwriter, director, author, journalist or anyone else, we need to ask the following general questions:

1. What are his fundamental beliefs about life?
2. What is he using to interpret the facts?
3. What are the practical implications of his worldview?
4. How consistent is his worldview?
5. What implications would it have for me personally?
6. What would it mean for the world in general?

We can also ask certain specific questions:

1. What does he believe is true about himself and his place in history?
2. How does he treat, or mistreat, his body?
3. How does he interact with friends and enemies, the rich and the poor, the strong and the weak?
4. What is his motivation in work and how does he spend his money?
5. What moral guidelines and obligations direct his thinking about justice and righteousness?

"Choose for yourselves this day whom you will serve . . . but as for me and my household, we will serve the Lord" (Josh. 24:15).

"Do not conform any longer to the pattern of this world, but be transformed by the renewing of your mind. Then you will be able to test and approve what God's will is—his good, pleasing and perfect will" (Rom. 12:2).[11]

How a Person's Theology Shapes Worldview

Here are some key doctrinal questions for you to use to evaluate different worldviews.[12]

The Doctrine of Man

- Is man a product of chance? Are we part of God or distinct creations of God?
- What distinguishes humans from the rest of creation?
- What is the image of God? Do people still possess that image even if they aren't Christians? What does this mean for the arena of life we share in common with non-Christians (work, play, etc.)?
- Are humans basically good or evil? How are we dead in our sins? How are we cut off from God? What does original sin mean?
- What does this mean for government and law? How do we balance liberty and justice? Can we expect to build an ideal society?

The Doctrine of Salvation

- Is salvation eternal or temporal?
- Do people really need saving? From what?
- Of what does the Christian doctrine of salvation consist?
- Is salvation the work of God entirely?
- How can man save himself? If man can save himself, why did Jesus Christ need to die on the cross and be resurrected?

The Doctrine of the Church

- Are we saved *from* the world or saved *in* the world?
- Is the Church a community that is separated from the world or to God in the world?
- Is the Church a community of only those who are truly saved, or is it a mixed body of Christians and hypocrites who will only be sorted out on the last day?
- How important are the earthly sacraments of bread, wine and water in our Christian experience?
- What are my responsibilities to the church as well as to my calling?

The Doctrine of History and the Future

- Is God's history of salvation, from Genesis to Revelation, a story of escape from this world and normal human history, or a story of providence and redemption in real time and space history?
- Are we wasting our time getting involved in this world when it is going to pass away at our Lord's return?

The Doctrine of the Nature of Reality (Ontology)

- Do we live in a real world—ontological realism?
- Or do we live in a great thought or imaginary world that can be shaped by magical thinking—ontological nominalism?

The Doctrine of Knowledge—Epistemology

- Can we know that something exists, such as a tree falling in the forest—epistemological realism?
- Or can we never know with certainty anything and so must make believe that reality exists—epistemological nominalism?

What Must We Do?

- We must think and behave biblically in all areas. We start with prayer, asking God to forgive us for being short-sighted and of little faith. We ask Him to equip us for the battle of life.
- Read books on Christian worldview thinking. Also read of the Christian impact on the founding of our nation. This is history that is being denied to students in public schools. Examples of the providence of God have been systematically removed from text books for the past several decades.
- Support Christian education, financially and/or as a volunteer on a committee of a local Christian school.
- Support a mature Christian candidate for a political office.
- Introduce others to Christian worldview studies, start a study group in your church.
- Most important, thank the Lord for your life in Him. Thank Him for redeeming you and the opportunity to work in His Kingdom.

- Then, take joy in knowing that at the end of a productive life, formed by a Christian worldview, you will hear, "Well done, good and faithful slave . . . enter into the joy of your master" (Matt. 25:21, *NASB*).

Conclusion

Christianity is superior to all other worldviews because it is logical, it explains many different kinds of phenomenon, and it fits the facts. As such, it provides a rational justification for judging what is good or evil, right or wrong, true or false and proper or improper. It also gives human beings a meaningful love and provides us with a document, the Bible, which can be empirically and rationally verified. By perceiving the worldview in a work of literature, cinema, video or television, we can determine the level that work reaches with regard to truth, justice, goodness, love and beauty, as depicted in the Bible, the Word of God, which is embodied in Jesus Christ, and in the divine traditions that the one true God has inspired.

CHAPTER 10

Who Stole Our Culture?

William S. Lind[1]

Sometime during the last half-century, someone stole our culture. Just 50 years ago, in the 1950s, America was a great place. It was safe. It was decent. Children got good educations in the public schools. Even blue-collar fathers brought home middle-class incomes, so moms could stay home with the kids. Television shows reflected sound, traditional values.

Where did it all go? How did that America become the sleazy, decadent place we live in today—so different that those who grew up prior to the sixties feel like it's a foreign country? Did it just happen?

It didn't just happen. In fact, a deliberate agenda was followed: to steal our culture and leave a new and very different one in its place. The story of how and why is one of the most important parts of our nation's history—*and it is a story almost no one knows.*

What happened, in short, is that America's traditional culture, which had grown up over generations from our Western, Judeo-Christian roots, was swept aside by an ideology. We know that ideology best as "political correctness" or "multiculturalism." It really is cultural Marxism, Marxism translated from economic into cultural terms in an effort that goes back not to the 1960s but to before World War I. Incredible as it may seem, just as the old economic Marxism of the Soviet Union has faded away, a new cultural Marxism has become the ruling ideology of America's elite. The number one goal of that cultural Marxism, since its creation, has been the destruction of Western culture and the Christian religion.

To understand anything, we have to know its history. To understand who stole our culture, we need to take a look at the history of political correctness.

Early Marxist Theory

Before World War I, Marxist theory said that if Europe ever erupted in war, the working classes in every European country would rise in revolt, overthrow their governments and create a new Communist Europe. But when war broke out in the summer of 1914, that didn't happen. Instead, the workers in every European country lined up by the millions to fight their country's enemies. Finally, in 1917, a Communist revolution did occur in Russia. But attempts to spread that revolution to other countries failed because the workers did not support it.

After World War I ended in 1918, Marxist theorists had to ask themselves the question: What went wrong? As good Marxists, they could not admit Marxist theory had been incorrect. Instead, two leading Marxist intellectuals, Antonio Gramsci in Italy and Georg Lukacs in Hungary (Lukacs was considered the most brilliant Marxist thinker since Marx himself) independently came up with the same answer. They said that Western culture and the Christian religion had so blinded the working class to its true, Marxist class interests, that a Communist revolution was impossible in the West, until both could be destroyed. That objective, established as cultural Marxism's goal right at the beginning, has never changed.

A New Strategy

Gramsci famously laid out a strategy for destroying Christianity and Western culture, one that has proven all too successful. Instead of calling for a Communist revolution up front, as in Russia, he said Marxists in the West should take political power last, after a "long march through the institutions"—the schools, the media, even the churches, every institution that could influence the culture. That long march through the institutions is what America has experienced, especially since the 1960s. Fortunately, Mussolini recognized the danger Gramsci posed and jailed him. His influence remained small until the 1960s, when his works, especially the "Prison Notebooks," were rediscovered.

Georg Lukacs proved more influential. In 1918, he became Deputy Commissar for Culture in the short-lived Bela Kun Bolshevik regime in Hungary. There, asking, "Who will save us from Western civilization?" he instituted what he called "cultural terrorism." One of its main components was introducing sex education into Hungarian schools. Lukacs realized that if he could destroy the country's traditional sexual morals, he would have taken a giant step toward destroying its traditional culture and Christian faith.

Far from rallying to Lukacs's cultural terrorism, the Hungarian working class was so outraged by it that when Rumania invaded Hungary, the workers would not fight for the Bela Kun government, and it fell. Lukacs disappeared, but not for long. In 1923, he turned up at a "Marxist Study Week" in Germany, a program sponsored by a young Marxist named Felix Weil who had inherited millions. Weil and the others who attended that study week were fascinated by Lukacs's cultural perspective on Marxism.

The Frankfurt School

Weil responded by using some of his money to set up a new think tank at Frankfurt University in Frankfurt, Germany. Originally it was to be called the Institute for Marxism. But the cultural Marxists realized they could be far more effective if they concealed their real nature and objectives. They convinced Weil to give the new institute a neutral-sounding name: the Institute for Social Research. Soon known simply as the Frankfurt School, the Institute for Social Research would become the place where political correctness, as we now know it, was developed. The basic answer to the question "Who stole our culture?" is the cultural Marxists of the Frankfurt School.

At first, the Institute worked mainly on conventional Marxist issues such as the labor movement. But in 1930, that changed dramatically. That year, the Institute was taken over by a new director, a brilliant young Marxist intellectual named Max Horkheimer. Horkheimer had been strongly influenced by Georg Lukacs. He immediately set to work to turn the Frankfurt School into the place where Lukacs's pioneering work on cultural Marxism could be developed further into a full-blown ideology.

To that end, he brought some new members into the Frankfurt School. Perhaps the most important was Theodor Adorno, who would become Horkheimer's most creative collaborator. Other new members included two psychologists, Eric Fromm and Wilhelm Reich, who were noted promoters of feminism and matriarchy, and a young graduate student named Herbert Marcuse.

Advances in Cultural Marxism

With the help of this new blood, Horkheimer made three major advances in the development of cultural Marxism. First, he broke with Marx's view that culture was merely part of society's superstructure, which was determined by economic factors. He said that on the contrary, culture was an independent and very important factor in shaping a society.

Second, again contrary to Marx, he announced that in the future, the working class would not be the agent of revolution. He left open the question of who would play that role—a question Marcuse answered in the 1950s.

Third, Horkheimer and the other Frankfurt School members decided that the key to destroying Western culture was to cross Marx with Freud. They argued that just as workers were oppressed under capitalism, so under Western culture, everyone lived in a constant state of psychological repression. Liberating everyone from that repression became one of cultural Marxism's main goals. Even more important, they realized that psychology offered them a far more powerful tool than philosophy for destroying Western culture: psychological conditioning.

Today, when Hollywood's cultural Marxists want to "normalize" something like homosexuality (thus "liberating" us from "repression"), they put on television show after television show where the only normal-seeming white male is a homosexual. That is how psychological conditioning works; people absorb the lessons the cultural Marxists want them to learn without even knowing they are being taught.

The Frankfurt School was well on the way to creating political correctness. Then suddenly, fate intervened. In 1933, Adolf Hitler and the Nazi Party came to power in Germany, where the Frankfurt School was located.

Since the Frankfurt School was Marxist, and the Nazis hated Marxism, and since almost all its members were Jewish, it decided to leave Germany. In 1934, the Frankfurt School, including its leading members from Germany, was reestablished in New York City with help from Columbia University. Soon, its focus shifted from destroying traditional Western culture in Germany to doing so in the United States. It would prove all too successful.

New Developments

Taking advantage of American hospitality, the Frankfurt School soon resumed its intellectual work to create cultural Marxism. To its earlier achievements in Germany, it added these new developments.

Critical Theory

To serve its purpose of negating Western culture, the Frankfurt School developed a powerful tool it called Critical Theory. What was the theory? The theory was to criticize. By subjecting every traditional institution, starting with family, to endless, unremitting criticism (the Frankfurt School was careful never to define what it was for, only what it was against), it hoped to bring them down. Critical Theory is the basis for the "studies" departments that now inhabit American colleges and universities. Not surprisingly, those departments are the home turf of academic political correctness.

Studies in Prejudice

The Frankfurt School sought to define traditional attitudes on every issue as "prejudice" in a series of academic studies that culminated in Adorno's immensely influential book *The Authoritarian Personality*, published in 1950. They invented a bogus F-scale that purported to tie traditional beliefs on sexual morals, relations between men and women, and questions touching on the family to support for fascism. Today, the favorite term the politically correct use for anyone who disagrees with them is "fascist."

Domination

The Frankfurt School again departed from orthodox Marxism, which argued that all of history was determined by who owned the means of production. Instead, they said history was determined by which groups, defined as men, women, races, religions, etc., had power, or dominance, over other groups. Certain groups, especially white males, were labeled "oppressors," while other groups were defined as "victims." Victims were automatically good, oppressors bad, just by what group they came from, regardless of individual behavior.

Though Marxists, the members of the Frankfurt School also drew from Nietzsche (someone else they admired for his defiance of traditional morals was the Marquis de Sade). They incorporated into their cultural Marxism what Nietzsche called the "transvaluation of all values." What that means, in plain English, is that all the old sins become virtues, and all the old virtues become sins. Homosexuality is a fine and good thing, but anyone who thinks men and women should have different social roles is an evil fascist. That is what political correctness now teaches children in public schools all across America. (The Frankfurt School wrote about American public education. They said it did not matter if school children learned any skills or any facts. All that mattered was that they graduate from the schools with the right "attitudes" on certain questions.)

Media and Entertainment
Led by Adorno, the Frankfurt School initially opposed the culture industry, which they thought "commodified" culture. Then, they started to listen to Walter Benjamin, a close friend of Horkheimer and Adorno, who argued that cultural Marxism could make powerful use of tools like radio, film and later television to psychologically condition the public. Benjamin's view prevailed, and Horkheimer and Adorno spent the World War II years in Hollywood. It is no accident that the entertainment industry is now cultural Marxism's most powerful weapon.

The Growth of Marxism in the United States
After World War II and the defeat of the Nazis, Horkheimer, Adorno and most of the other members of the Frankfurt School returned to Germany, where the Institute reestablished itself in Frankfurt with the help of the American occupation authorities. Cultural Marxism in time became the unofficial but all-pervasive ideology of the Federal Republic of Germany.

But hell had not forgotten the United States. Herbert Marcuse remained here, and he set about translating the very difficult academic writings of other members of the Frankfurt School into simpler terms Americans could easily grasp. His book *Eros and Civilization* used the Frankfurt School's crossing of Marx with Freud to argue that if we would only "liberate non-procreative eros" through "polymorphous perversity," we could create a new paradise where there would be only play and no work. *Eros and Civilization* became one of the main texts of the New Left in the 1960s.

Marcuse also widened the Frankfurt School's intellectual work. In the early 1930s, Horkheimer had left open the question of who would replace the working class as the agent of Marxist revolution. In the 1950s, Marcuse answered the question, saying it would be a coalition of students, blacks, feminist women and homosexuals—the core of the student rebellion of the 1960s, and the sacred "victims groups" of political correctness today. Marcuse further took one of political correctness's favorite words, "tolerance," and gave it a new meaning. He defined "liberating tolerance" as tolerance for all ideas and movements coming from the left, and *in*tolerance for all ideas and movements coming from the right. When you hear the cultural Marxists today call for "tolerance," they mean Marcuse's "liberating tolerance" (just as when they call for "diversity," they mean uniformity of belief in their ideology).

The student rebellion of the 1960s, driven largely by opposition to the draft for the Vietnam War, gave Marcuse a historic opportunity. As perhaps its most famous "guru," he injected the Frankfurt School's cultural Marxism into the baby boom generation. Of course, they did not understand what it really was. As was true from the Institute's beginning, Marcuse and the few other people "in the know" did not advertise that political correctness and multiculturalism were a form of Marxism. But the effect was devastating: a whole generation of Americans, especially the university-educated elite, absorbed cultural Marxism as their own, accepting a poisonous ideology that sought to destroy America's traditional culture and Christian faith. That generation, which runs every elite institution in America, now wages a ceaseless war on all traditional beliefs and institutions. They have largely won that war. Most of America's traditional culture lies in ruins.

A Counter-Strategy

Now you know who stole our culture. The question is, What are we, as Christians and as cultural conservatives, going to do about it?

We can choose between two strategies. The first is to try to retake the existing institutions—the public schools, the universities, the media, the entertainment industry and most of the main-line churches—from the cultural Marxists. They expect us to try to do that, they are ready for it, and we would find ourselves, with but small voice and few resources compared to theirs, making a frontal assault against prepared defensive positions. Any soldier can tell you what that almost always leads to: defeat.

There is another, more promising strategy. We can separate ourselves and our families from the institutions the cultural Marxists control and build new institutions for ourselves, institutions that reflect and will help us recover our traditional Western culture.

Several years ago, my colleague Paul Weyrich wrote an open letter to the conservative movement suggesting this strategy. While most other conservative (really Republican) leaders demurred, his letter resonated powerfully with grassroots conservatives. Many of them are already part of a movement to secede from the corrupt, dominant culture and create parallel institutions: the home schooling movement. Similar movements are beginning to offer sound alternatives in other aspects of life, including movements to promote small, often organic family farms and to develop community markets for those farms' products. If Brave New World's motto is "Think globally, act locally," ours should be "Think locally, act locally."

Thus, our strategy for undoing what cultural Marxism has done to America has a certain parallel to its own strategy, as Gramsci laid it out so long ago. Gramsci called for Marxists to undertake a "long march through the institutions." Our counter-strategy would be a long march to create our own institutions. It will not happen quickly or easily. It will be the work of generations—as was theirs. They were patient, because they knew the inevitable forces of history were on their side. Can we not be equally patient, and persevering, knowing that the Maker of history is on ours?[2]

CHAPTER 11

Where Are We Going?

Pat Buchanan's book *State of Emergency: Third World Invasion and Conquest of America*, begins as follows:

> As Rome passed away, so, the West is passing away, from the same causes and in much the same way. What the Danube and Rhine were to Rome, the Rio Grande and Mediterranean are to America and Europe, the frontiers of a civilization no longer defended. The children born in 2006 will witness in their lifetimes the death of the West.[1]

Buchanan illustrates that the fall of a civilization results from its own self-destruction. The Bible tells us to hold fast to what is good, yet history records that God-fearing nations first failed to hold to the life-sustaining foundation of biblical precepts that sustained their social order and moral fiber. Only then, after they became vulnerable through their self-inflicted decadence, were their enemies able to trespass.

What's undermining our sure foundation? While the mass media carries messages of an ideology of politically correct liberalism through our culture, the popular response is to elect politicians and legislators who replace existing standards with a faulty set of laws and subsequently appoint those who execute and interpret those laws to the detriment of society. Further, these leaders are largely responsible for the curriculum and public school administration that provide an ill-advised education to our children.

What if the mass media creates a culture that is so distracted, dumbed-down and polluted with explicit sex, graphic violence, obscene language and perversity that the majority of Americans lose their initiative to ensure sensible leaders are in place to preserve healthy communities, even when there's a critical need for leadership? Distracted by liberalism, moneymaking opportunities and emotionally charged agendas, constituents may neglect to fill influential positions with an informed, intelligent electorate.

Sobering Statistics

This situation now faces the United States. According to a recent poll conducted by Zogby International, 74 percent of Americans can name the three Stooges, but only 42 percent can name the three branches of our government. While 60 percent can name Bart as Homer's son on the TV show *The Simpsons*, less than 21 percent can name *The Iliad* or *The Odyssey* as one of the Greek poet Homer's epic poems. Finally, the poll showed that about 75 percent of Americans know the names of at least two of the Seven Dwarves, but only 25 percent can name two of the nine Supreme Court Justices.[2]

This poll demonstrates the low levels of intellectual sophistication and competence being delivered by our public education as well as the unworthiness of those entrusted to maintain our foundational beliefs and values. The mass media and our educational systems are filled with very intelligent and capable individuals. Yet their knowledge lacks the power of reason to be salt and light in a world prone to deterioration. They no longer ponder the apostle Paul's justification by faith in the book of Romans and other New Testament documents. And how many of them can name even half of the Ten Commandments? Without moral substance or standards, what distinguishing honor can they aspire to attain?

Instead, a prevailing ignorance of even the modern works of Russell Kirk, the founder of the conservative movement, undermines the values and traditions that formed the cultural foundation of Western civilization, in particular the republic that salutes the flag of the United States of America. While rejection of the God of the Bible and the gospel of Jesus Christ is presumed to be an informed and logical decision, it's more a lack of knowledge compounded with propaganda that has created prejudice against biblical principles. Our indulgence in data acquisition and management has blinded great minds to the difference between what knowledge is substantial and what is trivial or detrimental to civilization. As Proverbs 19:2 states, "It is not good to have zeal without knowledge."

Virtual Abuse

We often forget there is a war being waged inside our minds with eternal stakes for our souls. Our adversary allures our minds through materialism, secularism, humanism and all the other "isms" that conflict with Christianity. Unless we hold to our values, our moods and desires will be easily baited by the mass media of entertainment. Once hooked, the burden of guilt will drag us toward the hell intended only for God's adversary.

Many parents have forsaken the guard posts of their homes and have permitted open access for an indiscriminate flow of movies and television programs to occupy their children's minds. These parents assume that if a child's attention is being held, the content of all these programs meets a need for communication or at least is appropriate for their viewing. This permissive exposure to "virtual reality" overlooks the susceptibility of children and the potential for the mass media to provide instruction.

Only animals need to get caught in a trap in order to comprehend what a trap is. Human beings can be taught to avoid traps through dialog, images, the written word or another secondary source *before* they step into it. Thus, people's realm of knowledge is as broad as every message their brain receives. No one relies on personal experience alone to know if something is right or wrong. What is deduced from messages constitutes what behavior might be considered to be acceptable and normal. Because all human experiences construct a basis for social progress or regress, media must be reviewed for its content apart from how well it may engage a person's attention.

Truth or Consequences

As first mentioned in chapter 1, since 1966 (the year the Church abandoned Hollywood), violent crime, illegitimate births and teenage suicide rates have skyrocketed in the United States. While there are many factors that have contributed to our cultural decline, it is clear that the mass media have had a significant influence on behavior. A report by the Washington, D.C., based Children's Defense Fund states that every day in the United States:

- 2,781 teenage girls get pregnant (an increase of about 500 percent since 1966)
- 5,314 teenagers are arrested
- 135,000 children bring a gun to school[3]

Researchers affiliated with the National Bureau of Economic Research and Stanford University wrote in the journal *Science* that America's children are less physically fit, more suicidal, more violent, and score lower on standardized tests in recent years than in the 1960s.[4]

Europe Deconstructs

In a more global view, Peter Hammond notes that Europe could be in danger of falling to Islam. The only sure hope is a vital and permeating new spiritual revival, because only true biblical Christianity can defeat either radical Islam or secular hedonism. Hammond points out:

> Europe is committing cultural and economic suicide. By intermarrying with Muslims and building mosques and madressas [religious schools] throughout the continent, Europe is betraying future generations to bondage. The decline of Christianity in Europe is catastrophic. . . . Like Esau, they have sold their birthright for a mess of pottage. Now young Europeans are taught: "You come from nothing, you're going nowhere, life is meaningless!"[5]

The gospel of Jesus Christ once inspired productivity and innovations in Europe that brought blessings to the whole world. Christendom, as the Western world was known, developed medical science that saved lives and extended life expectancy. By applying the biblical principles of good stewardship, agricultural productivity and innovations, famines were ended. Christian missionaries spread literacy to societies that never had a written language, along with an understanding of republican forms of government and social law. Wisdom drawn from the Word of God and the good news of Jesus Christ established a culture of diversity that knew unprecedented blessings and prosperity.

Now, by abandoning its Christian roots and missionary calling, Europe is in a state of deterioration. As Peter Hammond notes, "Like a cut flower the beauty can only abide for a short time—because it is cut off from the source of its life. Soon the petals will fade and crumble and only the thorns will remain."[6] Europe aborts her future along with her babies, and confuses her youth with secular and pagan thought, while succumbing to the tidal wave of Muslim immigration. Europe may appear as frantic as a chicken with its head cut off; however, its head, Jesus Christ, remains willing to infuse this spiritually dead chicken with new life.

Muslim Invasion

In A.D. 330, Constantine chose Byzantium as the capital of the new Christian Roman Empire and renamed it "Constantinople." By 1453, Constantinople was the greatest city in the world. Then Muslim forces attacked by land and sea, battered its walls, massacred the congregation in the Hagia Sophia, the greatest ancient church building, sold 60,000 captives into slavery and buried the last of the Roman emperors in a heap of slaughtered countrymen and rubble.

What was at the time the Muslim Ottoman Empire (today the nation of Turkey) had been the land of the seven churches of Revelation. The Muslims eradicated the Christians until they were a minority in their own lands. In 1915, the Muslim Turks massacred 1.5 million Christian Armenians. In 1922, Smyrna, the last Christian city in Asia, was destroyed by the Muslim Turkish army. The biblical city of 300,000 people, where the apostles John and Paul had ministered, was annihilated.

Moderate Muslims?

On August 18, 2006, journalist Don Feder posted the following article on his "Cold Steel Caucus Report" website:

I was in London last week, where I gained a renewed appreciation for the religion of peace [Islam] and insights into the war we are in.

Thursday evening, I was lying in bed in my hotel room in Russell Square, less than 24 hours after MI-5 and the British police foiled a plot to blow up as many as 10 trans-Atlantic flights—with a potential death toll of 4,000. Officials described it as attempted "mass murder on an unimaginable scale." On the show I was watching, a BBC reporter interviewed a neighbor of one of the 24 terrorism suspects arrested—all British-born Muslims.

When someone is arrested for plotting a suicide attack or terror bombing, we're often told he recently became very interested in Islam—as opposed to really getting into Kaballah or the I Ching. When a Christian is reborn, he usually does good deeds and begins witnessing about Jesus. A newly observant Jew might keep kosher, become Sabbath-observant or start studying Torah.

When a devotee of the religion of peace feels the spirit move him, he quite naturally starts planning ways to commit "mass murder on an unimaginable scale." Again, like the London underground bombers of a year ago (who managed to kill 52 infidel commuters and injure over 700), those arrested last week all were native-born Muslims. Three were converts to Islam (like American Taliban John Walker Lind and shoe-bomber Richard Reid). When was the last time a Catholic convert tried to blow something up?

Winston Churchill, who encountered the business end of the scimitar in the Sudan as a young cavalry officer, observed in his 1899 book *The River War*: "Individual Muslims may show splendid qualities. Thousands become brave and loyal soldiers of the Queen; all know how to die; but the influence of the religion paralyses the social development of those who follow it. . . . Far from being moribund, Mohammedanism is a militant and proselytizing faith. It has already spread throughout Central Africa, raising fearless warriors at every step."

Britain's great wartime leader cautioned another generation of appeasement-bent Brits: "If you will not fight for right
when you can easily win without bloodshed; if you will not
fight when your victory is sure and not too costly; you may
come to the moment when you will have to fight with all the
odds against you and only a precarious chance of survival.
There may even be a worse case. You may have to fight when
there is no hope of victory, because it is better to perish than to
live as slaves."

The dismal prospect of those words coming to pass in
another century, in another conflict, were in my thoughts as I
departed London on another trans-Atlantic flight.[7]

Turning Europe into Eurabia

According to Peter Hammond, if the Muslims attain a majority, they will
persecute and ultimately exterminate all minorities. Hammond observed
that Muslims openly talk about turning Europe into "Eurabia." In fact,
the number of Muslim communities in Europe is growing significantly:
in Denmark Muslims make up 75 percent of convicted rapists and consume more than 40 percent of social welfare spending, though only 4
percent of the population; in France, 6 million Muslims make up 70 percent of convicted criminals in prison, although they are 10 percent of the
population; in Germany, Muslims number 2 million; in Italy, Muslims
make up 95 percent of convicted rapists; and in Sweden, there are
400,000 Muslims and a massive increase in anti-Semitic attacks.

Additional facts from recent intelligence reports note that of 48 countries with a Muslim majority, 46 are dictatorships. The Saudi Arabian government has financed the building of 1,500 mosques, 210 Islamic centers,
202 colleges and 2,000 religious schools in non-Muslim countries—mostly in Europe. And while the average European woman has 1.5 children, the
average Muslim woman in Europe has 7 children.

Epidemics

God-given prosperity has not led to praise and worship but to a selfish
pursuit of sensual pleasure that created an epidemic of sexually trans-

mitted diseases. While sanctified marriages resulted in births perceived to be gifts from God, illicit sexual relations present a child as unwanted burdens on licentious solipsistic adults, an unpleasant side effect to prevent or treat with abortion.

The consequence is a birth dearth—a population decline that results in a disastrous economy with a shortage of both labor, consumers and tax contributors. The orgy of Western hedonism cannot last. History proves that the future belongs to the fertile, but diminishing populations signal cultural collapse. As Peter Hammond warns:

> By abandoning its Christian heritage, aborting its babies, embracing hedonism and perversion, demanding unlimited personal freedoms, Europe is heading towards the repression of Islamic Sharia law. By rejecting Christianity, Europe is in danger of falling under Islamic totalitarianism.
>
> The combined effects of affluence and a rapidly falling birthrate have made Western Europe a magnet for millions of impoverished Muslims from North Africa and the Middle East. And with most Europeans embracing a practical atheism or a fuzzy new age spirituality, they are incapable of comprehending, let alone effectively dealing with, radical Islam. That, in a nutshell, is the problem.[8]

Called to Remember

Throughout the Bible, God called the Jews to remember. He called them to remember when He led them out of Egypt. He called them to remember when He led them through the Red Sea. He called them to remember when He fed them in the desert and when He brought them into the Promised Land. Regrettably, His chosen people, the Jewish nation, repeatedly forgot their Lord and their heritage.

Thus, the answer is revival, renewal and reformation of the Christian faith. Europe faced a similar threat of Islamic expansionism in the sixteenth century. Europe experienced a similar renaissance of paganism before in the fifteenth century. Peter Hammond notes,

"The threat is the same. And the solution is the same today as it was then. We need Reformation!"[9]

We need to recognize and eradicate the false gods of our age: secular humanism and radical Islam. Our sword and shield remain available through studying the Word of God and praying in the name of our Savior, Jesus Christ. As watchmen, we must identify the problems presented by our rebellion against God and help others to understand that being trapped by sin inevitably reaps tremendous trouble. We must proclaim the good news of victory through the gospel: that our Deliverer has overcome sin and death. As Peter Hammond notes:

- We are called to conquest. We must not merely survive—we need to thrive. We are called to be *more than conquerors.*

- We must conquer fear. "God has not given us a spirit of fear, but of power and of love and of a sound mind" (2 Tim. 1:7, *NKJV*).

- We must conquer cowardice. "Be strong in the Lord and in the power of His might. Put on the whole armor of God, that you may be able to stand against the wiles of the devil" (Eph. 6:10-11, *NKJV*).

- We must conquer ignorance. "My people are destroyed from lack of knowledge" (Hos. 4:6, *NKJV*).

- We must conquer unbelief. We must overcome the world by our faith (see 1 John 5:4).

- We need to be more courageous, more faithful and more effective in fulfilling the Great Commission. Humanism is self-destructive. Islam's days are numbered. Islam cannot survive freedom and the Quran cannot withstand critical academic scrutiny.

- We must win our enemies to Christ. David was a conqueror because he killed Goliath. Jesus Christ was more than a conqueror because He turned Saul the persecutor of the Church into Paul the great apostle of the Church. We are called to be more than conquerors. We must understand Islam and we must evangelize Muslims. "Every knee should bow . . . every tongue confess that Jesus Christ is Lord" (Phil. 2:10-11).[10]

As Charles Martel stopped the Muslim advance at the Battle of Tours in A.D. 732, so we need to rouse the Church to evangelize our Muslim neighbors and to stop the Muslim advance in Europe. As Christians liberated Romania, Hungary, Bulgaria and Greece from centuries of oppression by the Turks, so we need to free our neighbors from the deception of Islam and lead them to Christ.

The Need for Regeneration

America will self-destruct unless it can regenerate (or redeem) the pagan, anti-intellectual values of their culture with biblical principles that guide citizens to the recognition of the heavenly Father and the knowledge and wisdom to receive their Savior and Lord.

As Christians, we need to teach ourselves and our families about the impact of the mass media on the leaders and educators of our local and extended communities. We need to study the dynamic, profound truths found in the Bible and the gospel of Jesus Christ. Finally, we need to become informed thinkers so that we can withstand and disarm the harmful aspects of the mass media and restore the sublime beauty of our cultural history and traditions.

We need to wise up, America. Our minds and souls are at stake. This is not a job for Superman—and certainly not for Bart Simpson. It's a job for each and every one of us!

PART V

HOW TO DEVELOP

DISCERNMENT

CHAPTER 12

Asking the Right Questions About Media Influence

If you want to understand the power of pictures, stand in front of a group of friends, put your hand on your cheek, and then ask your audience to put their hand on their chin. Most, if not all, will mimic your visual statement rather than your verbal command and put their hand on their cheek, just as when children play Simon Says. That is the power of visual influence.

If a picture is worth a thousand words, as the Chinese proverb says, then the mass media of entertainment that combines pictures, music and other communication forms is the hydrogen bomb of influence. In order to manage this incredible influence as it relates to our families, we need to develop discernment and wisdom. How do we do this? By asking the right questions.

This chapter offers help on how you can develop wisdom and enjoy entertainment while avoiding the pitfalls of the media. These questions will help you penetrate the surface of the media through active viewing and listening so that you can avoid simply absorbing messages without awareness of the potential influence of a subtle message. Conscientious thought is crucial to filtering seemingly innocuous worldviews that can shape our culture. The Christian worldview is seeing the world as it is seen by God, who so loved the world that He gave us His Word, His Son, so that whosoever believes in Him should not perish but have everlasting life (see John 3:16).

Just How Powerful Is Media's Influence?

In 1994, the Discovery Channel aired *Selling Murder*, a documentary investigating how Dr. Joseph Goebbels, the Nazi propaganda minister from 1933 to 1945, used media to influence the acceptance of mass murder. At a time when a majority of German people rejected mercy killings (a euphemism for murder), Goebbels produced a movie called *I Accuse*, an emotive feature film about a beautiful, intelligent woman who was dying of an incurable disease and begged to be allowed to commit suicide.

After viewing the movie, a majority of the audience said they had changed their minds. After a few more of Goebbels's films about invalids and handicapped people, the German people became strong believers in the efficacy of mass mercy killings. Goebbels exploited the radio, press, cinema and theater in Germany to destroy the Jews, evangelical Christians, handicapped Germans and other groups.

As an insight into the power of the mass media, historian Paul Johnson writes the following in his book *Modern Times:*

> Hitler appears always to have approached politics in terms of visual images. Like Lenin and still more like Stalin, he was an outstanding practitioner of the Century's most radical vice: social engineering—the notion that human beings can be shoveled around like concrete. But in Hitler's case, there was always an artistic dimension to these satanic schemes. Hitler's artistic approach was absolutely central to his success. [Historians all agree] the Germans were the best-educated nation in the world. To conquer their minds was very difficult. Their hearts, their sensibilities, were easy targets.[1]

Indoctrination, with specific use of newsreels and films, was vital to Hitler's control of the new generation. Gerhard Rempel, in his book *Hitler's Children: The Hitler Youth and the SS*, wrote, "Each day began with a newsreel, followed by the various types of training. On Sunday mornings, an ideological program was substituted for church services, and Sunday nights were set aside for motion pictures."[2]

Two weeks before *Selling Murder* ran on the Discovery Channel, a network television program examined the current practice of killing patients by doctors in the Netherlands. The similarities between Nazi productions and television programs about Dr. Kevorkian, abortion and euthanasia were frightening. The exposure of rationalization in *Selling Murder* makes it a must-view for all who are concerned about the use of the mass media of entertainment to influence societal behavior.

How Does Madison Avenue Use the Media to Target Teenagers?

The 2001 *PBS Frontline* documentary *Merchants of Cool* shows exactly why and how the big corporations use the mass media to manipulate their target audience: teenagers. There has never been a generation that has experienced so much mass media of entertainment saturation.

The "why" is simple: Research shows that teens spent more than $100 billion in 1999 and influenced their parents to spend another $50 billion. The "how" is the distinguishing power of *Merchants of Cool*: The documentary reveals how corporate advertisers use influential teens to engineer stylistic trends or fads. *Merchants of Cool* points out that to remain cool, teens have to keep ahead of the curve. Interviews with marketing gurus, including those from MTV, Madison Avenue and the big corporations, are highly instructive. They demonstrate the intentionality and careful planning of manipulating the teenage audience.

Showing *Merchants of Cool* to a group of teenagers might be the most media-wise thing to do, as it unveils the workings of manipulators. Though it will enrage most teenagers, they'll start thinking of how they can develop the discernment, knowledge, understanding and wisdom to avoid being manipulated.

How Do Teenagers Feel About This Kind of Manipulation?

In fact, most audiences, including teenagers, want to avoid messages that manipulate or desensitize their feelings. A 2006 *Los Angeles Times* entertainment poll found that 58 percent of boys and 74 percent of girls age 12 to 17 are offended by sexual material.[3] The article about the poll quotes these words from 12-year-old Melina Erkan: "Sometimes in the music videos these days, the women they have dancing in the background, they dress really cheap, and women don't really look like that and act like that. . . . When I see that, I change the channel to something I like." Hannah Montes, a 21-year-old college student in Missouri, said,

"I get tired of hearing all the cussing and the sexual innuendoes."[4]

The poll included 839 minors aged 12 to 17, 811 young adults aged 18 to 24, and also a number of parents. Results from this poll showed that 80 percent of the parents surveyed did not think alcohol or marijuana were usually available at the parties their teenagers attended, but half of the teenagers who attended at least one party a month said alcohol, drugs or both were present.[5] Children want to make wise choices, but many parents are uninformed about how to provide appropriate support.

How Can We Teach Our Children to Be Media Savvy?

You may recall the analogy of blind men describing what they each perceived of an elephant. The one who took hold of the elephant's trunk said, "It's like a tree branch"; the one who took hold of its tail claimed, "It's like a rope"; and the one who grabbed its leg stated, "It's like a pillar." While difficult to get our arms around the beast of mass media, what we're viewing can be identified, compared and contemplated to determine how to bridle it without harm.

Parents can stimulate children to discover, discern and reflect on the messages of the media. Through guided discussions, media literacy develops the capacity to enjoy a positive cultural experience. Applying the Word of God sets the hand of the Master on the situation and engages families in discussions, which in itself redeems time (see Eph. 5:16). Further, overcoming ungodly influences through recognition of biblical precepts magnifies the power of the Word of God. Ultimately, time spent communicating biblical precepts uses God-given parental authority to lead our children in worship and spiritual growth.

Initially, parents must understand that they view entertainment differently than children. While parents are concerned over the amount of nudity and profanity, most children just watch the action and special effects. So parents and children must talk across a gap.

Though not always cognizant of the message, children's minds are open to receiving the messages that the media delivers. Often, children will mimic viewed behaviors or unwittingly ask for advertised products. In these instances in which children's minds are at stake, parents must ensure that biblical values enter the picture so that intimidating, confusing or shameful images are met with redemptive grace and dignity.

Media literacy means teaching your children how to identify the elements that construct the messages and how to derive clear information. Media literacy helps them formulate their own well-informed responses so that they can determine what the message means to them. By having children review and critique what they see and hear, they will learn to choose appropriate movies, television, games, music and mass media information. They will become a media-literate audience and will be able to determine what effect the media has on their behavior. (The questions at the end of this chapter may be useful conversation starters for parents in discussing with their children what is acceptable or objectionable material.)

How Can We Teach Our Children to Uncover a Movie's Message?

The process of becoming media literate involves three stages: ascertainment, discernment and reflection. The basic rudiments used to construct a message include stand-alone facts about at least one interesting character, a believable environment, and a motivation for his or her action despite increasing obstacles.

The first step is to identify these key elements so that you can then analyze the characters' traits, the rules that govern the characters' environment and behaviors, and the consequences for their actions, which all together involve an audience in the ensuing drama. Whether intentional or not, every story depicts a point of view by how these elements comprise the final outcome. Through a series of story events, seeds of thought are planted regarding a broader worldview.

Every movie has a *premise*. A premise is a concise statement of the thematic message that the story illustrates. In any context, the premise drives the story to a logical conclusion, which gives credence to the message. Thus, discovery of the premise identifies the basic idea that the media will plant in the mind of its audience. If the premise is good triumphs over evil, the drama will engage the audience in viewing how the good hero triumphs over the evil villain.

As a general rule, there is one main premise for the sake of clarity, and most premises do not express a universal truth. For example, poverty does not always lead to crime, but if that is the premise, the story will present believable circumstances to support that statement. In *Luther* and *Lady Jane*, faith triumphs over death; in *Macbeth* and *Collateral*, ruthless ambition destroys itself.

With a little practice, the premise can be found by analyzing the story. For example, in *Driving Miss Daisy*, a woman alienates everyone by her cruelty until her Christian chauffeur overlooks her demeaning barbs so that in the end she discovers true friendship. This heart-warming story proves the incredibly powerful premise that Christian virtues bring reconciliation. Another way of finding the premise is to ask, What happened to the hero and villain at the very end? How did that happen? Why?

Finding the premise will also help your children develop cause and effect thinking, which is so important in understanding a story. Once you have discovered the premise, the next step in the ascertainment stage is to address traits of the character and the story environment.

How Can We Help Our Children Recognize Worthy Heroes?

Even if a premise appears biblically correct, the method for proving the statement may not be. In popular entertainment, there is one hero who is the main focus, and this hero can be easily identified by children as the one to root for. Yet it is important to analyze the appropriateness of the hero's behavior. In both *The Lord of the Rings* and *The Chronicles of Narnia*, the hero is helped by supernatural forces that depict an act of God. In *Chariots of Fire* and *Invincible*, the heroes triumph not only because they are superior but also because they do the right thing. In *Shrek* or *Forrest Gump*, the hero triumphs because of quirks of fate. The Judeo-Christian worldview can also show that a hero is overwhelmed by adversity, such as in *The Diary of Anne Frank*, to illustrate the difference that faith makes to enter eternity with hope and dignity.

A hero who triumphs through acting out devious, privileged or paranormal behavior presents a view that denies having ultimate accountability to our heavenly Father. Pursuits that focus on self-ish, materialistic or purely emotional gratification present an anti-Christian worldview that is detrimental to the development of Christlike traits such as integrity and diligence, which precede attaining any goal of lasting value. For instance, as we have mentioned, Harry Potter's best qualities are overshadowed by his propensity to play tricks that are enhanced by an interest in the occult. In contrast, Frodo, the humble hobbit, is motivated by loyalty and succeeds by grace and mercy. Spiritual gifts in the Christian worldview are given to enable faithful servants to do good work. Even a child can recognize the correctness of rooting for a hero who benefits his community and the error of rooting for a self-serving liar.

How Can We Help Our Children Understand an Antagonist's Motivation?

Note that many dramatists refer to the main character who forces the action, whether good or bad, as the protagonist, whereas the antagonist opposes the outcome that is pursued by the protagonist.[6] Both the protagonist and antagonist construct the dynamics of the story, and their characteristics must be closely analyzed. Thus, it is equally important to identify the characteristics of the antagonist. A Christian worldview represents villains as characters that compensate for a lesser degree of true power by using deception and aggression against the hero. In the news, business leaders, conservative Christians and political leaders are often cast as the villains. It is necessary to discern what characteristics are attributed to the hero and the villain.

In the first two Harry Potter books and movies, the initial villains are Harry's non-magical repulsive relatives, who are terribly cruel to him, but the real villain is the wizard Voldemort, who is clearly rotten to the core. There is no distinction between the sources of good and evil since wizardry is used against wizardry. However, in *The Lord of the Rings*, Saruman and Sauron are clearly evil in the classic biblical sense of Lucifer. That is, they are filled with pride, greed and envy.

How Can Parents Teach Children What's Real and What's Not Real in Media?

For movies and television programs, success depends on premise, image and effect. Images and special effects capture and influence an audience.

In research on the relative influence of the visual and the audio, the producers of *Sesame Street* showed a test audience an animated short that explained why an ant could not grow to the size of an elephant. The sound track informed the audience that the ant's external skeleton could not sustain such weight, while the animated picture showed the ant growing to the size of the elephant and then exploding. Over 90 percent of the test audience said ants could grow to the size of an elephant. People remember about 60 percent of the visual and 40 percent of the audio.

Every communication impacts an audience not only by what it includes but also by its omissions. These omissions can create powerful secondary messages in the mind of the audience. Electronic media are more prone to distortion of reality than other communications because editing, close-ups, shadow shots, reverse shots and other camera techniques can cover any appearance of tampering with the truth.

Since a camera excludes everything outside its field, the viewer will interpret what he sees as a broader image. During my junior year at Dartmouth College, there was a small student takeover of the administration building. The TV news team shot the scene so tight that although the landscape was empty except for a handful of National Guardsmen, 30 students who had occupied the building and a few observers, the television news made the operation look like a major military maneuver.

As Gerry Mander states in his book *Four Arguments for Elimination of Television*, "There is a widespread belief that some things on television are 'real' and some things are not real. . . . Our society assumes that human beings can make the distinctions between what is real and what is not real, even when the real and not real are served up in the same way, intercut with one another, sent to us from many different places and times and arriving one behind the other in our houses, shooting out of a box in our living rooms straight into our heads."[7]

Is the Setting and Background of a Movie Significant?

To develop awareness of how the environment sends a message, children can be shown that props and scenery are used to set a story in a particular time and place. A horse and carriage may signal that a story is set in the past. As children learn to notice details, reading and viewing will become a richer experience. Misconceptions about the environment will send you distinct messages that influence how you look at the world and the subject matter of the entertainment product. In other words, the camera does lie—and so do the microphone and the computer.

Closely related to the background environment issue is the question of how language is used in a mass media product. A definitive study by professor Timothy Jay titled "Cursing in America" found that only 7 percent of American people curse on the job and only 12 percent in their leisure time, yet many movies and television programs would lead us to believe that Americans curse all the time.[8] One school of Marxist thought considered language as a weapon with which to attack the bourgeois society in which we live (several avant garde playwrights belong to this school).[9] Ironically, in the years that Movieguide® has researched audience preferences, evidence was found that the more foul language included in a movie, the worse it does at the box office.

Any social issue in any environment—from modern inner-city turmoil to intergalactic science fiction—contains environmental elements to be recognized for their impact on the story. Even a fictional universe needs stabilizing laws that maintain order under the best of circumstances, and threats that upset the balance create conflict. The environment should provide some degree of predictability and logic. Although supernatural gifts may be introduced, they are used to serve the greater good, when evil elevates conflict to a level that is humanly impossible to overcome. A Christian worldview shows the environment is ordered by stabilizing laws, with justice and mercy manifested through the consequences of actions, even if that order is known as a paradise lost.

What Worldview Does a Particular Movie Show?

When the premise of a movie is in agreement with the biblical worldview but the way that premise is shown is anti-Christian, immoral or evil, then the media product is problematic viewing for Christians committed to their faith. For example, if good triumphs over evil but only by means of magic, the method by which the premise is solved (magic) is anti-biblical. These movies are suspect for anyone who does not understand that all nominal occult magic is evil. The premise can be perfectly biblical, while the solution is not.

Why Is a Biblical Worldview Important?

A worldview should square with biblical precepts. If behaviors are exhibited that our heavenly Father finds objectionable—such as trickery, witchcraft, sex outside of a heterosexual life-long commitment, or unnecessary violence—those behaviors should be recognized as a cause for suffering and be viewed with some possibility of redemptive love to introduce the hope of salvation as much as possible. If simply condoned as normative, the message is clearly deviant from the Word of God.

Concern for the poor doesn't justify rooting for the condemnation of those who were better off, or the use of thievery to provide for the less fortunate. The Bible provides guidance for social change and compassion. Jesus talks about many who claim to have served Him, to whom He'll say, "I never knew you" (see Matt 7:22-24). Therefore, heroes who appear to be righteous must be examined for Christlike characteristics of humility, mercy and social responsibility. Biblical traits and characteristics in no way detract from entertainment experiences that can thrill our imaginations. Many of the greatest movies ever made are Bible-based stories.

For Christians and Jews, the biblical view toward reality is that we live in a real world, created by the real God, wherein there are real problems, pain and suffering that we cannot ignore or wish away. For those of us who are Christians, our Creator has saved us from the real consequences of sin through the real death and resurrection of His Son, the Christ, who was really God and really man. Any other ontology, or view of the nature of being, puts the mind out of touch with reality. As in the days of Noah, life may appear to go on as normal, yet only up to the point where, ultimately, reality is revealed.

Can Children Be Taught Discernment About Media?

Every mass media product reflects a view or opinion about reality and the laws that govern it. Some take an existentialist perspective that basically implies that people cannot find answers, so life is essentially meaningless. Other media products have an evolutionary view that implies there is no divine plan governing creation, so nothing is certain and, ultimately, everything is pointless. Thus, it is important to understand the nature of a media product to make discerning entertainment choices.

Heretical doctrine can most often be traced to misunderstanding the problem of evil. The humanistic view that man is basically good denies the impact of sin and the need for rebirth. New Age religions see evil as an illusion, eliminating any need to oppose ungodly agendas or to accept the atonement that Christ provided on the cross. Occultism supposes that evil is as strong as, and not subject to, the authority of a higher good, namely Christ. It is critical for a Christian worldview to present evil as what it is—actually and actively real, the negation of all that is truly good, in personal rebellion against the authority of God. Only by recognition of evil can appropriate remedial actions be taken.

Additional data about an environment is received through the media's sound-image schema. With a little practice, you can discover recurring themes and underlying principles in the media product. It may be difficult to name the most frequent sound or image, yet once identified, this information unveils any message that might be recited in the mind like an unwanted mantra. Children repeat songs from commercials such as McDonald's advertisements. Ask them to think about what the lyrics mean. Once conscious of these ideas, children will choose whether or not they want to carry them in their hearts and minds. You can help your children realize that they can command unwanted images to leave.

How Can We Know What Children Think About Movies They See?

Discernment questions address the dynamic interfaces between the readily identified elements and the philosophical and theological messages being communicated that are critical to making personal decisions about what is stored in the memory for future contemplation. By contemplating the entertainment experience together with your children, you can determine the lasting impact of the message. What becomes known through the presentation of evidence of a worldview creates memories that lead to actions, which construct the culture we live in. This is the fundamental reason that we must make culture-wise choices to fill our minds with the good, the true and the beautiful. If desensitized by poor media choices, we may justify or ignore ungodliness and then slowly be conditioned to condone a non-Christian point of view.

Children usually think about the character they would most like to be and are prone to accept the underlying belief systems that their favorite character models. Through discussion, a parent can share insight to expose inconsistencies in the message with a Christian worldview and expose the potential dangers of emulating those characters. Children often like or dislike a character based on outcomes of his or her behavior, so it's important to invite your child to consider the motivation and plausibility of characters' actions and whether or not the consequences of those actions are realistic. Viewing actions with discernment can diffuse the temptation to lose touch with God's will when tempted to mimic a role model.

Some media communicates positive values of honesty, courage and other positive traits. So, hopefully, your child will respond to questions about why he or she likes a character with answers such as, "Well, she was a good friend to him and believed in him no matter what," which will convey to you that your child is picking up on values such as friendship and loyalty. Together, you can also discuss alternative solutions to the problems a character faced that may be more in accordance with biblical guidance.

Children should be encouraged to put a name to their feelings. Asking children questions after seeing a movie will help them identify the source of their emotions, and it will also boost their self-esteem. Any time you ask children their opinion, you build their confidence tremendously about participating in the real world. It is important to set a tone that supports the child's responses and creative impressions of the story.

How Is the Family Portrayed in the Movies You See?

For a time, movies presented homosexuality and uncommitted sex as normative while mocking marriage and presenting psychotic moms and irresponsible dads. These types of movies attacked the basic building block of our society: the family. Now, however, contemporary mass media of entertainment and news that build up the family—such as the pro-life, pro-family, pro-marriage, pro-fatherhood *Father of the Bride* and *Cheaper by the Dozen*—are increasing. Box office successes such as *The Incredibles, Glory Road* and *Cars* continue this trend of portraying family and community in a positive way.

When you read the news or go online, pay attention to how the family is portrayed and whether or not the article or media product in question respects all four types of government: self-government, family, Church and civil government. The Christian Church is frequently not shown as a source of benefit, but rather as restrictive and ineffective in the community.

Always remember that the media product is a cacophony of ill-conceived religions such as materialism, eroticism, hedonism, humanism, cynicism, violent cults and a multitude of other modern variations on pagan practices. These religions, many of which can trace their roots back to long-discredited ancient cults, have their beliefs and ultimate meanings played out with ritualistic regularity. At any time, we may find happy Hollywood stars touting the virtues of astrology or other belief systems opposed to Christianity.

Is a Movie's Humor Appropriate?

Apart from misrepresenting the reality of moral and social interactions, the media often sets unrealistic expectations of psychological excitement in relationships, even without sexual or violent content. A sense of humor is a precious gift, yet expectations to find a spontaneous, comic solution to every problem may develop a lack of interest in maintaining relationships that require Christlike patience and encouragement to work through difficulties or misunderstandings. Discernment can prevent false expectations of friendship and marriage by noting that highly elevated emotional events are normally short-term, acute situations within a broader, more stable context.

The written Word of God has established the revelation of God to humanity. There's no limit to the humor found in mankind's limitations and misunderstandings with regard to trying to do what's right or wise. We are all children in the sight of our heavenly Father who alone possesses goodness, righteousness and true wisdom that is beyond human comprehension. Yet we are able to discern humor from mockery and right from wrong.

It is never appropriate behavior to mock religion. The Christian Church is often portrayed as weak, obsequious, rotten or foolish. Mockery is a sign of hubris and not of a desire to lift up the Truth. As written in Psalm 1:1, blessed is the man who doesn't sit among the mockers. History has proven that mockery leads to disaster. For example, Hitler began his campaign against the Jews by using grotesque cartoons.

These considerations can also be applied to politicians, cultural heroes and celebrities to ascertain their character and how well they serve role models. Discuss how the hero could succeed while abiding by the rules and what motivation compels him. Also, discuss what was at stake and whether or not the risks taken were appropriate, such as the hero risking possessions or his life to protect family and friends.

What Should Parents Do About Violent Content?

With regard to violent content, the emotive heart of drama is conflict, and the highest level of conflict is violence. The Gospel story contains the most violent scene imaginable: the crucifixion of Jesus Christ. Violence is not always bad, but in fact is sometimes critical to promote the good and the true. Ron Maxwell, director of *Gettysburg*, said that while violence was essential in the portrayal of the Civil War, he avoided excessive blood, guts and gore. His discretion made *Gettysburg* a movie that could reach a broader audience.

Many contemporary movies and television programs push the limits of violence. A longitudinal study released in May 2004 led by psychologist Dr. Douglas A. Gentile of Iowa State University found that children who consumed more media violence early in the school year were more verbally aggressive, relationally aggressive and physically aggressive later in the school year. Regrettably, TV news stories focus on violence as a result of the effort to get higher ratings by following the marketing rule: If it bleeds, it leads. This appeal to the lust of the eyes has well-researched detrimental consequences for susceptible children.

What About Sexual Content?

Besides violence, the absence of genuine story dynamics is often filled with an abusive sexual content. Actually, sex does not sell that well. In 1995, 36 movies were produced that had excessive sexual content. Two of the biggest budget Hollywood sex films, *Showgirls* and *Striptease*, lost millions of dollars despite mammoth advertising campaigns. Each year from 2000 to 2005, movies with very strong Christian worldviews and moral content averaged earnings between 3 and 16 times the amount earned by movies with more sex, including graphic or excessive depictions. One has to wonder why the entertainment industry continues to try to force such products on the public, even if they garner applause from secular critics and film festivals around the world.

The most profitable movies involve carefully crafted characters in a wholesome pursuit of moral values, such as *The Sound of Music, Beauty and the Beast, Tender Mercies, Sense and Sensibility* and *My Big Fat Greek Wedding*. A positive portrayal of real love entails giving, caring and life-long commitment in a monogamous, biblically sound, heterosexual marital relationship. The beauty of God's love is illustrated wonderfully in the Bible, so any media that desecrates acts of love in uncommitted sexual relationships or homosexual coupling should be anathema to His people. Many all-time great movies clearly involved biblical history.

Movieguide®'s annual study of the major movies released by Hollywood shows that people clearly do not like to see strong public displays of homosexual behavior—such as that portrayed in *Brokeback Mountain, Kinsey,* and *Tying the Knot*—no matter what they think of how the Bible strongly condemns homosexual behavior. In 2005, none of the top 25 movies at the box office had strong homosexual content, and 88 percent had no homosexuality. In 2004, only one movie in the top 25 movies at the box office had any strong homosexual content (*Dodgeball*). For 2004 and 2005, the stronger the homosexual content, the worse the box office results. The box office figures suggest that homosexuals either do not support movies or they are less than 1 percent of the population. Studies show that many who try homosexuality turn away from it and many that are in that lifestyle abhor it.

Should Christian Children Be Kept from Fantasy?

Children can be unsettled by even seemingly innocent things in an entertainment media product, so it is important to emphasize that some movies are pretending, as in a game of make-believe. The use of special effects or fantasy makes it possible to state a premise that could be too sensitive to address on familiar terms, such as *Shrek*'s inferiority complex about his appearance. If your child is very young, you might ask, "What pretend things were the characters doing?" A lot of young children want to mimic what they see, so it is wise to point out to them what is not real.

What Should Parents Say When History in a Movie Has Been Revised?

Media makers generally use stories to express their ideas through a well-formulated premise.[10] An inadequately developed premise will force the mass media maker to fill space with irrelevant material to make the plot entertaining.[11] It is popular to discredit authority or the government, another form of mockery. Most of these attacks are aimed at conservative governments, which protect free enterprise, in favor of socialism and communism.

The Lichter, Rothman and Lichter studies showed a majority of media makers believe that the state, not God, is the savior of mankind.[12] This view is a negation of three of the Ten Commandments: the First, since the state is elevated to a position higher than God; the Eighth, because the redistribution of property by the state takes property from individuals without consent; and, the Tenth, because the whole premise of socialism is based on covetousness. Asking how government and private enterprise are portrayed will help us to cut through any hidden political agendas.

When the media revises the past, a precarious situation is created for the future of our civilization. Much revisionism has been devoted to whitewashing the memory of the Holocaust from the annals of history by claiming that World War II gas chambers could not have killed so many people and that the death camps were actually work camps with good sanitary conditions. While *Schindler's List* accurately portrays the horror of the Holocaust, *The English Patient* whitewashes the real history of its Nazi hero, extols adultery and promotes euthanasia.

Equally perilous is the revision of history that supports our republican democracy and Christian heritage. Historian Catherine Millard has chronicled the removing of Christian quotes and information from our national monuments and the removal of the Christian writings of our Founding Fathers from the Library of Congress in her book *The Rewriting of America's History*. This book strives to preserve and enlighten America's Christian heritage with historical facts, while revealing attempts by revisionists to remove any trace of Christianity.

Is It Possible to Find Movies with Redemptive Qualities?

It is possible for a media product to have errors in its worldview and still be redemptive. *Nothing in Common* starts out with a young executive who pushes everyone around and plays with every woman he meets, but it ends with him giving up his job and his fast life to restore a relationship with his ailing father. Surprisingly, his boss lets him leave work with the insight that "there has been only one perfect Son." Therefore, *Nothing in Common* has a very redemptive message. Some children's films such as *Everyone's Hero* or *The Dirt Bike Kid* treat negative parts with a lack of conviction, while the redemptive element of love, courage or integrity is emphasized. We need to be aware of the good in the message along with our rebuttal of the elements that may be detrimental.

Developing a biblical worldview involves defining your approach to all areas of thought, including mass media, education, politics, religion, family, law, business and government. You must pierce through messages that are inconsistent with biblical principles. The mass media evades criticism by appealing to the First Amendment and by claiming appropriateness in the context of our culture. Clearly, these are specious evasions. Children need to be educated to view the world through God's perspective, not God's Word as perceived by the eyes of the world.

Questions Your Children Can Ask

In conclusion, the following is a list of questions that you can ask your children when viewing films, television shows or any other form of media.

Suggested Ascertainment Questions
  • Who were the hero and the villain?
  • What makes them worth rooting for or against?
  • What motivates them and how do they face their problems?
  • Was there any violence or sex that wasn't needed to tell the story?
  • What was gained at the end of the story? How? Why?

Suggested Discernment Questions
  • Was the hero someone you could trust?
  • Were the rules fair and was there accountability for keeping them?
  • Is the hero's behavior realistic? Are the consequences fair? How do events make the hero grow in character? Do those changes make the hero more like Christ?
  • Was there anything that would be embarrassing to share with family or authority figures? Is there respect shown to all people?
  • Were the actions appropriate and were the results what should be expected?

Suggested Reflection Questions
  • Were the characters good or bad examples to follow?
  • Would you be comfortable living in the hero's environment? Why or why not?
  • Were actions properly rewarded or punished? Would you do what the hero did? How did the actions affect important relationships such as with family, friends and God?
  • Was sexual behavior modest and dignified? Was any violence necessary for solving a problem? Was the language appropriate?
  • Was the hero's success or failure important? To whom? Why?

Suggested General Questions
  • What was your favorite part?
  • Who was your favorite character?

- Did good stand against evil?
- Who would you like to be in the story? Why?
- What could change the way you feel about the ending?

Conclusion

If we care about others being inundated by media messages and about the Lord Jesus, we will take a stand against any communication that undermines a biblical worldview and mocks our Lord and Savior Jesus Christ. Anything less than standing on His written Word denies our relationship with Him.

In previous centuries, entertainment was a once in a while thing. Someone might read aloud or play a musical instrument, and there might be an occasional visit to the theater. Today's use of the media has no relationship to those occasional happenings. It is not separate from the daily routine; it *is* the daily routine.

Regular discussions regarding the character traits and social interaction that are presented in media can have a positive impact on our culture by developing sharp minds. Instead of a subconscious influence, media messages can serve to develop discernment and appreciation of God's unchanging standards of behavior.

By bringing every thought into captivity, we live up to God's expectations and redeem the times, resisting the devil's schemes through the Word of God. Christ has already won the war. As we learn of Him and walk as guided by our true compass, the Bible, and unite our hearts to revere His Name, He makes us "more than conquerors."

CHAPTER 13

Seeing Connections of Contemporary Art and Biblical Faith

Doug Adams[1]

Our knowledge of biblical stories and characters will provide insights into all forms of artistic expression. When we look at a painting or sculpture and try to understand contemporary art, we need to do so through the perspective of what we know about the Bible. The Bible is the great code of Western culture.

During the first half of the twentieth century, many artists became more abstract and dropped connections with biblical and other historic subject matter. However, during the last few decades, some major contemporary artists have reconnected to biblical subjects. In the 1980s, George Segal included Abraham and Isaac, Adam and Eve and even the Crucifixion in his Holocaust memorial and other sculptures. Jasper Johns included references to the crucifixion and resurrection from Grunewald's "Isenheim Altarpiece" in 30 of his paintings.[2] In the following pages, we will explore the biblical and theological relations in the very recent work of Christo and Jeanne-Claude, "The Gates, Central Park, New York, 2005," and Kiki Smith's exhibition "A Gathering" that was on tour at major museums.

Perceptions of Freedom: Christo and Jeanne-Claude

Through four decades of collaboration, Christo and his wife, Jeanne-Claude, have presented art with biblical, theological and political perceptions of freedom, which most art critics have failed to understand.

Several of their major works, beginning with "Valley Curtain, Grand Hogback, Rifle, Colorado, 1970-72," culminate in "The Gates, Central Park, New York City, 1979-2005." These works express freedom in biblical and theological terms of exodus and resurrection as well as in political terms of the falling Iron Curtain and Berlin Wall and the permanent opening of the Brandenburg Gate.

Christo and Jeanne-Claude opened "The Gates" in New York's Central Park on February 12, 2005. Spaced along 23 miles of walkways, the 7,503 saffron-colored gates were 16 feet tall, ranging in width from 5-and-a-half feet to 18 feet. The free-hanging nylon panels of the gates dropped down to within 7-and-a-half feet above the ground. I spent several days passing through those many gates under the billowing fabric, while taking more than 400 slides and talking with the artists and others. I saw how "The Gates" freed people to explore all areas of the park and to interact with those who came from around the world to view this art with its emphasis on artistic, political and religious freedom.

In my interviews with Christo and Jeanne-Claude, their political and theological insights became evident. Born in 1935 in Bulgaria, Christo was reared first under Hitler's domination of Eastern Europe and then under Stalin's puppets. Christo escaped to Austria and later met Jeanne-Claude while he was doing portraits for her mother in Paris. Married in 1962, the couple have lived in New York City since moving to the United States in 1964.

In my initial telephone interview with Jeanne-Claude on April 12, 1988, we were puzzled over how many people miss the theological relationship of her husband's art, when he has emphasized his name: Christo (he had dropped his last name, Javacheff, so that he would simply be known as "Christo"). A few days later when the couple were at the Graduate Theological Union Library for their exhibition, we explored theological and political dimensions of "Running Fence, Sonoma, and Marin Counties, California, 1972-76" and "Umbrellas, Japan-U.S.A., 1984-91." We discussed their plan for "The Gates" when they returned in 2003 to present "Wrapped Snoopy House" to the Charles M. Schulz Museum in Santa Rosa, California.

The Significance of "The Gates"

Most writers missed the biblical and theological significance of "The Gates" and other of Christo and Jeanne-Claude's previous projects. The word "gate" originally meant "a path" or "the way." Passageways (gates and doors) are central images as thresholds of transcendence in religions such as Judaism and Christianity. In Judaism, every door helps us remember the Exodus through which God brought His people out of slavery in Egypt to freedom. In Christianity, Christ is the doorway (or He knocks at the door or sits in the doorway) as our way to freedom from death to resurrection.[3] In some religions the *axis mundi*—or place where seen and unseen worlds connect—invites one repeatedly to circumnavigate a cyclical pattern, but the door or gate in historical faiths such as Judaism and Christianity is a threshold to transcend what is known and to make a pilgrimage into a new territory.[4]

"The Gates" relate to a series of Christo and Jeanne-Claude's earlier art works. For example, their 1972 "Valley Curtain" was of a similar shape and color to the saffron Gates. The rust color of "Valley Curtain" was part of its parody of the iron curtain. By stringing 142,000 square feet of nylon polyamide curtain across a valley where they knew the winds would tear it to pieces, they affirmed that the spirit of freedom would not allow the iron curtain to stand for long. Now the iron curtain and the Berlin wall have been torn down, as they envisioned. In their places, Christo and Jeanne-Claude presented 7,503 gates through which people were free to move through 23 miles of New York's Central Park.

Freedom of movement through these gates is akin to the movement possible through the Brandenburg Gate, now permanently open between the eastern and western portions of a reunited Berlin. Their 1995 "Wrapped Reichstag, Berlin" signaled the death of the old divided Germany, with half under communist domination, and the birth of the new free united Germany. The Reichstag was associated with a more democratic tradition that was eclipsed by the communist occupation of East Germany, because it was closed by fire early in Hitler's reign and not used. So it was untainted by most totalitarian acts of the Nazi and the Communist regimes. More than five million Germans went to see a shimmering "Wrapped Reichstag" standing close to the previous site of the Berlin Wall. It appeared as a promising birthday present for a more democratic Germany.

Freedom to Create in the Most Unlikely Places

I remembered those Germans celebrating in Berlin when, a decade later, I was walking through "The Gates" in New York and met many Germans who had come to see this new work. The multitudes who visited Central Park during February 2005 to see "The Gates" felt safe in every area of the park. Writing for *Newsweek*, Cathleen McGuigan called Christo and Jeanne-Claude's presentation "a work with amazing power to transform. It redefines the rolling curves and contours and vistas of Frederick Law Olmstead's 19th Century romantic parkscape. And more important, it redefines civic life by creating a rare, if brief, exuberant communal experience. For a city on permanent orange alert, we welcome that."[5]

Christo chose to reveal the possibility for freedom and communal experience in sites that presented seemingly impossible bureaucratic or legal barriers. Placing thousands of gates in Central Park required Christo and Jeanne-Claude to work for 26 years to gain the necessary political support, which finally came together when Michael Bloomberg became mayor. They could have placed the gates in another location more quickly and with fewer problems.

"Wrapping the Reichstag" required Christo and Jeanne-Claude to wait until Germany was reunited and had a Speaker of the Assembly who was supportive. To string "The Running Fence" 24 and a half miles across dozens of different jurisdictions raised political problems that could have been avoided by building the fence on one ranch or within one county. Yet an important agenda for Christo is to demonstrate that freedom to create is possible even in the most unlikely places. In our April 16, 1988, interview, Christo emphasized that "freedom is most important to me and my work."

Gaining permission to construct the artwork reveals both the possibilities for freedom and the processes for interrelations in distinct communities. Revealing these interrelations is part of the art process and experience. As people tried to support or to oppose construction of

"The Running Fence," many realized for the first time not only their own distinct political jurisdiction but also the views that their neighbors expressed at meetings of different townships and county commissions. In this way, the art process led some people to come to know their neighbors. Christo and Jeanne-Claude have developed lasting friendships in many communities as they have sought permissions and then carried out each of their projects. Their art is usually installed on a site by long-term residents of that region.

Relationship and Community

On several occasions, I have witnessed the strong relationships between Christo, Jeanne-Claude and members of communities in which their art works were created. Many ranchers, whose land "The Running Fence" extended across in 1976, came together in 1988, a dozen years later, as the artists hosted a dinner in conjunction with our Graduate Theological Union Library retrospective. The ranchers explained that the artists had given them much time and patient thought so that they would understand and give permission for the project. Further, the artists had stayed in touch with them through the following years.

Cartoonist and evangelical Christian Charles Schulz, a close friend of Christo and Jeanne-Claude, substantially aided the process of gaining permissions for "The Running Fence." Schultz had introduced the artists to others in the Santa Rosa area, and I heard his wife and friends express deep appreciation for their friendship, even after Schulz's death, when the artists presented "Wrapped Snoopy House" to the Schulz Museum in 2003. In 2005, I talked with dozens of persons who worked on "The Gates" project and learned that many of them still appreciated thoughtful conversations with the artists.

Under the "Umbrellas"

Several other Christo and Jeanne-Claude art works elaborate their political and religious views. In their 1991 "Umbrellas," they raised 3,100 umbrellas, 28 feet 5 inches in diameter, in California and Japan. Historically, one umbrella was lifted above the head of the political and religious leader in Japan or in Europe. However, by lifting 3,100 huge umbrellas, Christo and Jeanne-Claude affirmed more democratic politics and the priesthood of all believers.

In Church art, there are often canopies lifted over the heads of important persons of significant biblical figures. This is the case with the north entrance of the thirteenth-century Chartres Cathedral, in which canopies are lifted over the heads Melchizedek, Abraham and Isaac, Moses, Samuel and David. In the worship services of that period and later, fixed canopies were located above the seats of the bishop and other major leaders of Church and state.

When such an important person proceeded inside or outside the church, an umbrella was held over his head by a person who followed.[6] During the time when "Umbrellas" project was displayed, thousands of persons came to picnic under many of the 1,760 yellow umbrellas along an 18-mile valley through which Interstate 5 runs, 60 miles north of Los Angeles, California, and under many of the 1,340 blue umbrellas along a 12-mile valley 75 miles north of Tokyo, Japan.

Similarly, in Christo and Jeanne-Claude's 1976 exhibit "The Running Fence"—a 24-and-a-half mile fence that rose from a gully east of Highway 101 and dipped into the Pacific Ocean near Bodega Bay— was not only a satire on the Berlin Wall (which was 24 kilometers) but also an affirmation of the earth as a gift from God. Christo and Jeanne-Claude called the fence "a ribbon of light" as other works such as "Wrapped Coast, Little Bay, Australia" (1969) wrapped the earth as a gift.

By seeing the earth or a building, like "Wrapped Kunsthalle, Bern, Switzerland, 1968," wrapped in a white shroud for three days, or three weeks, and then seeing it again after the removal of that fabric, one senses a death and resurrection experience.[7] Transformations are evidenced in Christo and Jeanne-Claude's art through alterations of sunlight and of wind. The sun, behind a cloud the color of "The Gates," was a dark orange, but it changed to a bright yellow when the sun came out. When there was no wind, the fabric in the "The Gates" hung down within a foot or two of peoples' heads; but when the winds were blowing strongly, the bottom of those panels fluttered 10 feet overhead at or above the top of the frame. As with "Valley Curtain" in 1972 and with "Running Fence" in 1976, "The Gates" in 2005 made visible the wind, which is often associated with the Holy Spirit.

Expanding the Vision

To maintain their artistic freedom, Christo and Jeanne-Claude never accept any government or corporate funds but finance all their projects, including their 21-million-dollar exhibit "The Gates," by selling drawings and collages ahead of time and films afterward. The dates associated with the works indicate how long their process artwork takes to secure permissions from the many constituencies needed: "The Running Fence" (1972-1976), "Umbrellas" (1984-1991), "Wrapped Reichstag" (1971-1995), and "The Gates" (1979-2005). Christo and Jeanne-Claude are persistent. They saw the fulfillment of "The Gates" project in February 2005, 26 years from conception to birth. Further, all materials in "The Gates" are being recycled, as were all the materials in "Umbrellas" (except for one blue umbrella and one yellow umbrella, which were closed and given to The Smithsonian).

While the impact of these art projects may take time to realize, their brief duration of actual exhibition (two or three weeks) emphasizes mortality, as Christo noted to those of us gathered for a briefing about "Umbrellas."[8] Art in a museum may give the illusion of immortality, but in reality, no work of art will last forever. "Umbrellas" question the permanence or importance of national boundaries. They lift our vision over the limits of boundaries, as Christ led Early Christians to see beyond their national boundaries with stories and actions that included Samaritans, centurions and other non-Jews. While some politicians bashed Japan as an economic enemy, Christo and Jeanne-Claude raised umbrellas north of both Tokyo and Los Angeles to lead us to overlook national differences. Christo noted, "The entire idea is to expand your vision by seeing the project in these places together. Everything about that project is determined to highlight that vision."[9]

For the future, Christo and Jeanne-Claude continue planning for "Over the River, Project for the Arkansas River," in which they will place a blue-colored cloth canopy above a 17-mile stretch of that river in Colorado. That planning was begun in 1992 and is listed as "in process."

Christo and Jeanne-Claude's transforming political and theological artistic explorations will thus continue into the future.

Portrayals of Strength: Kiki Smith

Born in 1954 to actress and opera singer Jane Smith and to sculptor and painter Tony Smith, Kiki Smith has developed into one of the major artists of our day. She brings together her Catholic appreciation of matters spiritual and sacramental with biblical insights and concern for the role of the body in knowing. A national exhibition of her work began at the Museum of Modern Art in San Francisco in late 2005 and moved to the Walker Art Center in Minneapolis in Spring 2006. Throughout the summer, the exhibition showed at the Contemporary Art Museum in Houston before appearing at the Whitney Museum in New York, November 16, 2006 to February 11, 2007.

Kiki Smith gives us perceptions into the strength of biblical women through her works such as "Mary Magdalene" (1994), "Lilith" (1994) and "Eve" (2001). Some of her works, such as "Mary Magdalene," are cast in bronze, but others are fragile in beeswax, or stitches on muslin. Silkscreen on Thai tissue paper, which moves as one passes by, was used for her portrayal of over a hundred babies, which may remind viewers of how children are so easily destroyed—whether by Pharaoh who killed the male children in Moses' day, by Herod who slaughtered the innocents in Jesus' day, or by others today who find children to be inconvenient.

Some works, like the flayed "Virgin Mary," show Smith's empathetic suffering deeply incised into the beeswax body, which makes Mel Gibson's *The Passion of the Christ* appear tame, but her "Untitled" crucifixion in methyl cellulose reveals a strength as the figure bends over deeply at the waist so the hair falls to the feet and the arms rise upward and outward as the horizontal beam of a cross. Smith's resurrection "Ice Man" is profoundly uplifting as the left arm and leg twist to hurl the figure upward. This resurrection sculpture reminds one of resurrection drawings by Michelangelo.

A liberating gospel is suggested in "Mary Magdalene" through several means. Attached to her right ankle is a broken chain, and her left foot strides forward. Her arms are at her sides with palms facing backward, as if she is pushing away from the past. Her head is raised up so she faces forward and upward. Such emancipation links Mary Magdalene, as the new Miriam, to Jesus, as the new Moses, while the Lord's Supper becomes the new Passover Seder and the Resurrection becomes the new Exodus.[10] The hair covering most of her body is a tradition in art, as she was portrayed in later life like a pious hermit who devoted herself to prayer in the wilderness. We see this covering throughout Donatello's "Magdalene" (c. 1455) in Florence, like the earlier "John the Baptist" (c. 1453) in Venice, both carved of wood.

While the body of Donatello's "Magdalene" seems youthful from the back or side, she appears very old from the front when we see her aged face. However, Smith's "Mary Magdalene" seems more youthful when we view her frontally and see her protruding firm round breasts. Breasts provide a primary source of nourishment for young lives in most cultures and, in many Christian art works, Mary the Mother offers one of her breasts to the Christ child or to the viewer as a source of sustenance. America's leading eighteenth-century Calvinist theologian, Jonathan Edwards, wrote that God's grace was exemplified by "a taste of honey" or "milk from a woman's breast." The "land of milk and honey" is a biblical description of the Promised Land and relates to Kiki Smith's choice of media and subject matter, such as beeswax and the female breast.

Contemporary Art and Biblical Faith

We can see deep biblical relations in the contemporary works of Christo, Jeanne-Claude, Kiki Smith and many other artists. These works are receiving significant attention in the press and at major museums, although the pervasive biblical dimensions of the works are often missed. When looking at contemporary art, let us bring all that we know about biblical characters and stories, for contemporary art and biblical faith now often deeply inform each other.

CHAPTER 14

Impressing God's Commands on Our Children

Dyonette Mayer[1]

One of the most important steps that we take to lead our children in the way of discernment is to become very aware of what we believe. It is impossible for any of us to teach something we don't comprehend. God challenges and directs parents very clearly to teach our children not only to obey, but how to obey. Our goal as Christian parents is to help our children develop strong Scripture-based beliefs that transform how they live and interact within modern day culture, as they grow and mature. One of the most important ways that we can do this is by developing a clear and strong picture of what we believe—in other words, by understanding a Christian worldview. When we understand what it is that we want to teach, the path ahead becomes much clearer.

Many books are available to parents that teach how to discipline our children. Discipline without a wholesome relationship equates to rebellion. Our goal as parents, as the Scripture says in Deuteronomy, is to begin with God's commands on our hearts and then to impress them on our children as we walk and live in our environment and culture. Scripture also says, "Do not exasperate your children: instead bring them up in the training and instruction of the Lord" (Eph. 6:4). This starts with a clear understanding of the instruction and law of the Lord. I can't emphasize enough the importance of first understanding what it is that we believe. Then, transferring our Christian worldview to daily situations and experiences becomes a much easier task. We often hear parenting experts say that the "do as I say, *not* as I do" approach doesn't work. Children rely on their parents to teach them in action as well as word.

Understanding the Impact of Media Influence

What is clear is that the mass media is a source of major influence in the lives of our children. As technology continues to move forward, the influence and impact of media on our children also continues to increase. What is interesting is that the new technologies are actually making it much more difficult for parents to supervise their children.

I often see parents in my office who are struggling not only with keeping up with the technology but also with managing the actual information to which their children have access. Some examples of this include iPods and Internet availability. Just look for a middle schooler, high schooler or preadolescent that doesn't know what an iPod is. My eight-year-old already knows how to download music to her much cheaper imitation of the iPod.

Our kids have easy access to free music, and it takes serious time and effort to manage to hear all of the songs they are downloading. With the headphones on iPods, we don't even hear the music as they listen to it. Subsequently, our children are listening to types of music that we don't know about. In the past, a parent's complaint was that nasty and harsh music was blaring from their child's rooms. It took virtually *no* effort to hear the quality and lyrics of music. It takes much more time and effort for parents to be a part of their child's decision making in this area today.

Many parents also express having difficulty managing their children's Internet usage. Most junior high and high schools provide access in computer labs and libraries that allow our youth to go to websites such as My Space, where they can develop and maintain an account totally unsupervised. These new advances in technology only increase our need to teach our children how to use discernment. As parents, we need to trust our children's choices outside of our direct influence more and more and at earlier and earlier stages of development.

Kids aged 2 to 7 average nearly 25 hours per week of mass media intake; the figure balloons to almost 48 hours each week among those aged 8 to 13.[2] The Internet is also becoming the medium of choice for 54 percent of children under the age of 8 and 73 percent of children aged 8 to 12 years.[3] Based on these statistics, the direction of the entertainment industry and technological developments—along with our children's growing interest, ease of access and ability in computers— I only see these statistics rising. Now more than ever, we need to be purposeful in training and equipping our children for discernment.

How Do You Begin?

Your first step is to examine yourself and identify your purpose clearly. In order to do this, examine Scripture, as well as available research, and identify what your goals are. Determine that God has established your position as a parent and that He will provide wisdom and authority as you seek to glorify Him for the sake of His name. He has commanded that children honor their parents in order to live a rewarding life.

Next, take a serious look at how the media has influenced your life and your choices. Seek to understand the ways that you utilize discernment in your media choices. You might be surprised at what you find. For example, I never see horror films or films with the intent to scare. I know that I don't like to be scared and that numerous times in Scripture, God commands us to fear not. Not only does this make my media choices easy, but it also is a pretty easy line of reasoning to follow and explain to my children.

You might also find that some of the media choices you make do not represent your belief system. It is important to realize that you cannot ask your children to be discerning without first using discernment in your choices. Your children must see you as being responsible and purposeful in your life. Your example is one of the loudest ways that you will communicate your values to your children. They are watching more closely than you may realize. Some easy questions to ask include the following:

1. What am I drawn to in my media choices? Are these choices a positive or negative influence in my life? Do they represent my belief system?

2. Where am I tempted in the media world? Is it a type of movie, television program, genre of music, Internet?

3. What do I do when faced with this temptation?

4. What have I done in the past that has helped me to be successful in making wise choices for myself?

Defining Your Parenting

In order to be an on-purpose parent, we need to identify those things that are most important to teach our children. Our current culture likes to be very diffuse in its boundaries, which can lead children to believe that they can and should bend and flex their beliefs and values to fit in with their peers.

It is important that your children see you standing firm. Be prepared to have an answer for parenting choices. So many parents struggle with how to set limits with their children. So many of these parents suffer from "on the fly" parenting, which is characterized by merely reacting to problems when they come up.

This year, my oldest child, Alexandra, asked for permission to be a vegetarian. My response was that I would have to get back to her. It's okay to take time in getting back to your children with an answer. They deserve a well-thought-out response and, in fact, need to learn that it's not wise to just shoot out an answer before considering the consequences. I knew immediately that I would not allow her to be a vegetarian, but I wanted to be able to clearly communicate my reasoning to her.

When I had carefully thought through the situation, I returned to my daughter and said, "Alexandra, my job as a parent is to raise you to adulthood. This includes making sure that you can make wise choices, get a good education, and understand the Lord and His commandments. It also means that I make sure that you will have the healthiest body possible. Your developing brain needs protein and your body needs iron. I have spoken with our pediatrician, and she agrees that becoming a vegetarian is not a good choice for you. When you are an adult you are free to make a choice, but while you live at home and are under my care, you will need to eat your meat."

Her response was, "Okay, Mom." The issue was over; my child understood my love, care and responsibility in parenting. She saw that my decision for her was not rash or unloving and therefore she was able to accept it—even though it was not what she originally wanted. My expectations are also clear and easy for her to understand and meet. Some easy questions to ask in this regard include:

1. What are the most important lessons that I want my children to take with them as they grow into adulthood?

2. What do I think about my children's use of the Internet or iPods? What do I think about their music choices or the time they spend playing video games?

3. Have I seen the impact of media on my children? Do they have a harder time sleeping after watching certain movies? Are they more disrespectful after listening to certain music? Do they dress more provocatively and wear more make-up when going to certain concerts? Do they act more aggressively after playing certain video games?

4. How do these choices promote and inhibit my establishment of the lessons and values that I am working to establish?

Understanding who you are and what your purpose is will help you to set good examples and be more prepared when issues arrive. It will also help you engage in meaningful discussion and relate to the difficulty of living a purposeful life that represents your Christian worldview in a fallen world.

One of the mistakes you can make as a parent is to be afraid to share some of the ways you have personally struggled with sin or temptation and how you were able to overcome that temptation. It helps children feel comfortable communicating when they feel that their parents understand and relate on some level with their struggles. Living discerning and culture-wise lives involves personal sacrifice. It is rarely the popular or easy choice. When you stand up for what you believe, you can face the consequences of rebuke or exclusion from the group. Sharing your struggles is an excellent way to bond with your children.

Just this morning, my eight-year-old daughter, Helena, shared her fear that "bad thoughts" sometimes were in her mind that tempted her. She wondered if God would punish her for those thoughts. I was able to explain to her that Christ was tempted, but that He remained pure because He did not sin, even though He was tempted. A person is not sinning just because he or she is tempted; rather, that person sins when he or she acts on that temptation.

Helena and I then talked about what things made temptation seem worse or harder. She shared that sometimes she was tempted to give me "sassy" answers. I asked her where she had seen others giving sassy remarks. Helena gave the typical responses, stating that she heard kids at school, at camp, at church and sometimes on television shows give sassy remarks under their breath.

What resulted from this discussion is that we were able to look at what her responsibility is in making good choices. Helena learned that she has to guard her heart above all else. It helped her to understand she was accountable for living as she believes. She could relate to Christ in what it felt like to be tempted. She understood her responsibility to stand against temptation, and through this discussion we were able to put into practice ways that she could do this.

Fun Ways to Develop Spiritual Muscles

Your job as a parent is to help your children develop the spiritual muscles that will help them stand firm. In order to do this, you must first have a relationship with your kids in which they will feel safe to share their sinful thoughts and urges. Then you need to understand your enemy.

I suggest many games to help with this. One game we play in the car and at the dinner table is "scenarios." We present a scenario in which someone might be tempted and then ask the kids what they would do in the situation.[4] Next, we ask what they think Christ would do in that same situation and look up Scripture. This exercise helps us develop scripts of behavior so that we will know how to respond if a sticky situation should ever arise in real life.

Another game that can be played at the dinner table or in the car involves asking each child if there was anything he or she had to do that day that required sacrifice. For example, I once shared how I wanted to say something bad to my friend because she was being mean to me, but instead I just prayed for her and went to be with some other friends. This game helps children understand that sometimes doing the right thing can be hard.

I like to define maturity as "doing what is right, despite how we feel." We live in a culture that strongly promotes doing whatever feels good at the moment. This is not a scriptural value, nor is it healthy, because our feelings are constantly changing. Therefore, it is important to establish our basis for action on something more constant and secure.

Another fun activity is to spend time discussing media influences with your children. One way to do this is to establish a movie night. You could go to a movie (if there is a good one out) or stay home and rent a good family DVD. When the movie is over, discuss what was good and not so good about the film. We ask questions such as, Was there a point to this film? Was there a story line that made sense? Were there any negative messages that you saw in the film? What were the positive messages about the film?

I like to ask about what they didn't like first and then what they did like. My five-year-old son, Christian, watched *Toy Story 2* last night. When he woke up this morning, he said, "There's a good message in this movie." I said, "What was it?" He responded, "Good friends help their friends when they are in trouble!" I laughed, but then we talked about good friends versus not-so-good friends and how you can tell the difference. It's amazing what insights you can glean from your little ones. Older kids also learn to be discerning and identify messages that are good and bad.

The Importance of Relationship

I love the story that circulates around the Internet about a father of three teenage kids who had the rule that they could not attend PG-13 or R-rated movies. His teens wanted to see a particular movie that was rated PG-13. They asked friends and some members of their church to find out what was offensive in the movie. They made a list of pros and cons about the movie to use to convince their dad to let them see it.

The cons were that the film contained three swear words, a scene of an exploding building (which you see that on TV all the time) and another scene that suggested a couple were having sex (you actually didn't "see" the couple in the movie having sex, it was just implied). The pros were that it was a popular movie—everyone was seeing it, and if the teenagers didn't see the movie, they would feel left out when their friends discussed it. In fact, many of the members of their church had seen it and said it wasn't bad. The movie also had a good plot, some great adventure and fantastic special effects. The movie's stars were among the most talented actors and actresses in Hollywood, and it probably would be nominated for several awards. Therefore, since there were more pros than cons, the teens said they were asking their father to reconsider his position on this one movie and to let them have permission to go see it.

The father looked at the list and thought for a few minutes. He said he could tell that his children had spent some time and thought on their request. He asked if he could have a day to think about it before making his decision. The next evening, the father called in his three teenagers, who were smiling smugly, into the living room. There on the coffee table he had a plate of brownies. The teens were puzzled. The father told his children that he had thought about their request and had decided that if they would eat a brownie, he would let them go to the movie.

Like the movie, the brownies had pros and cons. The pros were that they were made with good chocolate and yummy walnuts. They were moist and fresh and covered with chocolate frosting. He had made the brownies with an award-winning recipe and by his own loving hands. The brownies only had one con: He had added a little bit of dog poop. But he had mixed the dough well—the teens probably wouldn't be able to taste it—and he had baked it at 350 degrees so any bacteria or germs had probably been destroyed. The father stated that if any of his children could stand to eat the brownies that included just a "little bit of poop" and not be affected by it, he knew that they would also be able to see the movie with "just a little bit of smut" and not be affected. Of course, none of the teens would eat the brownies. The smug smiles disappeared.

Relationship is the most important tool that you will have in impacting and preparing your children to grow into discerning adults. As technology advances and parental controls become harder and harder to manage, the need for discernment will only increase. As parents, you will be inundated with different philosophies. One mother might strongly oppose "potty humor," while another might be fine with bodily noises but have strong feelings about violence. Even within the Church, different people will set different boundaries and limits.

The most important thing you can do is to be educated and aware. Ask questions, read books and talk with other parents whom you regard highly. Don't be afraid to share *yourself* with your kids and what has worked and what hasn't for you in your life. Discernment is a gift that you can give to your children that will span generations.

CHAPTER 15

Is the Mainstream Media
Fair and Balanced?

Fred Barnes[1]

Let me begin by defining three terms that are thrown around in debates about the media today. The first is "objectivity," which means reporting the news with none of your own political views or instincts slanting the story one way or another. Perfect objectivity is pretty hard for anyone to attain, but it can be approximated. Then there's "fairness." Fairness concedes that there may be some slant in a news story but requires that a reporter will be honest and not misleading with regard to those with whom he disagrees. And finally there's "balance," which means that both sides of an issue or on politics in general—or more than two sides, when there are more than two—get a hearing.

My topic is how the mainstream media—meaning nationally influential newspapers like the *Washington Post*, the *New York Times*, the *Wall Street Journal* and *USA Today*; influential regional papers like the *Miami Herald*, the *Chicago Tribune* and the *Los Angeles Times;* the broadcast networks and cable news stations like CNN; and the wire services, which now are pretty much reduced to the Associated Press—stacks up in terms of the latter two journalistic standards, fairness and balance. In my opinion, they don't stack up very well.

Twenty years ago I wrote a piece in *The New Republic* entitled "Media Realignment," and the thrust of it was that the mainstream media was shedding some of its liberal slant and moving more to the center. This was in the Reagan years, and I pointed to things like *USA Today*, which was then about five years old and was a champion of the Reagan economic recovery. CNN was younger then, too, and quite different from the way it is now; Ted Turner owned it, but he wasn't manipulating it the way he did later, which turned it into something quite different. Financial news was suddenly very big in the midst of the 401K revolution, and the stock market boom was getting a lot of coverage. *The New Republic*, where I worked, had been pro-Stalin in the 1930s, but by the 1980s had become very pro-Reagan and anti-communist on foreign policy. I also cited a rise of new conservative columnists like George Will. But looking back on that piece now, I see that I couldn't have been more wrong. The idea that the mainstream media was moving to the center was a mirage. In fact, I would say that compared to what I was writing about back in the 1980s, the mainstream media today is more liberal, more elitist, more secular, more biased, more hostile to conservatives and Republicans, and more self-righteous.

Liberal and Impenetrable

Liberalism is endemic in the mainstream media today. Evan Thomas—the deputy editor of *Newsweek* and one of the honest liberals in the media—noted this very thing with regard to coverage of the 2004 presidential race, which I'll discuss later. It was obvious, he said, that the large majority in the media wanted John Kerry to win and that this bias slanted their coverage. And indeed, every poll of the media—and there have been a lot of them—shows that they're liberal, secular and so on. Polls of the Washington press corps, for instance, about whom they voted for in 2004 always show that nine-to-one or ten-to-one of them voted Democratic. Peter Brown, a columnist who just recently left the *Orlando Sentinel*, conducted a poll a few years ago of newspaper staffs all around the country—not just at the big papers but also at midsize papers and even some small papers—and found that this disparity existed everywhere.

Nor is this likely to change. Hugh Hewitt, the California lawyer, blogger and talk-radio host, spent a few days recently at the Columbia Journalism School, supposedly the premier journalism school in America. He spoke to a couple of classes there and polled them on whom they had voted for. He found only one Bush voter in all the classes he spoke to. Steve Hayes, a fine young writer and reporter at *The Weekly Standard*, went to Columbia Journalism School and says that during his time there he was one of only two or three conservative students out of hundreds.

This is not to say that there aren't many fine young conservative journalists. But they aren't likely to be hired in the mainstream media. When I was at *The New Republic* for 10 years—and *The New Republic* was quite liberal, despite its hawkish foreign policy—any young person who joined the staff and wrote stories that were interesting and demonstrated that he or she could write well was grabbed immediately by the *New York Times* or other big newspapers, *Newsweek*, *Time* or the networks. But that doesn't happen at *The Weekly Standard*, where I work now. Some of our young writers are the most talented I have ever met in my 30-plus years in journalism. But they don't get those phone calls. Why? Because they're with a conservative magazine. Of course there has been one famous exception—David Brooks, who is now the conservative columnist with the *New York Times*. But he was probably the least conservative person at *The Weekly Standard*. Conservatives are tokens on most editorial pages, just as they are on the broadcast networks and on cable news stations like CNN and MSNBC. Of course, I have a vested interest, since I work for FOX News; but if you compare the number of liberal commentators on FOX—and there are a lot of them—with the number of conservatives on those other stations, you'll see what I mean.

The fact is that the mainstream media doesn't want conservatives. It doesn't matter whether they're good reporters or writers. They go out of their way not to hire them. This was true 20 years ago, and it's still true today. This impenetrability is why conservatives have had to erect the alternative media—talk radio, the blogs, conservative magazines and FOX News. Together, these form a real infrastructure that's an alternative to the mainstream media. But it's still a lot smaller, it's not as influential and it's largely reactive. It's not the equal of the mainstream media, that's for sure.

Powerful and Unfair

One way to see the unequaled power of the mainstream media is in how it is able to shape and create the stories that we're stuck talking about in America. A good example is Cindy Sheehan last summer. The

Sheehan story was a total creation of the mainstream media. And in creating the story, the media shamelessly mischaracterized Sheehan. It portrayed her as simply a poor woman who wanted to see President Bush because her son had been killed in Iraq. Well, in the first place, she had already seen President Bush once. Also, though you would never know it from the dominant coverage, she was in favor of the Iraqi insurgency—the beheaders, the killers of innocent women and children. She was on their side, and she said so. She was also filled with a deep hatred of Israel. Yet the media treated her in a completely sympathetic manner, failing to report the beliefs that she made little attempt to hide. In any case, the Cindy Sheehan story came to dominate the news for the latter part of the summer; only the mainstream media still has the power to *make* stories big.

To see how distorted the mainstream media's view of the world can be, one need only compare its coverage of the Valerie Plame "leak" story with its coverage of the NSA surveillance leak story. Plame is the CIA agent whose name was written about by reporter Robert Novak in a column, following which the media portrayed her as having been outed as an undercover CIA agent. The simple facts from the beginning were that she was not an undercover agent anymore; she was not even overseas. The story had no national security repercussions at all—none. But that didn't stop the media, which built the story up to great heights—apparently in the groundless hope that it would lead to an indictment of Karl Rove—and kept it front-page news, at least intermittently, for what seemed like forever. The NSA surveillance story, on the other hand, also created by the media—this time pursuant to a real leak, and one that was clearly in violation of the law—had tremendous national security implications. After all, it revealed a secret and crucial program that was being used to uncover plots to bomb and massacre Americans and probably rendered that program no longer effective. Not only was this important story treated on an equal basis with the non-story of Valerie Plame, but the media was not interested, for the most part, in its national security repercussions. Instead the media mischaracterized the story as a "domestic spying scandal," suggesting constitutional overreach by the Bush administration. Well, a domestic spying story is exactly what the story was *not*. Those being spied on were Al-Qaeda members overseas who were using the telephone. If some of those calls were with people in the U.S., they were monitored for that reason only. But the media's stubborn mischaracterization of the story continued to frame the debate.

This brings me to the use of unfair and unbalanced labeling by the media. How often, if ever, have you heard or read the term "ultraliberal"? I don't think I've ever heard or read it. You'll hear and see the term "ultraconservative" a lot, but not "ultraliberal"—even though there are plenty of ultraliberals. Another widely used labeling term is "activist." If people are working to block a shopping center from being built or campaigning against Wal-Mart, they are called "activists." Of course, what the term "activist" means is *liberal*. But while conservatives are called conservatives by the media, liberals are "activists." For years we've seen something similar with regard to debates over judicial nominees. The Federalist Society, with which many conservative judicial nominees tend to be associated, is always referred to as the *conservative* Federalist Society, as if that's part of its name. But the groups opposing conservative nominees are rarely if ever labeled as liberal—giving the impression that they, unlike the Federalist Society, are somehow objective.

Related to this, I would mention that conservatives are often labeled in a way to suggest they are mean and hateful. Liberals criticize, but conservatives hate. Have you noticed that the media never characterizes individuals or groups as Bush haters? There are Bush critics, but there are no Bush haters—whereas in the Clinton years, critics of the president were often referred to as Clinton haters. I'm not saying that there weren't Clinton haters on the fringes in the 1990s. But far-left groups like MoveOn.org have been treated as acceptable within the mainstream of American politics today by the media, while in truth they are as clearly animated by hatred as the most rabid anti-Clinton voices ever were.

Secular and Partisan Bias

With regard to religion, Christianity in particular—but also religious faith in general—is reflexively treated as something dangerous and pernicious by the mainstream media. Back in the early 1990s when I was

still at *The New Republic*, I was invited to a dinner in Washington with
Mario Cuomo. He was then governor of New York and had invited several reporters to dinner because he was thinking about running for president. At one point that night he mentioned that he sent his children to
Catholic schools in New York because he wanted them to be taught
about a God-centered universe. This was in the context of expressing his
whole-hearted support for public schools. But from the reaction, you
would have thought he had said that one day a week he would bring out
the snakes in his office and make policy decisions based on where they
bit him. He was subsequently pummeled with stories about how
improper it was for him, one, to send his kids to religious schools, and
two, to talk about it. It was amazing. The most rigid form of secularism
passes as the standard in mainstream journalism these days.

President Bush is similarly treated as someone who is obsessive
about his religion. And what does he do? Well, he reads a devotional
every day; he tries to get through the Bible, I think, once a year; and he
prays. Now, I know many, many people who do this. Tens of millions of
people do it. And yet the media treats Bush as some religious nut and
pursues this story inaccurately. Again, it is clear that partisan bias is
involved, too, because in fact, Bush talks publicly about his faith much
less than other presidents have. There is a good book about Bush's religion by Paul Kengor, who went back to every word President Clinton
spoke and found out that Clinton quoted Scripture and mentioned
God and Jesus Christ more than President Bush has. You would never
get that from the mainstream media.

The partisan bias of the mainstream media has been at no time
more evident than during the last presidential election. Presidential
candidates used to be savaged equally by the media. No matter who—
Republican or Democrat—they both used to take their hits. But that's
not true anymore. Robert Lichter, at the Center for Media and Public
Affairs in Washington, measures the broadcast news for all sorts of
things, including how they treat candidates. He's been doing it now for
nearly 20 years. And would anyone care to guess what presidential candidate in all those years has gotten the most favorable treatment from
the broadcast media? The answer is John Kerry, who got 77 percent

favorable coverage in the stories regarding him on the three broadcast news shows. For Bush, it was 34 percent. This was true despite the fact that Kerry made his Vietnam service the motif of the Democratic National Convention, followed weeks later by 64 Swift Boat vets who served with Kerry in Vietnam claiming that he didn't do the things he said he did. It was a huge story, but the mainstream media didn't want to cover it and didn't cover it, for week after week after week.

There was an amazingly well-documented book written by a man named John O'Neill—himself a Swift Boat vet—who went into great detail about why John Kerry didn't deserve his three Purple Hearts, etc. It might have been a right-wing screed, but if you actually read it, it wasn't a screed. It backed up its claims with evidence. Normally in journalism, when somebody makes some serious charges against a well-known person, reporters look into the charges to see if they're true or not. If they aren't, reporters look into the motives behind the false charges—for instance, to find out if someone paid the person making the false charges, and so on. But that's not what the media did in this case. The *New York Times* responded immediately by investigating the financing of the Swift Boat vets, rather than by trying to determine whether what they were saying was true. Ultimately, grudgingly—after bloggers and FOX News had covered the story sufficiently long that it couldn't be ignored—the mainstream media had to pick up on the story. But its whole effort was aimed at knocking down what the Swift Boat vets were saying.

Compare this with September 8, 2004, when Dan Rather reported on documents that he said showed not only that President Bush used preferential treatment to get into the Texas National Guard, but that he hadn't even done all his service. The very next morning, the whole story—because CBS put one of the documents on its website—was knocked down. It was knocked down because a blogger on a website called Little Green Footballs made a copy on his computer of the document that was supposedly made on a typewriter 30 years earlier and demonstrated that it was a fraud made on a modern computer. Then, only a few weeks after that embarrassment, CBS came up with a story, subsequently picked up by the *New York Times*, that an arms cache of 400 tons of ammunition in Iraq had been left unguarded by the American military and that the insurgents had gotten hold of it. Well, it turned out that they didn't know whether the insurgents had gotten that ammunition or not, or whether indeed the American military had possession of it. It was about a week before the election that these major news organizations broke this unsubstantiated story, something that would have been unimaginable in past campaigns. Why would they do that? Why would Dan Rather insist on releasing fraudulent documents when even his own experts recommended against it? Why would CBS and the *New York Times* come back with an explosive but unsubstantiated arms cache story only weeks later? They did it for one reason: They wanted to defeat President Bush for reelection. There is no other motive that would explain disregarding all the precautions you're taught you should have in journalism.

Fairing Well

I'll wind up on a positive note, however. Forty years ago, John Kenneth Galbraith—the great liberal Harvard economist—said that he knew conservatism was dead because it was bookless. Conservatives didn't publish books. And to some extent, it was true at the time. But it's no longer true. Conservatives have become such prolific writers and consumers of books that Random House and other publishing companies have started separate conservative imprints. Nowadays it is common to see two or three or four conservative books—some of them kind of trashy, but some of them very good—on the best-seller list. Insofar as books are an indication of how well conservatives are doing—at least in the publishing part of the media world—I would say they're doing quite well. They're not winning, but they're much better off than they were before—something that can't be said about how they are faring in the unfair and unbalanced mainstream media.

PART VI

UNDERSTANDING

THE ANSWERS

CHAPTER 16

More Than Conquerors

Now the adventure begins! As noted by many theologians, the Word of God sends us into all the world to transform the culture—first, by bringing people to a saving knowledge of Jesus Christ, and then by teaching His disciples through the insightful application of His Word written, the Bible. God sent us on this journey in Matthew 28:18:

> Then Jesus came near and said to them, "All authority has been given to Me in heaven and on earth. Go, therefore, and make disciples of all nations, baptizing them in the name of the Father and of the Son and of the Holy Spirit, teaching them to observe everything I have commanded you. And remember, I am with you always, to the end of the age" (*CSB*).

He also told us to go to the ends of the earth in Acts 1:8: "But you will receive power when the Holy Spirit has come upon you, and you will be My witnesses in Jerusalem, in all Judea and Samaria, and to the ends of the earth" (*CSB*). Not only does Christ equip us with the power of His Holy Spirit, but He also tells us in every single book of the Bible to "fear not" or "do not be afraid" of the adventure He has called us to undertake in His name.

Why does He say "fear not"? Because He tells us that "in all these things we are more than conquerors through him who loved us" (Rom. 8:37). Therefore, "neither death nor life, nor angels nor rulers, nor things present, nor things to come, nor powers, nor height, nor depth, nor any other created thing will have the power to separate us from the love of God that is in Christ Jesus our Lord!" (vv. 38-39, *CSB*).

We are continuously in a victorious status, as written in 2 Corinthians 2:14: "But thanks be to God, who always leads us in triumphal procession in Christ and through us spreads everywhere the fragrance of the knowledge of Him." One pastor illustrated this divine condition to the youth in his church with a story about the world heavyweight champion boxer George Foreman.

After retiring from boxing, George built a youth center to redeem young children and teenagers from bad neighborhoods in Houston through boxing. When he needed money, rather than beg, he decided to go back to the ring after 10 years of retirement. The sportscasters thought that George was too old and too out of shape, but he worked day after day to get back in condition. From 1987 to 1994, George worked his way back to another shot at the title. At the young age of 45, George knocked out 26-year-old Michael Moorer in the tenth round.

George took the prize money back to his youth center children and teenagers, who were more than conquerors. They did not need to train, or fight, but just receive the prize winnings. The same is true for all of us who have accepted Jesus Christ. Jesus suffered on the cross to win the victory so that He could give us the free gift of new life as the adopted sons and daughters of the Creator God who inherit His kingdom.

Thus, as you go into the entire world to redeem the culture, do not be afraid. You are a David against a Goliath, but God has made you more than a conqueror through Jesus Christ. Thus empowered, the apostles and Christians throughout the ages have changed the world.

For instance, many historians say that the only national charitable act in history was the abolishment of slavery in 1833 in the United Kingdom. Historians note that slavery had been present since the dawn of civilization in every country and that no one in England had an economic incentive to abolish slavery because everyone benefited by it. When William Wilberforce, a young parliamentarian, came to Jesus Christ at the age of 25, God called him to abolish slavery and reform morals in England. In 1791 the first vote to support his bill to stop the slave trade was roundly defeated. Forty-two long years passed before Parliament voted to abolish slavery. William Wilberforce wept as Parliament cheered. When asked why he wept, William Wilberforce said he was a sinful man, but Jesus Christ was a greater God. Subsequently, by God's sovereign grace, William Wilberforce helped instigate the second Great Awakening and the morals in England went from debauched to honorable with people caring for the sick, homeless and the needy, along with worshiping God in spirit and in truth.

Now, you, your friends and your family have a wonderful opportunity to accept God's challenge to go into the entire world to redeem the culture and revive civilization. As you do, remember that all things work for the good for everyone who loves God.

No Other Gods

Trendy dilettantes have the gall to say that movies and other mass media product are art and anything in the name of art is acceptable. Art, they say, is an expression of truth, and so all art is worthy of some audience.

The entertainment industry is a $100 billion-a-year business that appeals to people's visceral emotions to separate them from their hard-earned dollars. A portion of that money comes from media product with a heavy dose of perverse sex and violence, which some in the entertainment industry call "horny boy" movies because they target the hormones of teenage boys, who drag their dates along so that they can be desensitized to promiscuity.

All of the entertainment media use some artistic elements and some communicative elements, but sometimes these are employed only to enhance the moneymaking value of the product. Art per se is not truth. It is a product of man's creativity or, as Aristotle said, "Art is contrary to nature." Art is sometimes truthful, sometimes lies and often does neither.

Not only should we avoid sanctifying art as some holy object to be venerated, but we must stop setting the entertainment industry apart from God's law, as if it were beyond the standards of good and evil. Ignoring God's law in the name of art, speech or entertainment is the heresy of antinomianism (anti-law), which is abhorrent to God. Those who condone such lawlessness in the name of art are condoning the moral decay of our society.

Making art and entertainment our gods is undermining our society. Christians must resist the temptations of the world—the flesh and the devil—and stand up for what they believe. United we can influence media leaders by impacting the box office and the cash register.

Christophobia

Beside our misplaced veneration of entertainment, another reason the media are getting away with wasting our culture is the rampant growth of Christophobia in our society. The same phobia has diminished evangelism and led to so much ignorance about the biblical worldview. "Christophobia" is a term I coined many years ago in a Los Angeles newspaper to refer to those who have an irrational fear of and hostility toward Jesus Christ and anything Christian. The symptoms are quite simple and insidious. Some of these aberrant symptoms include:

- An unhealthy fear of using the name of Jesus as anything but a profanity in public
- A dread of discussing biblical principles in public
- A horror that someone would expose or discuss his or her Christianity in public
- An aversion to using biblical standards to make decisions and to determine right and wrong in any given situation
- A perverse fear of the Bible

There are many more symptoms of this dysfunctional condition and many other situations where Christophobia rears its ugly head in our schools, media and government. For example:

- Christmas is now called Winter Holidays.
- Easter vacation is avoided by school systems, even if it means skewing school calendars to create unbalanced terms.
- Newspapers ask Christians to edit out any biblical references.
- Courts refuse to consider the biblical point of view.

This destructive phobia has spread throughout our culture to the extent that Christians are often the most Christophobic members of our society. These Christophobic Christians:

- Get livid when you bring up a biblical perspective
- Apologize when the name of Jesus is used in reverence

- Complain when Christians stand together
- Worry that some Christians may be wearing their Christianity on their sleeves

Often these Christophobic Christians fret about using biblical standards to determine right and wrong. They are horrified that these standards might be applied to common "problems" such as murder, adultery, lying, sodomy, and the other evils condemned by the Word of God.

If this phobia continues at its current pace, it will become the most debilitating psychological aberration of our age. Christophobia causes many to hide their Christianity, others to deny it and still others to lash out at Christians. It may even inaugurate a widespread persecution of Christians and a denial of the Christian roots of our society. History will be revised to blame Christians for all the problems in the world, and the immorality that is condemned by the Bible will be acclaimed as the solution to our problems.

This abnormal psychological condition must be routed out of our national psyche before it is too late. Christians must help others understand the dysfunctional aspects of this disease. They must deliver those who suffer from it by introducing them to Jesus Christ and instructing them in the wholesome benefits of the biblical worldview.

Breeding Self-Hatred and Self-Destruction

While speaking to my class at a seminary at one of the top 10 universities in the United States, I found that most students seeking ordination, even the smartest and most gracious ones, have a hatred for their own culture. They hate white males, Christianity and Western civilization.

On September 1, 2006, the *Los Angeles Times* had a front page article entitled "The Enemies in Their Midst" about Britain's homegrown problem: militant Muslim converts "with British passports and the accompanying resources and western ways, as well as links to lethal [terrorist] networks in Pakistan." The article stressed that homegrown Muslim radicals in Europe result from "open borders, tolerant laws and social alienation."[1] Who would have thought that the politically correct *Los Angeles Times* would correctly perceive the source of the problem facing Christendom today?

Part of this social alienation comes from schools and universities that have been attacking the United States of America for the last 50 years. Another part is a steady stream of movies like *Talladega Nights, The Da Vinci Code, The Death of a President, The Last Samurai, Fahrenheit 9/11, Saved!, Gangs of New York, Jesus Camp* and *Kingdom of Heaven* that attack Western civilization and the United States, the Church, white men, business, and Christianity.

Herbert Marcuse, the left-wing teacher who invented Marxist tolerance and political correctness in the 1960s, would be delighted that the West is rearing children who hate themselves, hate their culture, hate their country, and will eventually bring the downfall of their own civilization. Marcuse developed the politically correct doctrine that asserts that these young alienated radicals should be tolerant of everybody, including sexual perverts and killers, with the exception of Christians. Too many of our children in the United States and in Europe have learned his lesson well.

The left-wing movies and television programs that are coming out of some segments of Hollywood and the entertainment industry are a part of the problem. Many of our young people are unwittingly buying into the evil propaganda and agendas being presented in these movies and programs. For instance, in Great Britain, a majority think their government is the cause of the underground London bombings, not militant Islam or terrorist nations like Iran.

Even more disturbing, earlier this year the *Sunday Times* in London reported that 14,200 of England's "elite," including top landowners, celebrities and offspring of major establishment figures, have recently converted to Islam. According to the *Times*'s study, carried out by Muslim convert Yahya (formerly Jonathan) Brit, the son of Lord Brit, the former Director-General of the BBC, many of the converts have been inspired by the writings of Charles Le Gai Eaton. Eaton is a former Foreign Office diplomat and author of *Islam and the Destiny of Man*.

"I have received letters from people," Eaton says, "who are put off by the wishy-washy standards of contemporary Christianity, and they are looking for a religion which does not compromise too much with the modern world."

C. S. Lewis, the great defender of the Christian faith, once observed that a watered-down Christianity is absolutely useless to anyone. He also urged the Church to go out and convert university intellectuals and other cultural leaders to the Christian faith, because those are the people that will train up the next generation in the way they should go.

The Church today, however, and many of our schools, are filled with untrained anti-intellectuals who do not have the necessary tools to capably defend their faith in the public square. Most Christians don't even believe in the inerrancy of the original Greek manuscripts of the New Testament documents. Neither do most Jews believe in the divine authority of the Torah, the Five Books of Moses.

That's why our young people are an easy prey for Muslim fanatics, Marxist radicals and sexual hedonists in our world, in our schools, and in the products of our ubiquitous mass media.

It's time that people in the West stop breeding self-hatred and boldly defend the biblical, religious, political, moral and cultural traditions that made Western civilization strong enough to allow the freedoms that are being so abused.

Censorship

Another fallacy, which is keeping Christians in bondage, is the phony cry of censorship every time someone speaks out against degrading entertainment. Censorship is prior restraint by the government and is not the same as a united effort to make obscenity and immorality unprofitable. Christians often fall for the cry of censorship and think the liberal press is uniformly opposed to all acts of censorship. The mass media are often only opposed to biblical morality—supporting an agenda to censor Christian speech, while promoting immoral speech. God calls us to be discerning and wise, not to be the dupes of semantic confusion.

Cast Your Vote

Patron sovereignty has traditionally been commended by Hollywood as the right of patrons to determine what they will choose to see or to avoid. In our free society, we can again exercise our freedom to influence the entertainment industry to produce moral, uplifting entertainment.

Despite their personal preferences that favor sex, violence and anti-Christian messages, the producers in Hollywood are ultimately concerned about the bottom line—how much money they can make. If Christians support the good and avoid the immoral, our impact will be quickly felt in Hollywood.

The adversary often convinces us that we are powerless—that there is not much left for us to do except complain, escape or avoid making choices about the media. The truth is that we have great power. We can change the nature of the entertainment.

God Is the Most Powerful Force in the World Today

Too many moral Americans believe we are facing overwhelming odds and unassailable power. Paul Klein, former vice president of NBC, said, "Television is the most powerful force in the world today."

Not even close. Television, nuclear power, communism, capitalism, the United States, sin, Satan, man and all other powers combined pale in importance and potency into shadowy insignificance when compared to the power of God: "Through him all things were made; without him nothing was made that has been made" (John 1:3).

The Answer

Not only is God the most powerful force in the universe, but also Jesus is the answer. He alone can deliver us from sin and death. Only the Sword of His Spirit, His Word written, can give us victory over the evil influences of this age.

Jesus Christ was the master of communications. His dramatic parable word pictures are as pertinent today as they were 2,000 years ago. Christ understood the power of communications and how ideas shape civilizations. His Word toppled one of the most powerful civilizations in history, the Roman Empire, and continues to transform the world today.

We Are His Body

The Good News is that God tells us that "Now ye are the body of Christ, and members in particular" (1 Cor. 12:27, *KJV*). And He affirms that thanks to Jesus Christ's victory on the cross, "We are more than conquerors through him who loved us" (Rom. 8:37).

Therefore, we can confidently respond to His instructions by standing in the whole armor of God against the wiles of the adversary—including immoral media. We not only have every right to unite to oppose evil communications, but we are called to and have the power to rebuke such evil in the love of Christ. Further, we are motivated by our care for our children and our neighbors.

Therefore, we must care enough about God and our neighbors to communicate His gospel with power throughout the world and to take every thought captive for Christ. We must learn the principles of powerful communication so that we can communicate the gospel through the mass media to reach every man, woman and child with biblical truth.

Furthermore, we must redeem the culture so that the good, the true and the beautiful—not vain imaginations—are proclaimed throughout the world. In obedience to His Word written, Christians need to reclaim the culture for Christ by advancing on several fronts:

- We need to raise the consciousness of Christians to impact the culture.
- We need to witness to and disciple everyone.
- We need to produce quality mass media of entertainment, art and culture.

So how can you make a difference? Choose to become informed about what is happening in Hollywood and the media (publications such as *Movieguide*® can help you gain discernment on the media). Spend your entertainment dollars wisely. Remember that every time you buy a movie ticket or other entertainment, it is a vote to the entertainment industry to make more of the same. Cast an informed vote. Also, voice your concerns to those responsible. Write to producers, distributors and sponsors. The only way they will know your objections is if you tell them. (*Movieguide*® provides those names and addresses.) Finally, actively participate in rejection of companies who act contrary to our biblical beliefs.

Signs of Revival

Though pessimistic voices say the golden age of Christianity is over and suggest that the Christian faith is being replaced by Islam and other beliefs, Christianity is the world's fastest growing religion. The Lausanne Statistics Task Force reports that the ratio of non-Christians to Bible-believing Christians now stands 6.8 to 1, the lowest ratio in history. The evangelical movement, worldwide, is growing three times faster than the world's population!

Furthermore, while the mass media tries to associate Christians with rednecks and rubes, the Barna Research Group says church attendance increases with education. Finally, leading researchers say that throughout the world there are signs of revival.

The great missionary and explorer Dr. Livingstone left England for Africa at a young age to bring the gospel to the Dark Continent and to deliver the people of Africa from the slave trade. He preached every day for years with little success. He suffered malaria attacks more than 60 times and lost the use of one of his arms to a lion while rescuing a black friend. Then he disappeared into the uncharted jungle.

A brash *New York Herald* reporter named Stanley was sent to find Dr. Livingstone. After one year, by the grace of God, he found Livingstone being cared for by the slave traders he had come to destroy. While on his death bed, Livingstone introduced the reporter to Jesus Christ.

Stanley's articles opened up Africa to the missionaries and within three years the king of Portugal signed an edict abolishing the slave trade. All Livingstone had set out to do was accomplished, but first he had to become the humble man of character who could serve as a vessel for the pure gospel of Jesus Christ. In a similar manner, we must first submit to Christ before we can reach the world with the good news of His salvation. Let us all pray that we are on God's side and that He does His will in and through us to the honor and glory of His holy name.

CHAPTER 17

For the Kids' Sake

Pat Boone

Ted Baehr is a gentle man, a good man.

As long as I've known him, for many years now, everything he does is somehow concerned with helping caring parents navigate their way, with their children, through the increasingly murky, polluted waters of today's culture. I can't count the times I've heard older parents say something like, "I pity folks today who bring children into this world, with the rampant immorality, drugs, violence and sexual permissiveness they'll all grow up in." Ted has been valiantly doing something about the mess, both to help parents and to convince media moguls to act responsibly. I admire him greatly.

I asked him if I could have the last word in this book, and he consented. I feel the need to speak to fathers (and mothers, too) more strongly perhaps than gentle Ted would. So please don't put this book down just yet, okay?

We're all getting closer each day to the moment when we'll stand before our Creator God and hear His judgment on how we've lived our lives. The Bible says so very clearly that each and every one of us must surely give an account for "the deeds done in the flesh." You'll have to do it, and so will I.

At that moment, God will not be impressed with movies I've made or gold records I've sung, with how much money I earned or whether I was well known or anonymous. His Word says He'll be primarily concerned with whether we received and obeyed His Son, Jesus—and how we discharged our responsibilities *as parents*.

And *you, fathers*, do not provoke your children to wrath, but bring them up in the training and admonition of the Lord (Eph. 6:4, *NKJV*, emphasis added).

I love *The Living Bible*'s paraphrase of that command: "Bring them [your children] up with the loving *discipline* the Lord Himself approves, with suggestions and *godly advice*" (emphasis added).

Friend, this is the Word of God, inspired and preserved and delivered to twenty-first-century parents. I can already hear Him asking me—and you—whether we set a godly example before our kids, whether we taught and demanded personal discipline in habits, language, behavior and morals.

It's not easy, I know. But if it's difficult where you live, imagine how it's been for my wife, Shirley, and me living and raising our kids right in the middle of Hollywood. Though I've made many movies and was once in the top 10 box office attractions, Shirley and I have gathered our four daughters and walked out of several big, popular films—several of them musicals, not in some huffy, self-righteous way. We just quietly left a big "entertainment" that we could see was going to be a rotten influence on our girls. They didn't complain either, because they saw we were right about it. We'd all have become increasingly uncomfortable with each passing minute, and it was just better to leave the theater.

Same with a lot of TV shows. Shirley's got the quickest remote in the West. As soon as the action heads in a raunchy direction or the language gets rough, that program is history! It has always been that way at our house. We've made lots of mistakes, like all parents, but we've really tried to set high standards in what we let pour into our house and into our kids' minds.

See, I really *believe* that moment is coming when I'll have to hear God's judgment on what kind of dad, what kind of husband I've been. I'll be judged on what I thought was okay for my kids to see and hear and absorb while they were under my care and supervision. I'll be judged on whether I diligently and prayerfully offered "suggestions and Godly advice," or like so many said, "Well, what can you do? Times have changed, and you can't police your kids all the time. Besides, they all talk about everything at school, and they're gonna have to deal with all that sooner or later anyway. Right?"

Right. But God expects us parents to teach our kids, in advance, *how* to deal with "all that," and *not* to just drift rudderless and defenseless into the corrupt pollution that so often disguises itself as "modern culture." If we abdicate that vital responsibility, we *will* answer to God.

So, don't make lame excuses. We have given you an overview and some guidelines in this book. Use them, and you will have an easier time as a parent helping your children navigate the murky cultural waters. And God knows that Ted Baehr and *Movieguide®* have gone to all the immense trouble of viewing and evaluating most of what our kids are likely to be exposed to. It's provided to you, it's provided to me, and we can use it to be better parents, better guides and companions to our kids and grandkids. To say to the Lord, "Hey, I couldn't do anything about it, it was everywhere" just won't cut it. We can do something about it. And we simply must. For our kids' sake. And our own.

Movieguide® Review of Amazing Grace

Quality: ★★★★
Acceptability: +4

Warning Codes:
Language: L
Violence: V
Sex: None
Nudity: None

Release Date: February 23, 2007
Time: 111 minutes
Genre: Historical Drama
Intended Audience: Older children to adults
Starring: Ioan Gruffudd, Albert Finney, Michael Gambon, Benedict Cumberbatch, Romola Garai, Ciaran Hands, Rufus Sewell and Tom Knight
Director: Michael Apted
Producer: Ken Wales
Writer: Stephen Wright
Distributor: Samuel Goldwyn Films and Roadside Attractions

Content: Very strong Christian worldview with very strong moral content about stopping slavery, feeding the hungry, taking care of the needy and a practical, deep Christianity that involves faith in action. The film contains some references to sedition, overthrowing tradition and cheating to achieve a goal, but most are not carried out and depend on one's view of government. There are six light obscenities and four light profanities; a scene where a man wrestles with physical pain and sickness; descriptions of the ill treatment of slaves; men beating a horse. There is no sex in the film, but there is upper male nudity and female cleavage, alcohol use, smoking (a man uses opium for his pain), and gambling.

Review: *Amazing Grace* is a gorgeous movie about a very Christian person: the abolitionist and reformer William Wilberforce. It has deep, soul-stirring Christian references to the sinfulness of people, the salvation of Jesus Christ and the divinity of Jesus Christ, with frequent renditions of the great hymn "Amazing Grace."

William Wilberforce led the fight to stop slavery in eighteenth-century England. After a young life of debauchery, William came to Christ at the age of 25. He believed that he was called by God to stop the slave trade and reform morals in England.

The movie begins with William talking to his friend Prime Minister William Pitt about the need to reform morals and stop slavery, and then flashes back in time to his conversion. It shows how a group of Christians, concerned about the abolition of slavery, were led by Wilberforce and inspired by the repentant ex-slave-trader John Newton (who wrote the lyrics to the hymn "Amazing Grace"). Together, they tirelessly work year after year to get the English Parliament to abolish slavery.

The movie is deeply concerned with faithfulness. It shows William's battles with his weak constitution and chronic pain, his struggles with laudanum (a medicinal form of opium), and the fierce opposition he faced in Parliament. In the midst of his fight for morality and against slavery, William's marriage brings joy and happiness to his life. His wife helps him transcend his problems.

Ioan Gruffudd ("Ian Griffith") does a wonderful job as Wilberforce. In fact, the directing and acting in this movie are superb. There are two anachronistic lines, however. For instance, Wilberforce says that his pet hare is a million years old, but nobody at that time thought of the earth as a million years old.

Amazing Grace is captivating to watch and inspiring in its Christian content. Since *The Passion of the Christ*, there has not been a movie with such strong Christian testimony. Best of all, the testimony is on the side of freeing the captives, feeding the hungry, taking care of the needy, and having a practical, deep Christianity that involves faith in action. It deserves four stars and deserves commendation.

That said, this is a historical movie, and the plot follows the history so closely that it has trouble fitting in the necessary dramatic plot points. A little judicious editing might give the movie a tighter, more dramatic storyline. Whether or not that happens, *Amazing Grace* is a great movie and will be an inspiration to all who see it.

Endnotes

Chapter 1: We Are Not in Kansas or Kiev Anymore

1. "Report on the Global AIDS Epidemic 2004," UNAIDS, 2004, no. 52. http://www.unaids.org/en/ (accessed December 2006).
2. Michael Specter, "Traffickers' New Cargo: Naïve Slavic Women," *The New York Times*, January 11, 1998.
3. Dr. Ken Boa and Bill Ibsen, *The Decline of Nations*, available at www.KenBoa.org.
4. Pontifical Council for Social Communications, Vatican City, June 4, 2000, World Communications Day (cf. Vatican Council II, Inter Mirifica, 3; Pope Paul VI, Evangelii Nuntiandi, 45; Pope John Paul II, Redemptoris Missio, 37; Pontifical Council for Social Communications, Communio et Progressio, 126-134, Aetatis Novae, 11).
5. Leslie Moonves interview, Associated Press, May 19, 1999.

Chapter 2: Dare to Care

1. See George Barna, *The Frog in the Kettle* (Ventura, CA: Gospel Light Publications, 1990).
2. "Harry Potter's Influence Goes Unchallenged in Most Homes and Churches," *The Barna Update*, May 1, 2006. http://www.barna.org/FlexPage.aspx?Page=BarnaUpdate&BarnaUpdateID=237 (accessed December 2006).
3. David Kinnaman, "Teens and the Supernatural," The Barna Group, January 23, 2006. http://www.barna.org/FlexPage.aspx?Page=Resource&ResourceID=208 (accessed December 2006).
4. The Gallup Poll on Major Institutions, June 1-4, 2006. The sample size consisted of 1,002 adults nationwide with a margin of error of ± 3 percent.
5. "Congressional Testimony of Darrell Scott, Father of One of the Columbine Shooting Victims—Truth!" *TruthOrFiction.com*. http://www.truthorfiction.com/rumors/d/darrellscott.htm (accessed December 2006).
6. Darrell Scott, Congressional testimony before the subcommittee on crime of the House Judiciary Committee, May 27, 1999. http://www.truthorfiction.com/rumors/d/darrellscott.htm (accessed December 2006).

Chapter 3: Salt and Light

1. George Barna, "Americans Draw Theological Beliefs from Diverse Points of View," *The Barna Update*, October 8, 2002.
2. Ibid.
3. John Ross and Jerold Aust, "World News and Trends: An Overview of Conditions Around the World," *Good News*. http://www.gnmagazine.org/issues/gn52/worldnewstrends52.htm (accessed December 2006).
4. H. Richard Niebuhr, *Christ and Culture* (London: Faber and Faber, Ltd., 1952).
5. Terry Lindvall, *The Silents of God* (Lanham, MD: Scarecrow Press, 2001).
6. The Motion Picture Production Code of 1930 (Hays Code), *Wikipedia.com*. http://en.wikipedia.org/wiki/Production_Code (accessed December 2006).
7. Margaret H. DeFleur, Ph.D. and Melvin L. DeFleur, Ph.D., "The Next Generation's Image of Americans: Attitudes and Beliefs Held by Teenagers in Twelve Countries: A Preliminary Research Report," 2003, College of Communication, Boston University.
8. Ibid.
9. Ibid.
10. Also note that each medium is composed of one or more tools from pencil and paper which compose a note to the sophisticated cameras, recorders, editing machines, satellites and other hardware and software which are necessary to produce and broadcast a television program.

Chapter 4: Snapshots of Our Culture

1. Jerome Kern and Dorothy Fields, "The Way You Look Tonight," © Aldi Music Company and Universal Polygram International, 1936.

2. Terrence Dashon Howard, "It's Hard Out Here for a Pimp," © Atlantic/Wea, 2005.

3. Dana Blanton, "Fox Poll: Courts Driving Religion Out of Public Life; Christianity Under Attack," *Fox News,* December 1, 2005. http://www.foxnews.com/story/0,2933,177355,00.html (accessed December 2006).

4. Neil Young, "Let's Roll," Silver Fiddle Music, © 2001.

Chapter 5: The Eyes of Innocence

1. James Scott Bell, Op-Ed piece in the *Los Angeles Times,* October 19, 2002. James is a writer and novelist in Los Angeles (see www.jamesscottbell.com). Reprinted with permission.

2. Jennifer Loven, "Survey: Teens Crave Family, *Ventura County Star,* August 8, 2001.

3. "70 Percent of U.S. Teens Find a Correlation Between the Bible's Messages and Their Own Lives," American Bible Society press release, July 17, 2006; The American Bible Society, *Weekly Reader Research,* Christian Post, July 18, 2006.

4. Bell, *Los Angeles Times.*

5. Jim Impoco, "TV's Frisky Family Values," *U.S. News and World Report,* April 15, 1996, pp. 58-62.

6. Ibid.

7. Data from the Teenage Research Institute, Wheaton, Illinois, reported in *Movieguide®* vol. IX, no 3 and 4.

8. Ted Baehr, *What Can We Watch Tonight?* (Grand Rapids, MI: Zondervan, 2004), pp. 19-20.

9. Jean Piaget, *The Origins of Intelligence in Children,* Margaret Cook, tr. (New York: W.W. Norton Co., 1963), David Elkind, *Children and Adolescents: Interpretive Essays on Jean Piaget* (New York: Oxford University Press, 1970) and Robert Morse, cited in Ted Baehr, *Media-Wise Family* (Colorado Springs, CO: Chariot Victor Publishing, 1998), pp. 115-117.

10. Piaget refers to this stage as the sensorimotor period.

11. Piaget refers to this stage as the preoperational period.

12. Dr. Donna Mumme, Tufts e-news, January 22, 2003.

13. The following information is taken from Barbara J. Wilson, Daniel Lynn and Barbara Randall, "Applying Social Science Research to Film Ratings: A Shift from Offensiveness to Harmful Effects," *Journal of Broadcasting and Electronic Media,* Fall 1990, vol. 34, no. 4, pp. 443-468. Reprinted by permission in *MovieGuide®* vol. VII, no. 14 and 15, 920724.

14. Ibid., citing C. Hoffner and J. Cantor, "Developmental Differences in Responses to a Television Character's Appearance and Behavior," *Developmental Psychology,* 1985, vol. 21, pp. 1065-1074.

15. Ibid., citing P. Morison and H. Gardner, "Dragons and Dinosaurs: The Child's Capacity to Differentiate Fantasy from Reality," *Child Development,* 1978, vol. 49, pp. 642-648.

16. Ibid., citing G. G. Sparks, "Developmental Differences in Children's Reports of Fear Induced by Mass Media," *Child Study Journal,* 1986, vol. 16, pp. 55-66.

17. Ibid., citing W.A. Collins, "Interpretation and Inference in Children's Television Viewing" in J. Bryant and D. R. Anderson, eds., *Children's Understanding of Television: Research on Attention and Comprehension* (New York: Academic Press, 1983), pp. 125-150.

18. Ibid., citing G. Comstock and H. J. Paik, *Television and Children: A Review of Recent Research* (Syracuse, NY: Syracuse University, 1987), report no. XX.

19. Ibid.

20. Ibid., citing A. Bandura, "Influence of Models' Reinforcement Contingencies on the Acquisition of Imitative Responses," *Journal of Personality and Social Psychology,* 1965, vol. 1, pp. 589-595; A. Bandura, D. Ross and S. A. Ross, "Vicarious Reinforcement and Imitative Learning," *Journal of Abnormal and Social Psychology,* 1963, vol. 67, pp. 601-607; and M. A. Rosekrans and W. W. Hartup, "Imitative Influences of Consistent and Inconsistent Response Consequences to a Model on Aggressive Behavior in Children," *Journal of Personality and Social Psychology,* 1967, vol. 7, pp. 429-434.

21. Ibid., citing A. Bandura, "Influence of Models' Reinforcement Contingencies on the Acquisition of Imitative Responses," pp. 589-595.

22. Ibid., citing Potter and Ware, 1987. The following information is taken from Barbara J. Wilson, Daniel Lynn and Barbara Randall, "Applying Social Science Research to Film Ratings:

A Shift from Offensiveness to Harmful Effects," *Journal of Broadcasting and Electronic Media,* Fall 1990, vol. 34, no. 4, pp. 443-468. Reprinted by permission in *MovieGuide*® vol. VII, no. 14 and 15, 920724

23. Ibid., citing A. Bandura, "Influence of Models' Reinforcement Contingencies on the Acquisition of Imitative Responses," pp. 589-595.

24. Ibid., citing W. A. Collins in J. Bryant and D. R. Anderson, eds., *Children's Understanding of Television: Research on Attention and Comprehension,* pp. 125-150.

25. Ibid., citing C. K. Atkin, "Effects of Realistic TV Violence vs. Fictional Violence on Aggression," *Journalism Quarterly,* 1983, vol. 60, pp. 615-621, and S. Feshbach, "The Role of Fantasy in the Response to Television," *Journal of Social Issues,* 1976, vol. 32, pp. 71-85.

26. Ibid., citing A. Bandura, *Social Foundations of Thought and Action: A Social Cognitive Theory* (Englewood Cliffs, NJ: Prentice-Hall, 1986).

27. Ibid., citing L. R. Huesmann, K. Lagerspetz and L. D. Eron, "Intervening Variables in the TV Violence-aggression Relation: Evidence from Two Countries," *Developmental Psychology,* 1984, vol. 20, pp. 746-775.

28. Ibid., citing W. A. Collins in J. Bryant and D. R. Anderson, eds., *Children's Understanding of Television: Research on Attention and Comprehension*, pp. 125-150.

29. Ibid., citing L. Berkowitz, "Some Aspects of Observed Aggression," *Journal of Personality and Social Psychology,* 1965, vol. 2, pp. 359-369, and T. P. Meyer, "Effects of Viewing Justified and Unjustified Real Film Violence on Aggressive Behavior," *Journal of Personality and Social Psychology,* 1972, vol. 23, pp. 21-29.

30. Ibid., citing M. A. Liss, L. C. Reinhardt and S. Fredricksen, "TV Heroes: The Impact of Rhetoric and Deeds," *Journal of Applied Developmental Psychology,* 1983, vol. 4., pp. 175-187.

31. Ibid.

32. Ibid., citing A. Bandura, *Social Foundations of Thought and Action: A Social Cognitive Theory.*

33. Ibid.

34. Ibid.

35. Ibid.

36. John Rosemond, "Pre-schoolers Who Watch TV Show Symptoms of Learning Disabilities," *The Atlanta Constitution,* November 16, 1983, p. 12-B.

37. Lawrence Kohlberg, "Stage and Sequence: The Cognitive-Developmental Approach to Socialization," *Handbook of Socialization and Research* (New York: Rand McNally, 1969), p. 391.

38. Robert W. Morse, *The TV Report* (New York: The Regional Religious Educational Coordinators of the Episcopal Church, 1978) and Baehr, *Media-Wise Family,* p. 107.

39. "The UCLA Television Violence Monitoring Report," UCLA Center for Communication Policy, September 1995.

40. Victor Cline, "Pornography Effects: Empirical and Clinical Evidence" (Paper delivered at the NFF Media Workshop, Pittsburg, PA, November 1990).

41. "The UCLA Television Violence Monitoring Report," UCLA Center for Communication Policy, September 1995.

42. Walter Reich, "The Monster in the Mists," *New York Times* Book Review, Sunday, May 15, 1994. This issue of the *New York Times* had at least four articles on the subject, including a lengthy cover page critique of three new books on the subject and a report in the news section entitled "Father Wins Suit Against Memory Therapists." The *Atlanta Journal/Constitution* followed suit with several articles, as did other papers around the country.

43. V. B. Cline, R. G. Croft and S. Courrier, "Desensitization of Children to Television Violence," *Journal of Personality and Social Psychology,* 1973, cited in The UCLA Television Violence Monitoring Report, UCLA Center for Communication Policy, September 1995.

44. National Institute of Mental Health news release, May 29, 2006.

45. Ibid.

46. William J. Bennett, "Quantifying America's Decline," *Wall Street Journal,* March 19, 1993.

47. Quoted in *MovieGuide*® vol. VII, no. 3, 920214.

48. Data based on a 1994 UCLA Center for Communication Policy/*U.S. News and World Report* survey mailed to 6,300 decision makers in the entertainment industry with a 13.76 percent response rate.

Chapter 6: Child's Play

1. Edward E. Ericson, Jr., "Solzhenitsyn—Voice from the Gulag," *Eternity*, October 1985, pp. 23-24.
2. Peter H. Klopfer, Shameet N. Bakshi, Richard Hockey, Jeffrey G. Johnson, Patricia Cohen, Elizabeth M. Smailes, Stephanie Kasen and Judith S. Brook, "Kids, TV Viewing, and Aggressive Behavior," *Science*, July 5, 2002; 297: 49-50.
3. Ted Baehr, *Media-Wise Family* (Colorado Springs, CO: Chariot Victor Publishing, 1998), p. 63, citing an Associated Press report dated July 7, 1992.
4. Baehr, *Media-Wise Family*, pp. 64-65, citing *The New York Guardian*, December 1993.
5. *Movieguide®* vol. VII, no. 10, 920522.
6. Baehr, *Media-Wise Family*, p. 67, citing an Associated Press report dated March 26, 1992.
7. Ibid., p. 68, citing *The Vancouver Sun*, September 29, 1993.
8. Mark Yerkes, "The Effects of Sex and Violence on Captive Minds: An Insider's Perspective," *Movieguide®* vol. VII, no. 21, 921102.
9. Stephen Farber, "Why Do Critics Love These Repellent Movies?" *Los Angeles Times*, March 17, 1991.
10. Michael Medved, "Hollywood's 3 Big Lies," *Movieguide®* vol. XI, no. 1, 960101, January A, reprinted from *Reader's Digest*, October 1995.
11. American Psychological Association, "Big World, Small Screen: The Role of Television in American Society" (Lincoln, NE: University of Nebraska Press, 1992).
12. Ibid.
13. Bill Moyers, "World of Ideas: David Puttnam," PBS television, April 7, 1990.
14. Robert Kubey, "Media Use and Its Implications for the Quality of Family Life," paper delivered at the NFF Media Workshop, November 1990.
15. Baehr, *Media-Wise Family*, p. 83, and David Pearl, chief of the Behavioral Sciences Branch of Extramural Research Programs at the National Institute of Mental Health (NIMH), quoted in "Under the Gun: Hill Examines TV Violence," *Broadcasting*, October 29, 1984, p. 33.
16. Rebecca L. Collins, Marc N. Elliott, Sandra H. Berry, et al, "Watching Sex on Television Predicts Adolescent Initiation of Sexual Behavior," *Pediatrics*, vol. 114, no. 3, September 2004.
17. Jube Shiver, Jr., "Television Awash in Sex, Study Says," *Los Angeles Times*, November 10, 2005.
18. Susan J. Landers, "Doctors Can Bridge Sex Knowledge Gap for Teens," *American Medical News*, August 23/30, 2004.
19. Ibid.
20. Ridgley Ochs, "Casual Sex, Serious Health Consequences," *Los Angeles Times*, March 8, 2004.
21. Kelsey Blodget, "Pornography Becomes More Socially Accepted," *The Dartmouth*, May 4, 2006.
22. Katharine DeBrecht, "Teens Emulate Hollywood Idols on MySpace Which Make Them Easy Prey for Predators," *Movieguide®*, vol. XXI, no. 18/19: 060912 = September A/B, 2006. Katharine DeBrecht is the author of *Help Mom! Hollywood's in My Hamper* (Los Angeles, CA: World Ahead Publishing, Inc., 2006).
23. Dr. Judith A. Reisman, *Soft Porn Plays Hardball* (Huntington House, LA: Need publisher name, 1991), p. 56.
24. Jesse J. Holland, "Groups Link Media to Child Violence," Associated Press, July 25, 2000.
25. The first international assessment of educational progress, 1989, Educational Testing Service of Princeton, New Jersey.
26. Abbie Jones, "When the Telly Is On Babies Aren't Learning," *Chicago Tribune*, March 10, 1996, section 13, p. 1.
27. Ibid.
29. Mother Teresa of Calcutta, National Prayer Breakfast, 1994.

Chapter 7: Behind the Scenes of Hollywood

1. Patrick J. Kiger "Chew. Spit. Repeat. The Movie Industry Consumes Carpetbagging Investors Like Prime-Cut Steak. What's the Appeal of Being Eaten Alive?" *Los Angeles Times,* February 29, 2004.
2. Patrick Goldstein, "The Big Picture: Where They Root for Failure," *Los Angeles Times,* August 7, 2001.
3. Dan Glaister, "Apocalypto Now: Gibson's Next Big Gamble," *Guardian News,* December 5, 2006. http://film.guardian.co.uk/news/story/0,,1964042,00.html?gusrc=rss&feed=1 (accessed December 2006).
4. William C. Taylor and Polly LaBarre, "How Pixar Adds a New School of Thought to Disney," *The New York Times,* January 1, 9, 2006.
5. Tom Flannery is a *Movieguide®* reviewer who has written opinion pieces for publications such as WorldNetDaily.com, *Newsday, The Los Angeles Times,* and *Christian Networks Journal,* and he has won numerous awards for his work, including the Eric Breindel Award for Outstanding Opinion Journalism from News Corp/The New York Post and six Amy Awards.
6. "Annual Survey of America's Faith Shows No Significant Changes in Past Year," *The Barna Update,* 1999. http://www.barna.org/PressNoSignificantChanges.htm; Laurie Goodstein, "As Attacks' Impact Recedes, a Return to Religion as Usual," *New York Times,* November 26, 2001. http://www.nytimes.com/2001/11/26/.
7. "Barna Identifies Seven Paradoxes Regarding America's Faith," *The Barna Update,* December 17, 2002. http://www.barna.org/FlexPage.aspx?Page=BarnaUpdate&BarnaUpdateID=128.
8. David Outten is the Managing Editor of *Movieguide®.* He formerly published a local newspaper, was an artist with Disney's Epcot Center and designed Filemaker software for prestigious clients.

Chapter 8: The Power of Parables

1. "Spellbook," Scholastic Books. http://www.scholastic.com/titles/twitches/spellbook.htm (accessed December 2006).
2. "Write Your Own Magic Spell," Scholastic Books. http://www.scholastic.com/schoolage/activities/3up/ magicspell.htm (accessed December 2006).
3. Walter Hooper, ed., "Bluspels and Flalansferes: A Semantic Nightmare," in *Selected Literary Essays* (London: Cambridge University Press, 1969), p. 426.
4. Abram Book, "The Lion, the Witch, and the Marketing Plan, *Christianity Today,* October 14, 2005. http://www.christianitytoday.com/leaders/special/narnia.html (accessed December 2006).

Chapter 9: Worldviews and Beyond

1. Dan Smithwick contributed to the first third of this chapter, which was adapted from his chapter in the *Media-Wise Family*™. In 1986, Dan founded Nehemiah Institute to provide Christian worldview assessment and training services to Christian educators. Dan is the author of The PEERS Test, an internationally used assessment program for evaluating comprehension of Christian worldview principles.
2. Ronald H. Nash, *Worldviews in Conflict* (Grand Rapids, MI: Zondervan Publishing House, 1992), p. 9.
3. David F. Wells, *No Place for Truth* (Grand Rapids, MI: Eerdmans Publishing Co., 1993) p. 293.
4. Ibid., pp. 293-294.
5. A recent example was the United Methodist's 1996 General Conference held in Denver, Colorado, which included a report by 15 dissenting bishops who expressed their pain about the Church's present standards on homosexuality.
6. Gary L. Railsback, "An Exploratory Study of the Religiosity and Related Outcomes Among College Students," dissertation for Doctor of Philosophy in Education, 1994.
7. *Engel vs. Vitale,* 370 U.S. 421 (1962).
8. Francis A. Schaeffer, *A Christian Manifesto* (Westchester, IL: Good News Publishers, 1981), p. 17.
9. Norman Geisler and William D. Watkins, *Worlds Apart: A Handbook of World Views* (Grand Rapids, MI: Baker Book House, 1989), p. 11.
10. Ibid., p. 246.

11. Dr. Peter Hammond is a South African missionary who has pioneered outreaches in the war zones of Mozambique, Angola and Sudan. He is the Founder of Frontline Fellowship and the author of *Faith Under Fire in Sudan; In the Killing Fields of Mozambique; Slavery, Terrorism and Islam, The Greatest Century of Missions* and *The Greatest Century of Reformation*. You can contact Dr. Hammond at Frontline Fellowship, PO Box 74, Newlands, 7725, Cape Town, South Africa, www.frontline.org.za.

12. Adapted by permission from Michael S. Horton, "My Father's World," *Movieguide*® vol. VII, no. 22, 921116.

Chapter 10: Who Stole Our Culture?

1. William S. Lind has a B.A. in History from Dartmouth College and an M.A., also in History, from Princeton University. He serves as Director of the Center for Cultural Conservatism of the Free Congress Foundation in Washington, D.C., and as a vestryman at St. James Anglican Church in his hometown of Cleveland, Ohio.

2. Those wishing to read more about the history of cultural Marxism and its creation of political correctness will find a short book on the subject on the Free Congress Foundation website (www.freecongress.org). Its last chapter offers an annotated bibliography. Free Congress also sells (for $20) an excellent video documentary history of the Frankfurt School. A new biography of Theodor Adorno by Lorenz Jäger, simply titled *Adorno*, is a superb and readable introduction to the Frankfurt School's most important thinker.

Chapter 11: Where Are We Going?

1. Pat Buchanan, *State of Emergency: Third World Invasion and Conquest of America* (New York: Thomas Dunne Books, 2006), opening paragraph.

2. Melissa DeLoach, "A Lesson on Civic Duty," Zogby Intenational, September 18, 2006. http://www.zogby.com/Soundbites/ReadClips.dbm?ID=13689.

3. William J. Bennett, "Quantifying America's Decline," *The Wall Street Journal*, March 15, 1993.

4. Quoted in *Movieguide*® vol. VI, no. 10, 910524.

5. Peter Hammond, "Reformation or Islamisation?" ReformationSA.org. http://www.reformationsa.org/articles/Reform%20or%20islam.htm (accessed December 2006).

6. Ibid.

7. Don Feder, "London Journal—Moderate Muslims Behaving Badly," *Cold Steel Caucus Report*, August 18, 2006. http// www.donfeder.com (accessed December 2006).

8. Peter Hammond, "Reformation or Islamisation?"

9. Ibid.

10. Ibid.

Chapter 12: Asking the Right Questions About Media Influence

1. Paul Johnson, *Modern Times: The World from the Twenties to the Nineties*, revised edition (New York: Harper Perennial, 1992), p. 130.

2. Paul Rempel, *Hitler's Children: The Hitler Youth and the SS* (Chapel Hill, NC: The University of North Carolina Press, 1989), p. 76.

3. Robin Abcarian and John Horn, "Underwhelmed by It All: For the 12-to-24 Set, Boredom Is a Recreational Hazard," *Los Angeles Times*, August 7, 2006.

4. Ibid.

5. *Los Angeles Times*/Bloomberg poll, published in the *Los Angeles Times*, August 18, 2006.

6. One such dramatist that holds this view is Lajos Egri, who wrote the definitive text about scriptwriting, *The Art of Dramatic Writing* (New York: Simon and Schuster, 2004), which is required reading at premier film schools.

7. Gerry Mander, *Four Arguments for Elimination of Television* (New York: Harper Perennial, 1978).

8. Timothy Jay, *Cursing in America* (Philadelphia, PA: John Benjamins Publishing Company, 1992).

9. The famous Marxist, Professor Marcuse at the Sorbonne, advocated using language as a

weapon. He inspired many of the most renowned Communist revolutionaries in the twentieth century. Even Jane Fonda studied with him.

10. See Lajos Egri, *The Art of Dramatic Writing*, p. 6.
11. Note that the term "media maker" is being used here to refer to all involved in making a movie, including the screenwriter, the director, the producer and the executive producer, as well as other participants in the entertainment industry.
12. Robert Lichter, Linda Lichter and Stanley Rothman, *The Media Elite* (Washington, DC: Adler and Adler, 1986). See also Donald Wildmon, *The Home Invaders* (Wheaton, IL: Victor Books, 1985), pp. 18-23, for an excellent analysis of the Lichter Rothman studies.

Chapter 13: Seeing Connections of Contemporary Art and Biblical Faith

1. Doug Adams is Professor of Christianity and the Arts at Pacific School of Religion and chair of the core doctoral faculty in "Art and Religion" at the Graduate Theological Union, Berkeley, California. He is the author of 8 books and editor of 20 books, including *Transcendence with the Human Body in Art: George Segal, Stephen De Staebler, Jasper Johns, and Christo* and *Eyes to See Wholeness: Visual Arts Informing Biblical and Theological Studies in Education and Worship Through the Church Year*.
2. These works are described in detail in Doug Adams, *Transcendence with the Human Body in Art: George Segal, Stephen De Staebler, Jasper Johns, and Christo* (New York: Crossroad Books, 1991.)
3. For a more in-depth exploration of these topics, see Doug Adams, *Eyes to See Wholeness: Visual Arts Informing Biblical and Theological Studies in Education and Worship Through the Church Year* (Prescott, AZ: Educational Ministries Inc., 1995).
4. Art historian Jo Milgrom details how the doorway and its associated menorah are central in Jewish art in her book *Art as Religious Studies*, edited by Doug Adams and Diane Apostolos-Cappadona (New York: Crossroad Books, 1987).
5. Cathleen McGuigan, "Orange Alert," *Newsweek*, February 21, 2005, p. 64.
6. See Doug Adams, *Eyes to See Wholeness*, chapter 24, "Uplifting Umbrellas and the Importance of All Persons."
7. For further discussion of this dynamic, see chapter 4 of Doug Adams, *Transcendence with the Human Body in Art: Segal, De Staebler, Johns, and Christo*. One other art historian who has been perceptive of references to resurrection in these wrapped works is Dominique Laporte, who discerned explicit connections with the Christian tradition through what she called "the shroud syndrome or the phantasm of resurrection." See Dominique G. Laporte, *Christo*, translated by Abby Pollak (New York: Pantheon Books, 1988), p. 67.
8. *The Bakersfield Californian*, October 6, 1991, page 46.
9. Ibid.
10. See "The Biblical Code Versus The Da Vinci Code," *Church Educator*, May 2006.

Chapter 14: Impressing God's Commands on Your Children

1. Dyonette "Dee Dee" Mayer is a licensed clinical social worker who has been committed to both the emotional and spiritual health of women, children, marriage and families for over 18 years. Dee Dee also serves as a leader, teacher and speaker for Club 31, a ministry of over 200 women at Calvary Community Church of Westlake Village. With this commitment and passion for children and families, Dee Dee is now cohost with Ted Baehr of a televised program that focuses on providing education and media wisdom in today's complex media world.
2. Henry J. Kaiser Family Foundation, "Kids and Media," November 1999.
3. EPM Communications, "Research Alert Yearbook," 2003, pp. 7-102, 317-326.
4. A great book for scenarios is *Sticky Situations* by Betsy Schmitt (Carol Stream, IL: Tyndale Kids, 2006).

Chapter 15: Leading Our Children out of Darkness

1. Ken Smitherman has served as the president of the Association of Christian Schools International for the past 10 years. Prior to that time, he served as a Christian school administrator in Idaho, Hawaii and Washington for 26 years. He currently also serves as the president of the board of the Council for American Private Education (CAPE).
2. Fran Sciacca, *Generation at Risk* (Minneapolis, MN: World Wide Publications, 1990).

3. Leo Reisberg, "Campus Witches May Wear Black, but Don't Look for Hats or Broomsticks," *Chronicle of Higher Education,* October 20, 2000. http://chronicle.com/free/v47/i08/08a04901.htm (accessed December 2006).

4. Gordon MacDonald, *The Life God Blesses* (Nashville, TN: Thomas Nelson Publishers, 1997).

5. Ron Kirk, a Christian educator, has studied and taught the biblically and historically identified applied-faith philosophy outlined in this essay since 1980. The principles he sets forth have now long proven themselves in the curriculum and methods of pioneering day and home schools. Gloriously married since 1971, Ron and Christina have five children and five grandchildren. Ron was ordained as a minister of the gospel in 1984. This article, originally titled "Get Wisdom! A Biblical Christian Philosophy and Method for Education," was published in *Chalcedon Report,* September 2001. It has been rewritten by permission.

6. One student of mine lost a brother in the fourth grade, causing him emotionally to close down for a time. He missed lessons in fractions, but his school passed him on. He never learned math beyond the third-grade level until he came to me in the ninth grade. He thought he was stupid and could not learn until we systematically reviewed the material on fractions. He caught on in about two weeks of special half-hour lessons and never looked back.

7. True knowledge *approximates* the world (properly guided by God's declaration of reality—His Word) within our minds. Our ability to *know* derives from forming associations in the mind between individuals of every kind into an increasingly complex understanding of reality.

8. A *homoousian* is a Christian who believes that Jesus Christ is of the same substance as God in accordance with the Council of Nicaea's definition of the Trinity.

Chapter 16: Is the Mainstream Media Fair and Balanced?

1. Fred Barnes is executive editor of *The Weekly Standard.* From 1985 to 1995, he served as senior editor and White House correspondent for *The New Republic.* He covered the Supreme Court and the White House for the *Washington Star* before moving on to the *Baltimore Sun* in 1979. He served as the national political correspondent for the *Sun* and wrote the Presswatch media column for the American Spectator. He is host, along with Mort Kondracke, of the Beltway Boys on FOX News, where he also appears regularly on Special Report with Brit Hume. Mr. Barnes graduated from the University of Virginia and was a Neiman Fellow at Harvard University. This chapter is adapted from a speech delivered in Palm Beach, Florida, on February 22, 2006, at a Hillsdale College National Leadership Seminar on the news media in the twenty-first century. This article is reprinted by permission from IMPRIMIS, the national speech digest of Hillsdale College (www.hillsdale.edu.)

Chapter 17: More than Conquerors

1. Sebastian Rotella, "The Enemies in Their Midst," *The Los Angeles Times,* September 5, 2006.

Appendix A: How Movies and Television Programs Are Constructed

1. Ben Wattenberg, editorial in *The Atlanta Journal/Constitution,* July 5, 1992.

2. David Outten, "The 21st Century Pulpit," *Movieguide®* vol. VIII, no. 12, 930607.

3. See Ted Baehr, "Behind the Myst: An Interview with the Creator of the Most Popular Computer Game," *Movieguide®* vol. XI, no. 13, 960617.

4. Samuel Goldwyn was a Hollywood film producer and one of the founders of Metro-Goldwyn-Mayer. His Western Union statement is quoted in the article "Lost in the Cosmos," *Newsweek,* December 10, 1984, p. 94.

5. On August 19, 1996, *USA Today* listed the top grossing movies of all time after adjusting for inflation and found that almost all of them were family movies, mostly G and PG, that had strong moral messages.

6. Lajos Egri, *The Art of Dramatic Writing* (New York: Touchstone, 1960), p. 263.

7. Also note that each medium is composed of one or more tools from pencil and paper that compose a note to the sophisticated cameras, recorders, editing machines, satellites, and other hardware and software that are necessary to produce and broadcast a television program.

8. John Berger, "Ev'ry Time We Say Goodbye," *Expressen,* November 3, 1990.

About *Movieguide*® and the Christian Film and Television Commission™

We publish *Movieguide®: A Biblical Guide to Movies and Entertainment* to provide people with a detailed review of each movie to help them choose those to see and those to avoid. Each review provides a biblical perspective, enabling viewers to discern based on a biblical worldview. *Movieguide®* equips people to confront ungodly communications and take every thought captive for Jesus Christ.

While some Christians choose not to watch any movies, more than two-thirds of the born-again, evangelical and/or charismatic Christians watch what non-Christians watch. And many parents have written us saying they had no idea what their sons and daughters were watching until they subscribed to *Movieguide®*. Now they talk about movies with their teenagers and discuss why they should not watch specific movies and videos. Other people thank us for making them aware of things they missed in a movie or video, which has helped them to be more discerning. Many teenagers have told us they did not notice the evil in films until they started reading *Movieguide®*. Many say they turned from those films and toward the Bible.

Through the Christian Film and Television Commission™, we have undertaken to reestablish the Church's presence in Hollywood. By God's grace, we are making a difference! In fact, we have seen great breakthroughs evidenced by the movies being released at the box office. When we started *Movieguide®* in 1985, the major studios in Hollywood released only one movie with any positive Christian content. In 2005, however, 132, or 49.3 percent, of the top movies released by Hollywood contained positive Christian content! Also, when we started there were only 6 movies aimed at families; in the past several years, there have been at least 40. Furthermore, when we started in 1985, 75 percent of the top Hollywood movies were R-rated, but now, less than 40 percent are R-rated.

The chairman of a major studio told me that he attributed these positive shifts directly to *Movieguide's®* influence as well as the Christian Film and Television Commission™'s box office analysis and Annual

Report to the Entertainment Industry. Every studio now has a Christian film division, and several studios are doing major films with strong Christian content. This does not mean that the studios are not still doing bad movies, but it does mean that there are less of the bad and an increasing number of the good.

Undergirded by the grace of God, the reasons we have had such success in the Hollywood entertainment industry are fivefold:

1. Through our extensive research, we have been able to demonstrate to Hollywood executives that family films and clean mature-audience films do better at the box office.

2. As the demographic profile of the American audience continues to get older (due to the aging of the baby boomers), this aging audience will select more family and wholesome fare in entertainment media. (The aging of America will continue until the year 2009, when the younger age groups will regain their ascendancy.)

3. Many of the Hollywood executives and talent now have families and want to produce movies and programs that their families can watch.

4. Many Hollywood executives and talent are now involved in their own causes and find it difficult to deny the influence of the media with regard to violence and sexual mores when they claim it influences people politically or environmentally.

5. Many Hollywood executives and talent are coming to know Jesus Christ as Lord and Savior and are going or returning to the Church.

You can make a difference by subscribing to *Movieguide*® or by joining the Christian Film and Television Commission.™ For more information, call or write the following:

Movieguide®
The Christian Film and Television Commission™
1151 Avenida Acaso, Camarillo, CA 93012
(800) 899-6684 · www.movieguide.org

Thanks

I especially want to thank my coauthor Pat Boone, our introducer Janet Parshall, and all the contributors: Doug Adams, Fred Barnes, Don Feder, Tom Flannery, Peter Hammond, Ron Kirk, Bill Lind, DeeDee Mayer, David Outten, Ken Smitherman, Dan Smithwick, and all those who permitted me to use excerpts from their articles.

I want to give a special thanks to Dale Lippman, who helped proof and improve, and to Dr. Tom Snyder, who contributes to every project.

Also, I want to thank the staff, directors, advisers and friends of the Christian Film and Television Commission/Good News Communications, Inc.

In His Name,
Ted Baehr

Raise Your Children to Love Jesus

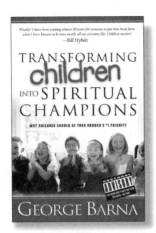
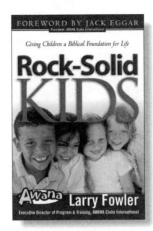
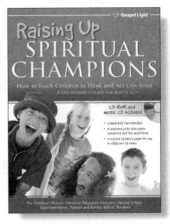
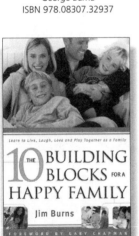
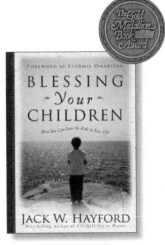
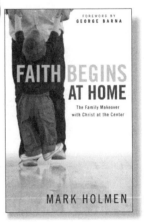